OCR Anthology for Latin AS and A Level Shorter Prose Authors

The following titles are available from Bloomsbury for the OCR specifications in Latin and Greek

Cicero *pro Roscio Amerino*: A Selection, with introduction, commentary notes and vocabulary by Neil Treble

OCR Anthology for Latin AS and A Level Shorter Prose Authors, covering the prescribed texts by Nepos, Tacitus and Apuleius, with introduction, commentary notes and vocabulary by Katharine Radice and Stuart R. Thomson

OCR Anthology for Latin AS and A Level Shorter Verse, covering the prescribed texts by Lucretius, Tibullus and Ovid, with introduction, commentary notes and vocabulary by John Godwin

OCR Anthology for Latin GCSE 2027–2028, covering the prescribed texts by Pliny the Younger, Aulus Gellius, Apuleius, Ovid and Virgil, with introduction, commentary notes and vocabulary by Tim Chambers and Declan Lawell

OCR Anthology for Classical Greek GCSE 2027–2028, covering the prescribed texts by Herodotus, Lysias, Homer and Euripides, with introduction, commentary notes and vocabulary by Christopher Burnand and Andy Mylne

OCR Anthology for Classical Greek AS and A Level 2026–2028, covering the prescribed texts by Aristophanes, Herodotus, Homer, Lucian, Plato and Sophocles, with introduction, commentary notes and vocabulary by Matthew Barr, John Claughton, Benedict Gravell, Rowena Hewes, Ellice Hetherington and Stuart R. Thomson

Virgil *Aeneid* IV: A Selection, with introduction, commentary notes and vocabulary by John Storey

Supplementary resources for these volumes can be found at
https://bloomsbury.pub/OCR-editions-2026-2028

Please type the URL into your web browser and follow the instructions to access the Companion Website. If you experience any problems, please contact Bloomsbury at onlineresources@bloomsbury.com

OCR Anthology for Latin AS and A Level Shorter Prose Authors

Selections from

Nepos, *Life of Hannibal* 1–13
(… *Baebio Tamphilo*)
Tacitus, *Annals* XIV.29–37 and
59 (… *et posito metu*)–65
Apuleius, *Metamorphoses* VI.7–21

With introduction, commentary notes and vocabulary by Katharine Radice (Nepos and Tacitus) and Stuart R. Thomson (Apuleius)

BLOOMSBURY ACADEMIC
LONDON • NEW YORK • OXFORD • NEW DELHI • SYDNEY

BLOOMSBURY ACADEMIC

Bloomsbury Publishing Plc, 50 Bedford Square, London, WC1B 3DP, UK
Bloomsbury Publishing Inc, 1385 Broadway, New York, NY 10018, USA
Bloomsbury Publishing Ireland, 29 Earlsfort Terrace, Dublin 2, D02 AY28, Ireland

BLOOMSBURY, BLOOMSBURY ACADEMIC and the Diana logo are trademarks of Bloomsbury Publishing Plc

First published in Great Britain 2025

Copyright © Katharine Radice and Stuart R. Thomson, 2025
Sections of the introduction to Apuleius (@ Stuart Thompson) are reproduced or adapted from *Apuleius* Metamorphoses *V: A Selection* (Bloomsbury, 2018) © Stuart R. Thomson

Katharine Radice and Stuart R. Thomson have expressed their right under the Copyright, Designs and Patents Act, 1988, to be identified as Author of this work.

Cover design: Terry Woodley
Cover image: Roman mosaic in Carmona, Spain © Manakin/istockphoto.com

All rights reserved. No part of this publication may be: i) reproduced or transmitted in any form, electronic or mechanical, including photocopying, recording or by means of any information storage or retrieval system without prior permission in writing from the publishers; or ii) used or reproduced in any way for the training, development or operation of artificial intelligence (AI) technologies, including generative AI technologies. The rights holders expressly reserve this publication from the text and data mining exception as per Article 4(3) of the Digital Single Market Directive (EU) 2019/790.

Bloomsbury Publishing Plc does not have any control over, or responsibility for, any third-party websites referred to or in this book. All internet addresses given in this book were correct at the time of going to press. The author and publisher regret any inconvenience caused if addresses have changed or sites have ceased to exist, but can accept no responsibility for any such changes.

A catalogue record for this book is available from the British Library.

A catalog record for this book is available from the Library of Congress.

ISBN: PB: 978-1-3503-8449-1
ePDF: 978-1-3503-8450-7
eBook: 978-1-3503-8451-4

Typeset by RefineCatch Limited, Bungay, Suffolk
Printed and bound in Great Britain

For product safety related questions contact productsafety@bloomsbury.com.

To find out more about our authors and books visit www.bloomsbury.com and sign up for our newsletters.

Contents

Preface	vii

Nepos: *Life of Hannibal* **1–13 (… *Baebio Tamphilo*)**

Introduction	3
Text	19
Commentary Notes	27
Vocabulary	57

Tacitus: *Annals* **XIV.29–37 and 59 (… *et posito metu*)–65**

Introduction	87
Text	103
Commentary Notes	111
Vocabulary	155

Apuleius: *Metamorphoses* **VI.7–21**

Introduction	191
Text	221
Commentary Notes	229
Vocabulary	273

Endorsement statement

The teaching content of this resource is endorsed by OCR for use with specification AS Level Latin (H043) and specification A Level Latin (H443).

All references to assessment, including assessment preparation and practice questions of any format/style are the publisher's interpretation of the specification and are not endorsed by OCR.

This resource was designed for use with the version of the specification available at the time of publication. However, as specifications are updated over time, there may be contradictions between the resource and the specification, therefore please use the information on the latest specification and Sample Assessment Materials at all times when ensuring students are fully prepared for their assessments.

Endorsement indicates that a resource is suitable to support delivery of an OCR specification, but it does not mean that the endorsed resource is the only suitable resource to support delivery, or that it is required or necessary to achieve the qualification.

OCR recommends that teachers consider using a range of teaching and learning resources based on their own professional judgement for their students' needs. OCR has not paid for the production of this resource, nor does OCR receive any royalties from its sale. For more information about the endorsement process, please visit the OCR website.

Preface

The text and notes found in this volume are designed to guide any student who has mastered Latin up to GCSE Level and wishes to read a selection of writing by Nepos, Tacitus and Apuleius in the original.

The edition is, however, particularly designed to support students who are reading these texts in preparation for OCR's AS or A Level Latin examinations in June 2026–June 2028. (Plase note this edition uses AS to refer indiscriminately to AS and the first year of A Level, i.e. Group 1.)

This edition contains a detailed introduction to the context of the ancient works, supported by lists of key characters, timelines and glossaries of stylistic devices as appropriate. The notes to the texts themselves aim to help students bridge the gap between GCSE and AS Level Latin and focus, therefore, on the harder points of grammar and word order. At the end of the book is a full vocabulary list for all the words contained in the prescribed sections, with words in OCR's Defined Vocabulary List for AS Level Latin flagged by means of an asterisk.

Katharine Radice
Stuart R. Thomson
July 2024

Nepos

Life of Hannibal 1–13
(… *Baebio Tamphilo*)

Introduction

Classical history: Poetry, prose and biography

Classical literature began with the great Greek epic poems. To a modern-day audience, these poems seem to be the stuff of fiction: they offer fantastical tales of heroic deeds in a semi-imaginary world where monsters exist and gods interact directly with humans. The Greeks, however, saw these poems as definitive of their heritage and the writing of Classical history, therefore, had its first roots in the imaginary content of these epic poems, the vivid construction of their main characters and the drama offered by the speeches and the characters' interactions with each other.

In the fifth century BC, the Greek historians Herodotus and Thucydides established the genre of prose history. Herodotus reported the information he found out on his travels, offering at least a degree of authenticity to what he wrote. He made no claim, however, that everything in his history was 'true' and his history is bulging with the weird and the wonderful. Thucydides did more to move history into the realm of fact and claimed that he was presenting an accurate analysis of the conflict between the Athenians and the Spartans. Even Thucydides, however, gave himself a degree of artistic licence and especially so when it came to reporting or recreating the great speeches of the day.

Roman writers were deeply influenced by these Greek precedents and authors such as Ennius and Virgil wrote Roman history through the medium of epic poetry. We should not, therefore, be surprised if Roman history seems closer to a historical novel (or melodrama) than to a modern-day history textbook. The Romans looked to the past to help them understand the present and they were particularly interested in the characteristics and speeches of the figures who had shaped their community. The enduring success of the Roman Republic (founded in 509 BC and in its last throes during Nepos' life in the first century BC) had established a power-sharing structure where Rome's elite men competed for political and military office. Within this, oratory was a central skill: an ambitious Roman needed to be able to inspire troops before battle, argue cases in the law courts, win popular support in elections and – crucially – be able to speak convincingly during senatorial debates. Roman history typically focuses, therefore, on personalities and tends to report not just what was done but also what was said, creating a persona for its central characters via selected anecdotes and reported speech. Inevitably, in recreating the speeches and characters of the past, Roman history was a blend of fact and imagination.

Within this, biography became a natural sub-genre of history. It offered the opportunity for authors to create a much shorter character sketch of significant historical figures, freed from the need for a broader overview of a set of events. If a reader is looking for facts and figures about the Punic wars, careful analysis of military strategy and a detailed account of the historical and political context of the time, these things will not be found in Nepos' biography of Hannibal. Instead, Nepos offers us a rapid summary of Hannibal's life, dashing through a selection of his military successes at breakneck speed and lingering instead on four anecdotes which provide the chance for him to dramatize his central character.

Biography would become established as a significant literary genre in the hands of authors such as Suetonius, but Nepos' biographies are the earliest Latin examples still in existence today. His most famous collection – *de viris illustribus* – is thought to have included accounts of 400 different individuals.

Nepos' life

Nepos was born in Cisalpine Gaul in *c.* 110 BC but by 65 BC he was living in Rome. Unlike many of Rome's elite, Nepos did not pursue a political career and he spent his time with literary men, such as the polymath and Hellenophile Atticus. Indeed, Nepos refers to Atticus' work as a source for his biography of Hannibal (see Chapter 13). The poet Catullus dedicated his book of poetry to him and famous Romans such as the orator Cicero were among his friends. Nepos' friendships with men such as Catullus and Cicero suggest that he was respected by the most prominent intellectuals of his day, but his written texts have been less admired by later readers than, for example, the great histories written by Livy and Tacitus. No doubt this is partly because of Nepos' much narrower focus, his sparse engagement with literary sources, and his sometimes congested prose style.

Hannibal and the Punic Wars

Hannibal was Rome's greatest enemy and a figure of enduring fascination for the Romans, used in Nepos' day as a literary trope to symbolize danger and typically characterized as an untrustworthy and ruthless military opponent. For approximately fifteen years, Hannibal and his army remained in Italy and the Romans had to endure the threat of a seemingly unbeatable opponent on their doorstep, even suffering the humiliation of having to abandon Rome temporarily when Hannibal marched on the city in 211 BC.

Direct conflict, however, between Carthage and Rome had begun in 264 BC with the First Punic War and would rumble on until Rome completely destroyed the city at the end of the Third Punic War in 146 BC. Carthage and Rome had become the dominant powers in the Mediterranean and both communities were keen to expand their territory. During the third century BC they began to compete for control of Sicily and then Spain. Under instruction from the Carthaginian rulers, Hamilcar, Hannibal's father, made peace with Rome in 241 BC, ending the First Punic War, but tensions continued. After Hamilcar's death, Hannibal resumed military operations in Spain and in 219 BC he attacked and conquered Saguntum, a town allied to Rome.

The loss of Saguntum sparked the beginning of the Second Punic War. Hannibal, no doubt expecting that Rome would respond forcefully, took the initiative and decided to attack. In 218 BC he gathered a force of 90,000 infantry and 12,000 cavalry and elephants and took up position between the river Ebro and Pyrenees mountains, no doubt expecting to fight against the Romans there. Then, with 50,000 infantry, 9,000 cavalry and thirty-seven elephants he marched to the river Rhône and onwards to the Alps. His daring decision to cross into Italy via the Alps – and the fact that he managed to do so within fifteen days – is one of the most famous moments of his military campaign, but it resulted in significant loss of life. After he arrived in Italy, he won his first major battle at Lake Trebia and then went on to ambush the consul C. Flaminius at Lake Trasimene. Flaminius and 15,000 Romans were killed, and a further 10,000 captured. In 216 BC, the Romans fielded their largest army to date against him, commanded by two consuls: Hannibal won a devastating victory against them at Cannae. Only 14,500 Romans escaped alive.

Hannibal's strategy rested on his belief that Rome's Italian allies would defect to him, but he was only partially successful in this. In addition, Rome had appointed one of their best military men – Quintus Fabius Maximus – as dictator in 217 BC and he instigated the policy that the Romans should avoid a major pitched battle against Hannibal at all costs. In the years that followed, various skirmishes took place, but the Roman policy of avoidance denied Hannibal the opportunity of the major victory necessary to secure his success. While the war dragged on in Italy and Hannibal was making little progress, the Romans were making significant gains against his brother, Hasdrubal, in Spain and in 207 BC Hasdrubal was defeated and died. The balance was tipping in the Romans' favour and – when the Romans made the controversial and daring decision to launch an attack on Carthage – Hannibal had little choice but to return on the backfoot to his home territory.

When Hannibal returned to Carthage, he was defeated at the Battle of Zama in 202 BC by Publius Cornelius Scipio (later known as Scipio Africanus to commemorate this victory). A peace treaty was agreed between Carthage and Rome, but it came at considerable financial cost to the Carthaginians and the Romans remained uneasy about the stability of the peace. Prominent Roman statesmen, such as the great orator M. Porcius Cato, repeatedly called for the total destruction of Carthage and in 149 BC fighting began again in the Third Punic War. Success for the Romans came comparatively quickly and in 147 BC, Publius Cornelius Scipio Aemilianus, the grandson by adoption of Scipio Africanus, laid siege to the city, capturing it in 146 BC. The Roman victory was total and brutal: the entire population of Carthage was sold into slavery and the city was completely destroyed.

Nepos' interpretation of Hannibal's life

As mentioned above, Nepos does not dwell on facts and figures. Some dates are given via the standard mechanism of referring to the Roman consuls for that year, but he offers no information about the size of the armies, the overall death toll in battle or even Hannibal's over-arching military strategy. There is no explanation of Hannibal's decision to invade Spain, the rationale for the march over the Alps, or Hannibal's belief that he would be able to achieve success on Italian soil by enlisting the support of disaffected Roman allies. Nepos also does surprisingly little to characterize the Roman response to Hannibal. He refers to the fact that, after Cannae, the Romans decided not to engage in a large-scale pitched battle against Hannibal, but he does not attribute this strategy to Quintus Fabius Maximus, Rome's famous dictator, nor does he offer any information about the startling change in tactics instigated by the younger Scipio. Chapter 6 opens with the information that Hannibal was recalled to Carthage, but Nepos does not explain that the Romans had decided to regain a military advantage by attacking Carthage while the Carthaginian army was in Italy. Moreover, Nepos offers a rather sweeping and seemingly unsupported claim that Hannibal's undoing was the *invidia* of his own countrymen and that – without this – he could probably have gone on to win against the Romans.

What Nepos does offer, however, is a clear-cut portrait, focused on Hannibal's undying hatred of the Romans and his intelligence. The biography opens with a bold, rhetorical contrast between the Romans' superiority over all other races in their *virtus*, and the idea that Hannibal surpassed all other military leaders in his *prudentia*. Nepos moves at pace through most of his material, but he slows down for four anecdotes which he uses to exemplify his characterization. The first anecdote recreates Hannibal's speech to king Antiochus of Syria, in which he tells Antiochus of the moment when Hannibal's father asked him to swear never to be a friend to the Romans. Hatred of the Romans is a continuing theme and, although Hannibal's military successes are condensed into just three chapters (Chapters 3 to 5), Chapters 7 to 12 all centre on Hannibal's ongoing attempts to whip up a fighting force against the Romans via alliances with Antiochus in Syria and Prusias in Bithynia.

Hannibal's *prudentia* is exemplified by the other three anecdotes: Hannibal's decision to escape from Q. Fabius Maximus' attack by the trick of tying branches to cattle's horns and setting them on fire (Chapter 5), his skill in hiding his wealth from the Cretans (Chapter 9) and his use of poisonous snakes in the sea battle against king Eumenes (Chapters 10 to 11). Nepos' interest in – and admiration for – Hannibal's trickery is clear. In Chapter 5, Nepos signals that he has no interest in a long summary of Hannibal's military success (*longum est omnia enumerare proelia*) but he is willing to offer these detailed vignettes to illustrate that Hannibal's defining characteristic was his cunning.

Key people in Nepos' account

- **Hannibal**: leader of the Carthaginian army and Rome's most dangerous enemy.
- **Hamilcar**: Hannibal's father and commander of the Carthaginian army during the latter years of the first Punic War.
- **Hasdrubal**: Hannibal's brother-in-law; appointed commander of the Carthaginian forces after Hamilcar's death (not to be confused with Hannibal's brother, Hasdrubal, who took command of the section of the Carthaginian army left in Spain when Hannibal decided to invade Italy).

- **Mago**: Hannibal's brother.
- **Antiochus, king of Syria**: Hannibal fled to Syria when he was first exiled from Carthage and enlisted Antiochus' support against the Romans. Antiochus was defeated by the Romans when they fought at Thermopylae.
- **Prusias, king of Bithynia**: After Antiochus was defeated, Hannibal fled to Bithynia and enlisted the support of Prusias and other kings. Hannibal lived in Bithynia for approximately seven years but he was betrayed by Prusias to the Romans. The Romans laid siege to Hannibal in his Bithynian castle and Hannibal committed suicide.
- **Eumenes, king of Pergamon**: Nepos gives a lengthy anecdote of Hannibal's military cunning in a naval battle against Eumenes during Hannibal's time in Bithynia.

Timeline of key events in Nepos' account

237 BC – Hannibal – aged nine – swears to his father that he would never enter into an alliance with the Romans; as a result of this oath, Hannibal joins his father on his campaign to Hispania (modern-day Spain). (**Nepos, Chapter 2**)

221 BC – Hannibal – aged less than twenty-five – is appointed commander of the Carthaginian army after his brother-in-law, Hasdrubal, dies. (**Nepos, Chapter 3**)

219 BC – Hannibal takes control of Saguntum, a city under Roman control. This leads to the outbreak of the Second Punic War between the Carthaginians and the Romans. (**Nepos, Chapter 3**)

218 BC – Hannibal leads his army over the Pyrenees, past the river Rhône, over the Alps and into Italy. Hannibal has major victories against Publius Cornelius Scipio near the river Rhône, the river Po and at Lake Trebia. (**Nepos, Chapter 4**)

c. **218/217 BC** – Hannibal makes for Etruria and – on the journey – suffers from an eye disease and loses sight in his right eye. In 217 BC,

Hannibal fights against (and kills) the consul C. Flaminius at Lake Trasimene.

216 BC – Hannibal routs the armies of two consuls (C. Terentius and L. Aemilius) in the Battle of Cannae, the worst defeat suffered by the Romans during this war.

216–203 BC – Hannibal continues to be undefeated in Italy. He kills the consul L. Aemilius Paulus and several others of consular rank (**Nepos, Chapter 4**). He advances to Rome (211 BC). He goes on to fight against Quintus Fabius Maximus (previously appointed as Roman dictator in 217 BC) and wins by the cunning decision to tie burning sticks to the horns of cattle and use these, at night, to terrify the Roman army. Hannibal wins against M. Minucius Rufus with a similar trick. Hannibal has victories against the consul Tiberius Sempronius Gracchus and the consul M. Claudius Marcellus (208 BC), ambushing each of their armies. (**Nepos, Chapter 5**)

203 BC – Hannibal is recalled to Carthage and tries – unsuccessfully – to agree a temporary peace treaty with Scipio Africanus (son of Publius Cornelius Scipio). Hannibal fights against Scipio at the Battle of Zama, loses and flees at pace to Hadrumentum. Numidians attack Hannibal as he flees. At Hadrumentum, Hannibal gathers new troops. (**Nepos, Chapter 6**)

201 BC – Carthage makes peace with Rome but Hannibal maintains command of the Carthaginian army. (**Nepos, Chapter 7**)

200 BC – Carthage tries to negotiate better terms with Rome, asking that their prisoners be returned. Rome demands that Hannibal and his brother Mago are stripped of their military command. (**Nepos, Chapter 7**)

196 BC – The Carthaginians recall Hannibal and Mago to Carthage and Hannibal is appointed to the most senior magistracy in Carthage. He demonstrates significant administrative and financial skill. (**Nepos, Chapter 7**)

195 BC – Hannibal, fearing that Roman envoys have been sent to capture him, flees from Carthage to King Antiochus in Syria. The

Carthaginians pursue him, confiscate his property, tear down his house and render him an exile. (**Nepos, Chapter 7**)

193 BC – Hannibal returns to Cyrene, Africa to see whether the Carthaginians will join with Antiochus in attacking the Romans. He summons his brother Mago to meet him. The Carthaginians punish Mago with exile. Hannibal and Mago, unable to return to Carthage, set sail for Syria. Mago dies. (**Nepos, Chapter 8**)

193-191 BC – Hannibal fights against the Rhodian fleet and loses (**Nepos, Chapter 8**)

191-190 BC – The Romans defeat Antiochus at Thermopylae. Hannibal, fearing that he will be handed over to the Romans, flees to Crete and hides his wealth there by a cunning trick. (**Nepos, Chapter 9**)

190 BC – Hannibal goes to Prusias, king of Bithynia, in Asia Minor, incites him to war against the Romans and enlists the support of other kings. Hannibal is unable, however, to secure the support of Eumenes, king of Pergamon, and fights against him. Aware that Roman support has given Eumenes superior resources, Hannibal defeats Eumenes by cunning and uses venomous snakes during a sea battle. (**Nepos, Chapters 10 to 11**)

c. **183 BC** – Envoys from Prusias to Rome reveal Hannibal's whereabouts to the Roman consul, Titus Quintius Flaminius. The senate sends Flaminius and a deputation to ask that Prusias surrender Hannibal. Prusias agrees, but on the basis that he is not asked to hand Hannibal over himself. The Roman forces surround Hannibal's castle; when Hannibal realises there is no escape, he commits suicide by poison. (**Nepos, Chapter 12**)

Reading Latin prose

Reading idiomatic prose brings with it various challenges: each author has their own idiosyncrasies and this means that readers need to be ready to encounter familiar words or structures used in unfamiliar ways. In addition, the grammatical rules taught in traditional courses explain how a language fits together, but reading Latin requires a readiness to notice things that are idiomatic to Latin, not to English, and then work out how to reshape them in a way that suits English idiom. The following offers a brief overview of some key things to bear in mind.

- **Concision and omissions**: even in the midst of the longest Latin sentence, Latin is naturally more concise than English. This is partly because English often needs multiple words to translate just one Latin word (compare verb forms, for example, such as *pugnabam* – 'I was fighting' or basic adverbs such as *diu* – 'for a long time'). More significantly, however, Latin's concision is also because Latin regularly leaves words out. As a reader, it is important to be ready to put these back in. The most frequent omissions are:
    - **subjects for verbs**: the person ending of the verb will make the subject clear, but English leans towards specifying the subject with a noun, and so it may be necessary to translate a verb with its subject specifically expressed – e.g. *congressus est* – 'Hannibal encountered …'.
    - **objects for verbs**: Latin will frequently omit the object if it is clear from context.
    - **the verb 'to be'**: this is routinely omitted and especially so for perfect passive indicatives and perfect passive/future active infinitives in an indirect statement.
    - **antecedents for the relative pronoun**: the noun that *qui, quae, quod* refers to is often left out in Latin, especially if it is a general reference to men, women or things. This means that it is important to be ready to translate *qui* as 'the man who', *quae* as 'the things which' and so on.
    - **nouns for adjectives**: Latin will frequently use a free-standing adjective, requiring the reader to infer the noun described from the number and gender of the adjective, e.g. *suos* – 'his own men'.

- **A preference for pronouns**: Latin routinely uses a pronoun where it would be more idiomatic in English to use a noun instead. This means that every time you encounter a pronoun in Latin, it is important to use its number and gender to identify the noun represented. For neuter pronouns, such as *id*, the thing represented may be the fact or event referred to in a previous clause and you may find it best to translate *id/hoc* as 'this fact, that event, this news' and so on.
- **Connecting pronouns**: in order to achieve a smooth flow from one sentence to another, Latin prose authors often included a word at the start of a sentence to link it to the previous sentence. Nepos has a particular preference to use pronouns to mark this connection. This means that he often promotes a pronoun ahead of the conjunction which leads into its clause, but in English it will be best to translate the conjunction first. In addition, Latin often uses a relative pronoun to provide this connection, but English rarely does: if you meet a connecting relative pronoun at the start of sentence it will be best to translate it as if it were a part of *is, ea, id* or *hic, haec, hoc* instead, or replace it with the noun it represents. For example, *cuius post obitum* – 'after his father's death'.
- **The genitive case**: the nominative, accusative, dative and ablative case typically connect a noun with a verb, but the genitive case is used to link one noun to another. The most common connection is possession, and so the genitive is often translated as 'of . . .'. In practice, however, English makes use of a much wider range of pronouns to link one noun to another (e.g. the signal **for** battle, power **over** Hannibal) and it is important, therefore, to translate a Latin genitive by using the English preposition that best suits the context.
- ***qui, quae, quod***: this is one of Latin's most important conjunctions and it is used in various different ways. As a reader, you will need to consider which of the following applies:
  - *qui, quae, quod* at the start of a sentence as a connecting relative – best translated as if it were *is, ea, id* or *hic, haec, hoc*
  - *qui, quae, quod* + indicative to express a straightforward relative clause

- *qui, quae, quod* + subjunctive to express one of the following:
  - generic *qui* clause – i.e. 'the sort of person who would …'
  - purpose *qui* clause – i.e. '[men] who were to …'
  - causal *qui* clause – i.e. 'in as much as he had …'
  - a relative clause embedded within indirect speech (see further below).
- *ut* is also a common conjunction which fulfils a number of different roles and it is important to notice whether it is used with a subjunctive or not.
  - *ut* + subjunctive = purpose ('so that …'), result ([with the result] 'that …'), indirect command or a clause acting as subject or object to another verb ('that …')
  - *ut* without a subjunctive = when, as, since, how

Advanced syntax

Nepos' text contains structures which are often not taught during GCSE or intermediate Latin courses. When these appear, they are detailed in the commentary to the text, but it is worth being alert to the following.

- **The rules of sequence**: the tense of subjunctive in a subordinate clause typically depends in part on the tense of the finite verb in the sentence's main clause. Sentences with a main clause set in past time will typically use only the imperfect or pluperfect subjunctive in a subordinate clause (a relationship known as *historic sequence*), but a present or perfect subjunctive will appear in a subordinate clause for a sentence where the main clause is not in past time (*primary sequence*).
- **Extended indirect speech** (*oratio obliqua*): English typically handles extended indirect speech by embedding it in a series of separate sentences, each one containing a verb which reminds the reader that the indirect speech is continuing (for example, '**She said** that it was raining. **She added** that she was surprised because the forecast had

been clear. **She asked** if she could borrow an umbrella.'). Latin, however, typically introduces the indirect speech only at the very beginning, and the constructions used for indirect statement, question, command etc. make it clear if the indirect speech continues for more than a sentence. As a reader, you will need to be ready to keep adding a verb of saying/thinking/asking such as those in bold above, and you will need to notice when an accusative + infinitive construction or a subjunctive verb indicates that the author is still reporting someone else's words, thoughts or instructions.

- **Aspect**: the choice of verb tense conveys the time of an action but it also conveys the *aspect*, i.e. how we think about an action. The perfect and imperfect indicatives, for example, both refer to actions in the past, but the imperfect encourages us to think of the action in process or as something not yet finished, whereas the perfect tense presents the action as completed. One of the most important principles of verb formation in Latin is that parts of the verb which share the same stem, share the same aspect: parts of the verbs formed from the present stem (i.e. the first principal part) all share the *not-yet-finished* aspect, whereas parts of the verb formed from the perfect or supine stems share a *viewed-as-finished* aspect. This is the reason why you will meet, for example, a pluperfect subjunctive used to represent in indirect speech what would have been a future perfect indicative in direct speech: the choice of verb in indirect speech has to represent the aspect of the verb in the original direct speech.

Further information about these constructions can be found in an advanced reference grammar such as *The Oxford Latin Grammar* by James Morwood.

Literary style

As noted above, Nepos' prose style is neither as flamboyant nor as distinctive as other authors such as Cicero, Livy or Tacitus, but he is able to add vigour or interest by the following means:

- **Demonstrative pronouns for emphasis**: it is easy to get used to translating *hic* as 'this' or *ille* as 'that' and to forget that their role is to point out or emphasize a key detail in a sentence. Put simply, the more demonstrative words there are, the more energetic or vigorous a text feels. In addition, it may be necessary to be flexible in how you translate these words since English adds emphasis in a variety of ways.
- **Adjectives** add colour and the more adjectives there are, the more colourful the writing. It is worth being alert to the quantity of adjectives within a sentence and especially when the adjective is emphasized by using a comparative or superlative form or because it has been separated from its noun and put in a prominent position in the sentence (such as at the beginning or end of a clause).
- **Vivid tenses**: the tenses with an unfinished aspect (see '**Aspect**' above) are naturally more vivid than the viewed-as-finished aspect because the unfinished aspect encourages us to imagine the action while it was/is happening. The imperfect, therefore, is often more vivid than the perfect tense. Most vivid of all is when authors choose to use the present tense (a technique often referred to as the *historic present*) to report past time events in a way which encourages the reader to imagine they are happening right now. English idiom, however, rarely does this, and it is often best to translate a historic present tense as if it were a past tense.
- **The impersonal passive construction**: forms of the verb such as *pugnatum est* feel very awkward in English but they usually add drama or emphasize the idea of the action. They are constructed by using the action itself as the subject (hence their 3rd sg. neuter form). Translated very literally, *pugnatum est* means 'the fighting was fought'. This focus on the action creates emphasis on the thing that was done rather than the people who did it. Often, the best English equivalent is to use a noun instead, e.g. 'There was a battle'.
- **Clause structure**: subordinate clauses sharpen an account because they make clearer the relationship between two events and they

also allow an author to distinguish between the most important event (the main clause) and events that are less important (subordinate clauses). Compare, for example, the following sentences:

- The soldiers fought bravely and the general was happy.
- Because the soldiers fought bravely, the general was happy.

The use of a subordinate clause in the second example highlights the causal relationship between these two events and highlights that the more important information is 'the general was happy'. In Latin, therefore, subordinate clauses were seen to add sophistication and clarity to a sentence. Like other prose authors such as Livy or Cicero, Nepos sometimes writes in long sentences with a large number of subordinate clauses. This shows narrative control but English is less comfortable with multiple subordinate clauses within one sentence. You may need, therefore, at times to translate one, long Latin sentence as a series of shorter sentences in English, but it is worth noticing how Nepos uses sentence structure to highlight which event is the most important and how other events are related to it.

- **Word order**: Latin's most important emphatic technique is word order. Latin's prose style embeds an expectation that words which work together will be next to each other (e.g. adjectives and their nouns, or adverbs and their verbs). Breaking with this expectation creates emphasis on the word which is out of place, and you will find that Nepos often emphasizes a word by promoting it to the start of a sentence or delaying it to the end.

Suggested further reading

Cassell's Latin Dictionary (1982), London: Cassell Ltd.
Garland, Robert (2010), *Hannibal*, Ancients in Action, London: Bristol Classical Press.

Hornblower, Simon, and Antony Spawforth, eds (1996), *The Oxford Classical Dictionary*, 3rd edn, Oxford: Oxford University Press.

Livy (2004), *The War with Hannibal: The History of Rome from Its Foundation Books 21–30*, trans. Aubrey Selincourt with an Introduction by Betty Radice, London: Penguin Classics.

Morwood, James (1999), *The Oxford Latin Grammar*, Oxford: Oxford University Press.

Mulligan, Brett (2015), *Cornelius Nepos, Life of Hannibal: Latin Text, Notes, Maps, Illustrations and Vocabulary*, Dickinson College Commentaries, Cambridge: Open Book Publishers.

Polybius (1979), *The Rise of the Roman Empire*, trans. Ian Scott-Kilvert, London: Penguin Classics.

Text

[**1**] Hannibal, Hamilcaris filius, Carthaginiensis. si verum est, quod nemo dubitat, ut populus Romanus omnes gentes virtute superarit, non est infitiandum Hannibalem tanto praestitisse ceteros imperatores prudentia, quanto populus Romanus antecedat fortitudine cunctas nationes. nam quotienscumque cum eo congressus est in Italia, semper discessit superior. quod nisi domi civium suorum invidia debilitatus esset, Romanos videtur superare potuisse. sed multorum obtrectatio devicit unius virtutem. hic autem velut hereditate relictum odium paternum erga Romanos sic conservavit, ut prius animam quam id deposuerit, qui quidem, cum patria pulsus esset et alienarum opum indigeret, numquam destiterit animo bellare cum Romanis.

[**2**] nam ut omittam Philippum, quem absens hostem reddidit Romanis, omnium his temporibus potentissimus rex Antiochus fuit. hunc tanta cupiditate incendit bellandi, ut usque a rubro mari arma conatus sit inferre Italiae. ad quem cum legati venissent Romani, qui de eius voluntate explorarent darentque operam consiliis clandestinis ut Hannibalem in suspicionem regi adducerent, tamquam ab ipsis corruptus alia atque antea sentiret, neque id frustra fecissent idque Hannibal comperisset seque ab interioribus consiliis segregari vidisset, tempore dato adiit ad regem, eique cum multa de fide sua et odio in Romanos commemorasset, hoc adiunxit: 'Pater meus' inquit 'Hamilcar puerulo me, utpote non amplius VIIII annos nato, in Hispaniam imperator proficiscens Carthagine, Iovi optimo maximo hostias immolavit. quae divina res dum conficiebatur, quaesivit a me, vellemne secum in castra proficisci. id cum libenter accepissem atque ab eo petere coepissem, ne dubitaret ducere, tum ille "Faciam", inquit "si mihi fidem, quam postulo, dederis." simul me ad aram adduxit, apud quam sacrificare instituerat, eamque ceteris remotis tenentem iurare iussit numquam me in amicitia cum Romanis fore. id ego ius iurandum patri

datum usque ad hanc aetatem ita conservavi, ut nemini dubium esse debeat, quin reliquo tempore eadem mente sim futurus. quare, si quid amice de Romanis cogitabis, non imprudenter feceris, si me celaris; cum quidem bellum parabis, te ipsum frustraberis, si non me in eo principem posueris.' hac igitur, qua diximus, aetate cum patre in Hispaniam profectus est.

[3] cuius post obitum, Hasdrubale imperatore suffecto, equitatui omni praefuit. hoc quoque interfecto exercitus summam imperii ad eum detulit. id Carthaginem delatum publice comprobatum est. sic Hannibal, minor V et XX annis natus imperator factus, proximo triennio omnes gentes Hispaniae bello subegit; Saguntum, foederatam civitatem, vi expugnavit; tres exercitus maximos comparavit. ex his unum in Africam misit, alterum cum Hasdrubale fratre in Hispania reliquit, tertium in Italiam secum duxit. saltum Pyrenaeum transiit. quacumque iter fecit, cum omnibus incolis conflixit: neminem nisi victum dimisit. ad Alpes posteaquam venit, quae Italiam ab Gallia seiungunt, quas nemo umquam cum exercitu ante eum praeter Herculem Graium transierat, quo facto is hodie saltus Graius appellatur, Alpicos conantes prohibere transitu concidit; loca patefecit, itinera muniit, effecit, ut ea elephantus ornatus ire posset, qua antea unus homo inermis vix poterat repere. hac copias traduxit in Italiamque pervenit.

[4] conflixerat apud Rhodanum cum P. Cornelio Scipione consule eumque pepulerat. cum hoc eodem Clastidi apud Padum decernit sauciumque inde ac fugatum dimittit. tertio idem Scipio cum collega Tiberio Longo apud Trebiam adversus eum venit. cum his manum conseruit, utrosque profligavit. inde per Ligures Appenninum transiit, petens Etruriam. hoc itinere adeo gravi morbo afficitur oculorum, ut postea numquam dextro aeque bene usus sit. qua valetudine cum etiam tum premeretur lecticaque ferretur C. Flaminium consulem apud Trasumenum cum exercitu insidiis circumventum occidit neque multo post C. Centenium praetorem cum delecta manu saltus occupantem. hinc in Apuliam pervenit. ibi obviam ei venerunt duo consules, C. Terentius et L. Aemilius. utriusque exercitus uno proelio fugavit, Paulum

consulem occidit et aliquot praeterea consulares, in his Cn. Servilium Geminum, qui superiore anno fuerat consul.

[5] hac pugna pugnata Romam profectus est nullo resistente. in propinquis urbi montibus moratus est. cum aliquot ibi dies castra habuisset et Capuam reverteretur, Q. Fabius Maximus, dictator Romanus, in agro Falerno ei se obiecit. hic clausus locorum angustiis noctu sine ullo detrimento exercitus se expedivit; Fabioque, callidissimo imperatori, dedit verba. namque obducta nocte sarmenta in cornibus iuvencorum deligata incendit eiusque generis multitudinem magnam dispalatum immisit. quo repentino obiecto visu tantum terrorem iniecit exercitui Romanorum, ut egredi extra vallum nemo sit ausus. hanc post rem gestam non ita multis diebus M. Minucium Rufum, magistrum equitum pari ac dictatorem imperio, dolo productum in proelium fugavit. Tiberium Sempronium Gracchum, iterum consulem, in Lucanis absens in insidias inductum sustulit. M. Claudium Marcellum, quinquies consulem, apud Venusiam pari modo interfecit. longum est omnia enumerare proelia. quare hoc unum satis erit dictum, ex quo intellegi possit, quantus ille fuerit: quamdiu in Italia fuit, nemo ei in acie restitit, nemo adversus eum post Cannensem pugnam in campo castra posuit.

[6] hinc invictus patriam defensum revocatus bellum gessit adversus P. Scipionem, filium eius, quem ipse primo apud Rhodanum, iterum apud Padum, tertio apud Trebiam fugarat. cum hoc exhaustis iam patriae facultatibus cupivit impraesentiarum bellum componere, quo valentior postea congrederetur. in colloquium convenit; condiciones non convenerunt. post id factum paucis diebus apud Zamam cum eodem conflixit: pulsus – incredibile dictu – biduo et duabus noctibus Hadrumetum pervenit, quod abest ab Zama circiter milia passuum trecenta. in hac fuga Numidae, qui simul cum eo ex acie excesserant, insidiati sunt ei; quos non solum effugit, sed etiam ipsos oppressit. Hadrumeti reliquos e fuga collegit; novis dilectibus paucis diebus multos contraxit.

[7] cum in apparando acerrime esset occupatus, Carthaginienses bellum cum Romanis composuerunt. ille nihilo setius exercitui postea

praefuit resque in Africa gessit itemque Mago frater eius usque ad P. Sulpicium C. Aurelium consules. his enim magistratibus legati Carthaginienses Romam venerunt, qui senatui populoque Romano gratias agerent, quod cum iis pacem fecissent, ob eamque rem corona aurea eos donarent simulque peterent, ut obsides eorum Fregellis essent captivique redderentur. his ex senatus consulto responsum est: munus eorum gratum acceptumque esse; obsides, quo loco rogarent, futuros; captivos non remissuros, quod Hannibalem, cuius opera susceptum bellum foret, inimicissimum nomini Romano, etiamnum cum imperio apud exercitum haberent itemque fratrem eius Magonem. hoc responso Carthaginienses cognito Hannibalem domum et Magonem revocarunt. huc ut rediit, rex factus est, postquam praetor fuerat, anno secundo et vicesimo. ut enim Romae consules, sic Carthagine quotannis annui bini reges creabantur. in eo magistratu pari diligentia se Hannibal praebuit, ac fuerat in bello. namque effecit, ex novis vectigalibus non solum ut esset pecunia, quae Romanis ex foedere penderetur, sed etiam superesset, quae in aerario reponeretur. deinde M. Claudio L. Furio consulibus Roma legati Carthaginem venerunt. hos Hannibal ratus sui exposcendi gratia missos, priusquam iis senatus daretur, navem ascendit clam atque in Syriam ad Antiochum profugit. hac re palam facta Poeni naves duas, quae eum comprehenderent, si possent consequi, miserunt, bona eius publicarunt, domum a fundamentis disiecerunt, ipsum exulem iudicarunt.

[8] at Hannibal anno tertio postquam domo profugerat, L. Cornelio Q. Minucio consulibus, cum quinque navibus Africam accessit in finibus Cyrenaeorum si forte Carthaginienses ad bellum Antiochi spe fiduciaque inducere posset, cui iam persuaserat ut cum exercitibus in Italiam proficisceretur. huc Magonem fratrem excivit. id ubi Poeni resciverunt, Magonem eadem, qua fratrem, absentem affecerunt poena. illi desperatis rebus cum solvissent naves ac vela ventis dedissent, Hannibal ad Antiochum pervenit. de Magonis interitu duplex memoria prodita est. namque alii naufragio, alii a servolis ipsius interfectum eum scriptum reliquerunt. Antiochus autem, si tam in agendo bello consiliis eius parere voluisset, quam in suscipiendo instituerat, propius

Tiberi quam Thermopylis de summa imperii dimicasset. quem etsi multa stulte conari videbat, tamen nulla deseruit in re. praefuit paucis navibus, quas ex Syria iussus erat in Asiam ducere, hisque adversus Rhodiorum classem in Pamphylio mari conflixit. quo cum multitudine adversariorum sui superarentur, ipse, quo cornu rem gessit, fuit superior.

[9] Antiocho fugato verens, ne dederetur, quod sine dubio accidisset, si sui fecisset potestatem, Cretam ad Gortynios venit, ut ibi, quo se conferret, consideraret. vidit autem vir omnium callidissimus in magno se fore periculo, nisi quid providisset, propter avaritiam Cretensium. magnam enim secum pecuniam portabat, de qua sciebat exisse famam. itaque capit tale consilium. amphoras complures complet plumbo, summas operit auro et argento. has praesentibus principibus deponit in templo Dianae, simulans se suas fortunas illorum fidei credere. his in errorem inductis statuas aeneas, quas secum portabat, omni sua pecunia complet easque in propatulo domi abicit. Gortynii templum magna cura custodiunt non tam a ceteris quam ab Hannibale, ne ille inscientibus iis tolleret secumque duceret.

[10] sic conservatis suis rebus Poenus illusis Cretensibus omnibus ad Prusiam in Pontum pervenit. apud quem eodem animo fuit erga Italiam neque aliud quicquam egit quam regem armavit et exercuit adversus Romanos. quem cum videret domesticis opibus minus esse robustum, conciliabat ceteros reges, adiungebat bellicosas nationes. dissidebat ab eo Pergamenus rex Eumenes, Romanis amicissimus, bellumque inter eos gerebatur et mari et terra; sed utrobique Eumenes plus valebat propter Romanorum societatem. quo magis cupiebat eum Hannibal opprimi; quem si removisset, faciliora sibi cetera fore arbitrabatur. ad hunc interficiundum talem iniit rationem. classe paucis diebus erant decreturi. superabatur navium multitudine; dolo erat pugnandum, cum par non esset armis. imperavit quam plurimas venenatas serpentes vivas colligi easque in vasa fictilia conici. harum cum effecisset magnam multitudinem, die ipso, quo facturus erat navale proelium, classiarios convocat hisque praecepit, omnes ut in unam Eumenis regis concurrant navem; a ceteris tantum satis habeant se defendere. id illos facile

serpentium multitudine consecuturos. rex autem in qua nave veheretur, ut scirent, se facturum. quem si aut cepissent aut interfecissent, magno iis pollicetur praemio fore.

[11] tali cohortatione militum facta classis ab utrisque in proelium deducitur. quarum acie constituta, priusquam signum pugnae daretur, Hannibal, ut palam faceret suis, quo loco Eumenes esset, tabellarium in scapha cum caduceo mittit. qui ubi ad naves adversariorum pervenit epistulamque ostendens se regem professus est quaerere, statim ad Eumenem deductus est, quod nemo dubitabat, quin aliquid de pace esset scriptum. tabellarius ducis nave declarata suis eodem, unde erat egressus, se recepit. at Eumenes soluta epistula nihil in ea repperit, nisi quae ad irridendum eum pertinerent. cuius etsi causam mirabatur neque reperiebat, tamen proelium statim committere non dubitavit. horum in concursu Bithynii Hannibalis praecepto universi navem Eumenis adoriuntur. quorum vim rex cum sustinere non posset, fuga salutem petit; quam consecutus non esset, nisi intra sua praesidia se recepisset, quae in proximo litore erant collocata. reliquae Pergamenae naves cum adversarios premerent acrius, repente in eas vasa fictilia, de quibus supra mentionem fecimus, conici coepta sunt. quae iacta initio risum pugnantibus concitarunt, neque, quare id fieret, poterat intellegi. postquam autem naves suas oppletas conspexerunt serpentibus, nova re perterriti, cum, quid potissimum vitarent, non viderent, puppes verterunt seque ad sua castra nautica rettulerunt. sic Hannibal consilio arma Pergamenorum superavit neque tum solum, sed saepe alias pedestribus copiis pari prudentia pepulit adversarios.

[12] quae dum in Asia geruntur, accidit casu ut legati Prusiae Romae apud T. Quintium Flamininum consularem cenarent atque ibi de Hannibale mentione facta ex his unus diceret eum in Prusiae regno esse. id postero die Flamininus senatui detulit. patres conscripti, qui Hannibale vivo numquam se sine insidiis futuros existimarent, legatos in Bithyniam miserunt, in his Flamininum, qui ab rege peterent, ne inimicissimum suum secum haberet sibique dederet. his Prusias negare ausus non est: illud recusavit, ne id a se fieri postularent, quod adversus

ius hospitii esset: ipsi, si possent, comprehenderent; locum ubi esset, facile inventuros. Hannibal enim uno loco se tenebat, in castello, quod ei a rege datum erat muneri, idque sic aedificarat, ut in omnibus partibus aedificii exitus haberet, scilicet verens, ne usu veniret, quod accidit. huc cum legati Romanorum venissent ac multitudine domum eius circumdedissent, puer ab ianua prospiciens Hannibali dixit plures praeter consuetudinem armatos apparere. qui imperavit ei, ut omnes fores aedificii circumiret ac propere sibi nuntiaret, num eodem modo undique obsideretur. puer cum celeriter, quid esset, renuntiasset omnesque exitus occupatos ostendisset, sensit id non fortuito factum, sed se peti neque sibi diutius vitam esse retinendam. quam ne alieno arbitrio dimitteret, memor pristinarum virtutum venenum, quod semper secum habere consuerat, sumpsit.

[13] sic vir fortissimus, multis variisque perfunctus laboribus, anno acquievit septuagesimo. quibus consulibus interierit, non convenit. namque Atticus M. Claudio Marcello Q. Fabio Labeone consulibus mortuum in annali suo scriptum reliquit, at Polybius L. Aemilio Paulo Cn. Baebio Tamphilo, Sulpicius autem Blitho P. Cornelio Cethego M. Baebio Tamphilo.

Commentary Notes

Chapter 1

Hannibal: the nominatives name the focus of this text. In English: 'This account is about Hannibal...'.

Carthaginiensis: it is worth preserving the emphasis of this word order: 'This account is about Hannibal, son of Hamilcar, the Carthaginian.'

verum est: the neuter 'noun' described by *verum* is the statement conveyed in the *ut* clause. In English: 'If the fact that... is true'.

quod: Latin often leaves out the antecedent for a relative pronoun but in English it is often useful to put it back in: 'something which...'.

ut... superarit: *superarit* is a shortened form of the perfect subjunctive *superaverit*. *ut* + subjunctive is often used in Latin to create a noun clause, i.e. a unit which functions as the subject or object of another verb, or which offers information which is then described by an adjective (as here). In English: '[the fact] that the Roman people overpowered...'.

virtute: the abstract noun *virtus* often refers to military excellence.

non est infitiandum: a gerundive of obligation followed by an accusative + infinitive – 'it must not be denied that...'.

tanto... quanto...: as a pair, these adjectives create a correlation in quantity – 'to that extent ... the extent to which ...'. In more idiomatic English, 'Hannibal surpassed ... to the same extent as the Roman people ...'.

antecedat: subjunctive because it is a subordinate clause in indirect speech. Translate as if it is a present indicative.

prudentia: ablative to express how Hannibal was superior – 'in his good judgement'.

cum eo: as is often the case, it is best to translate this pronoun with a noun in English: 'with the Roman people'.

congressus est: Hannibal is still the subject.

quod: an accusative of respect – 'in respect of which thing', i.e. 'in light of this fact'.

nisi . . . debilitatus esset: *nisi* + pluperfect subjunctive – 'if he had not been weakened . . .'.

domi: locative – 'at home' (i.e. in Carthage).

videtur superare potuisse: the Latin's literal equivalent here is 'he seems to have been able to conquer . . .' but the more idiomatic translation is 'it seems that he would have been able to conquer . . .'.

sed: Nepos lingers on the idea that Hannibal's downfall was because he became unpopular within his own community and not the result of any shortcoming in military skill.

hic: Nepos likes to open his sentences with a pronoun; in English it is more idiomatic to include a noun as well – 'this man'.

relictum odium paternum: one of the idiomatic differences between Latin and English is that Latin is more prone to use adjectives (including participles) than English. Here, it is best to convert the ppp. into a finite verb and the adjective *paternum* into a noun. Observing this idiom, the very literal translation 'the left behind paternal hatred' becomes '[Hannibal preserved] the hatred which had been passed down to him by his father'.

ut . . . deposuit: this result clause deals with a potential result: '. . . that he would have cast off his life sooner than [let go of] this hatred'. Notice that – again – the Latin pronoun *id* is best translated with a noun instead.

qui . . . destiterit: the subjunctive shows that this *qui* clause is a generic *qui* clause and so, in effect, another result clause; it shows that Hannibal was the sort of man to do something. English needs us to supply an antecedent for the *qui*: 'and indeed Hannibal became the sort of man who ... never stopped ...'.

cum: concessive in flavour here – 'although', 'even though'. Nepos is highlighting that Hannibal continued to imagine that he was at war with the Romans even when he had been driven out from Carthage and lacked the means to conduct a war.

cum patria pulsus esset: Hannibal was driven from his homeland in 195 BC. In Chapters 7 to 11, Nepos details his alliances first with King Antiochus III of Syria and then King Prusias I of Bithynia.

destiterit bellare: *desisto* + infinitive = 'stop doing something'. The infinitive is a verbal noun, i.e. it refers to the thing that is the action itself. Because of this, it is naturally used as subject or object of another verb.

Chapter 2

Nepos offers an anecdote to prove his previous claim about Hannibal's unending hatred of the Romans. Nepos jumps forwards in time to a conversation between Hannibal and Antiochus, king of Syria. Hannibal had been exiled from Carthage in 195 BC and spent several years with Antiochus. In this anecdote, Hannibal has realized that – after a visit from Roman envoys – Antiochus' enmity towards the Romans may be wavering and he attempts to shore it up by proving his unswerving hatred of them.

ut omittam Philippum: this compressed construction is equivalent to the English idiom 'leaving aside Philip'. *ut* introduces a purpose clause (with a present subjunctive for primary sequence) but requires us to understand a main clause from context. Uncompressed the meaning would be '[I am making the decision to mention ... next], so that I may leave out ...'.

Philippum: Philip V of Macedon.

absens: this present participle refers to Hannibal; Hannibal had negotiated an alliance with Philip at a distance.

rex Antiochus: Antiochus III of Syria.

tanta cupiditate ... bellandi: the gerund is genitive and depends, therefore, on the noun *cupiditate* – 'with such great desire of waging war', i.e. 'with such great desire to wage war'.

usque a rubro mari: 'all the way from the Red Sea'. The distance is impressive; the Red Sea is more than 1,000 miles from Italy. Note that *mare* has an ablative singular form ending in -*i*.

ad quem: the relative pronoun at the start of a sentence is best translated as 'he', 'she', 'it', 'they', 'this' etc. Here: 'to this man'. *ad quem* should be translated after *cum*.

qui ... explorarent darentque: the subjunctive verbs show that this relative clause expresses purpose: 'who were to find out ... and to give ...'.

ut ... adducerent: purpose clause.

regi: the dative is used to indicate a person affected by an action; here the idea is that the Roman envoys are intending to bring Hannibal under suspicion and that Antiochus is the king who will end up suspicious of Hannibal. In English: 'to make Hannibal into an object of suspicion for the king'.

tamquam ... sentiret: this clause gives the grounds for the suspicion, i.e. the Roman envoys spoke as if Hannibal had changed his mind and so could no longer be trusted by Antiochus as an ally. *ab ipsis* refers to the Romans: the implication is that the Romans have persuaded Hannibal to be disloyal to Antiochus. *alia atque antea*: very literally, this means '[as if Hannibal had been thinking] other things previously', i.e. 'as if Hannibal's thoughts were now otherwise than before'. Notice that the imperfect tense of *sentiret* is imperfect by aspect, i.e. it refers to an ongoing action in the past.

neque . . . fecissent: *neque* shows that this is a continuation of the *cum* clause: 'and when they had not done this in vain', i.e. when the Roman envoys had been successful in creating suspicion.

idque . . . comperisset: the *cum* clause continues; it is helpful in English to repeat the conjunction: 'and when Hannibal had found out . . .'.

seque . . . vidisset: the *cum* clause continues: 'and when Hannibal had seen . . .'.

se . . . ab interioribus consiliis segregari: an indication that Antiochus no longer trusted Hannibal to be in his inner circle.

tempore dato: 'when the opportunity arose'.

adiit: Hannibal is the subject. After a long list of subordinate clauses, Nepos uses the main clause to focus on the key action in this sentence, i.e. the moment when Hannibal went to Antiochus to prove his enduring hatred of the Romans.

cum . . . commemorasset: Nepos uses a shortened form of the pluperfect subjunctive *commemoravisset*.

puerulo me: *puerulus* is a diminutive form of *puer*: 'when I was just a little boy'. Both words are ablative, in effect working as an ablative absolute (verb *to be* understood).

Carthagine: note that Latin does not use prepositions to express motion towards, motion away from or position at a town or small island. The ablative case is used here (without a preposition) to mean 'from Carthage'.

Iovi optimo maximo: a standard honorific title for Jupiter: 'to Jupiter, greatest and best'. The polytheistic approach to religion meant that the Romans often associated the deities of a different culture with their own, and so Nepos uses a Roman name to represent the Carthaginian deity.

quae divina res dum: when the relative pronoun is used as a connecting relative at the start of a sentence it is best translated as 'this', 'that', 'he' etc. Note that here, as is often the case, the subject has been promoted ahead of the conjunction which introduces its clause: 'while this divine ritual ...'.

vellemne: *-ne* signals that this is an indirect question: '... whether I wanted ...'.

in castra profisci: 'to set out for the camp', i.e. to join him on his military campaign.

id cum: notice that the pronoun *id* has been promoted ahead of *cum*, the conjunction which opens its clause. This often happens either for emphasis or when the word promoted provides the connection with the previous sentence. Here, *id* refers to Hamilcar's offer to take Hannibal with him on his military campaign.

ne dubitaret: indirect command after *petere*.

ducere: supply an object – 'to take me'.

si ... dederis: *dederis* is future perfect indicative, as is common when the conditional clause refers to a future action which needs to have been completed before the main clause action takes place. It is best to translate it, however, as an English present tense, in keeping with the English idiom to use a present indicative in subordinate clauses which refer to future time.

tenentem: supply *me*.

fore: an alternative form for the future infinitive of *sum*.

id ... ius iurandum ... datum: all these words agree and are the object of *conservavi*; *ius iurandum* means a formal oath and so: 'I have kept that formal oath given ...'.

dubium ... quin ... sim futurus: *quin* + subjunctive explains the area of doubt: '... doubtful that I will be ...'.

reliquo tempore: ablative to show time within which: 'during my remaining time', i.e. 'for the rest of my life'.

quare: 'for this reason'.

quid: note that the pronoun *quis, quis, quid* means 'anyone, anything' when it is used after *ne, num, nisi* or *si*.

si quid amice ... cogitabis: very literally, 'if you think anything in a friendly way' but in more idiomatic English, 'if you have any friendly thoughts'.

si me celaris: *celaris* is the shortened form of the future perfect indicative, *celaveris*. The object needs to be understood from context – i.e. 'if you hide [your thoughts]'. *me* is an accusative of respect – 'as for me', i.e. 'as far as I am concerned'.

cum ... parabis: when *cum* introduces a clause that is purely temporal (i.e. it means 'when' without any flavour of 'since'), it is followed by an indicative.

te ipsum frustraberis: 'you will frustrate yourself', i.e. 'you will get nowhere'.

in eo: the pronoun picks up on *bellum*. Hannibal's point is that Antiochus will only be successful if he puts Hannibal in charge of any military campaign against the Romans.

hac igitur ... profectus est: Nepos wraps up his anecdote by returning to its beginning, i.e. the moment when Hannibal set out to Spain with his father (and swore eternal hatred of the Romans). This allows for a neat transition to Chapter 3, which begins with Hasdrubal's death.

Chapter 3

cuius: when *qui, quae, quod* is used to introduce a sentence, it is best translated as 'he', 'she', 'it', 'this' or as the noun it represents. Here: 'after Hamilcar's death'. Hamilcar died in 229 BC.

Hasdrubale: this refers to Hasbrubal, Hannibal's brother-in-law (not to be confused with Hasbrubal Barca, Hannibal's brother).

hoc quoque interfecto: Nepos uses pronouns more often than idiomatic English does; *hoc*, therefore, is more idiomatically translated with a noun instead: 'when Hasdrubal too had died'. Hasdrubal died in 221 BC.

id: the neuter pronoun here represents the event conveyed by the previous sentence: 'this decision was ...'.

Carthaginem: notice that the names of towns do not require a preposition when the meaning is motion towards, away from or position at. The accusative case shows that the meaning is 'to Carthage'.

minor V et XX annis natus: *natus* means 'aged ...' and so here, 'less than twenty-five years old'.

cum Hasdrubale fratre: Nepos includes the noun *fratre* to make it clear that this is Hannibal's brother (rather than his brother-in-law Hasdrubal, now dead).

foederatam civitatem: Nepos writes from the Roman perspective, and so this means a state allied to the Romans.

ad Alpes: these words have been promoted ahead of their clause's conjunction (*posteaquam*). In English, it is best to translate *posteaquam* first.

praeter Herculem Graium: the reference to the great mythical hero Hercules raises Hannibal's achievements to epic proportions. According to legend, Hercules had crossed into Italy after taking the sun god's cattle. While there, Hercules defeated the fire-breathing monster Cacus in the territory which would one day become the city of Rome. Sacrifices to honour Hercules for this were a significant ritual in the Roman religious calendar.

quo facto: this refers to Hercules' success in crossing the Alps. In idiomatic English, 'since he did this'.

is ... saltus: the demonstrative pronoun *is* is used to refer to *saltus*: 'that mountain pass is called the Greek pass'.

Alpicos: supply a noun from the number and gender of this adjective: 'the Alpine men'.

concidit: sentence returns to Hannibal and he is the subject of this verb.

effecit ut: *ut* + subjunctive here provides the object for *effecit*: 'he brought it about that . . .'.

ea . . . qua . . . hac: these are all feminine ablative singular and all require a noun like *via* to be understood: 'by that route', 'a route by which', 'by this route'.

elephantus ornatus: 'an equipped elephant', i.e. an elephant laden with military gear.

unus homo inermis: Nepos' point is that Hannibal opened up a route which made it possible for a whole military expedition to pass through (including elephants and all their equipment) in places where previously a man without any baggage at all (hence 'unarmed') could scarcely crawl his way through.

in Italiamque pervenit: *-que* is usually attached to the word before which it is to be translated; here, the prepositional phrase *in Italiamque* is taken as one unit, hence the position of *-que* at the end of the phrase. English idiom, however, does not require a preposition after 'reach', therefore the translation is 'and he reached Italy'.

Chapter 4

Nepos offers a fast-paced summary of Hannibal's initial victories in Italy. These were the battle at Lake Trebia in 218 BC, Lake Trasimene in 217 BC and then Cannae in 216 BC, where Hannibal defeated two consular armies.

cum hoc eodem: the pronouns refer to Publius Cornelius Scipio. Hannibal fought against him for a second time at Clastidium.

Clastidi: locative to show *place where* – 'at Clastidium'.

apud Padum: 'near the river Po'.

decernit . . . dimittit: note the dramatic present tenses. This technique is common in Latin prose and is often called the 'historic present tense'. Idiomatic English would more naturally use a past tense here.

saucium . . . fugatum: the number and gender of these words show that they describe Publius Cornelius Scipio; English requires us to add a pronoun: 'Hannibal dispatched him wounded and . . . routed'.

tertio: 'for a third time'.

cum collega Tiberio Longo: Scipio had been wounded in the previous battle and so is assisted here by his consular colleague, Tiberius Longus.

adversus eum: i.e. Hannibal.

conseruit: Hannibal is now the subject.

hoc itinere: the ablative denotes time within which – 'during this journey'.

dextro: understand *oculo* with this adjective.

qua valetudine: the relative pronoun used at the start of a sentence is often best translated by a demonstrative pronoun – 'by this ill health'.

cum: 'although'.

C. Centenium praetor: the accusative requires us to reuse the verb *occidit*.

cum delecta manu: Centenius had with him 4,000 elite cavalrymen.

duo consules: two consuls led the Roman forces at the battle of Cannae, commanding an army much bigger than Hannibal's. Hannibal's impressive victory was his greatest military success against the Romans.

The historian Livy estimates that 48,000 Romans were killed and 20,000 captured; Polybius estimates the death toll to be 70,000. Whatever the numbers, ancient sources agree that Hannibal annihilated the Roman army: Livy states that Terentius Varro, the surviving consul, fled with only fifty men.

exercitus . . . fugavit: *exercitus* is accusative plural and Hannibal is the subject of *fugavit*.

Paulum: i.e. the consul Lucius Aemilius Paulus.

consulares: supply a noun with this adjective from its number and gender: 'men of consular rank'. The accusative case requires us to re-use *occidit* from the previous clause.

Chapter 5

hac pugna pugnata: the battle of Cannae (previously described in Chapter 4).

profectus est: Hannibal is the subject.

reverteretur: notice that *reverto* is a transitive verb and typically therefore requires a direct object. When the meaning is intransitive (e.g. I turn back), the passive voice is used.

Q. Fabius Maximus, dictator Romanus: one of the most fundamental political principles of the Roman Republic was the idea that no one person should hold absolute power. In times of crisis, however, the Romans recognized the expediency of having a sole ruler and a dictator could be appointed. The role of dictator usually lasted for a maximum of six months and a dictator was expected to resign from the post as soon as the crisis was over. Quintus Fabius Maximus was appointed dictator in 217 BC in response to the threat Hannibal posed.

in agro Falerno: 'in the Falernian territory'.

ei: Hannibal.

se obiecit: 'he threw himself in the way of', and so, 'he encountered'.

clausus . . . expedivit: Hannibal is now the subject.

sine ullo detrimento exercitus: remember that the role of the genitive case is to bind one noun to another and, although 'of' is the most common meaning of the genitive, sometimes a different preposition is needed in English. Here, 'without any harm to his army'.

callidissimo imperatori: *callidissimus* because Fabius had managed to trap Hannibal in a confined space, a clever move which should have resulted in significant harm to Hannibal's army.

dedit verba: literally, 'he gave words' but, in meaning, 'he evaded action'. The implication is that Hannibal chose not to engage in battle and this left Quintus Fabius Maximus with words rather than deeds.

namque: Nepos now explains how Hannibal managed to escape from Quintus Fabius Maximus' army, despite his difficult position.

dispalatum: a supine of purpose. The supine can be used in this way after verbs of motion/sending: 'he set a great number of this type loose to wander about'.

quo: when *qui, quae, quod* is used to open a sentence (rather than a subordinate clause), it is best translated as 'this', 'that', 'he', 'she' etc. Here, 'when this unexpected sight had been thrown upon them'.

sit ausus: = *ausus sit*.

non ita multis diebus: 'within not so many days'.

magistrum equitum: the Master of the Horse was a dictator's deputy.

pari ac dictatorem imperio: 'with power equal to the dictator'. *imperium* means the power to command; it was unprecedented for the Romans to appoint – in effect – a co-dictator and the level of power given to Minucius Rufus shows the scale of the crisis facing the Romans. Notice that the adjective – *pari* – has been promoted for emphasis. *dictatorem* is an accusative of respect.

dolo: Nepos highlights again Hannibal's tactical skill in outwitting the Roman commanders.

fugavit: Hannibal is the subject.

absens . . . sustulit: Hannibal was away from his army during this battle, but Nepos makes him the subject of *sustulit*, suggesting that he was still responsible for his army's success. *tollo* usually means 'I lift, raise' but here the meaning is 'dispatch'.

in insidias: Gracchus is believed to have been ambushed while bathing.

M. Claudium Marcellum: Marcellus was one of the most successful military leaders of this period. He won the *spolia opimia*, the highest military honour, for killing a Gallic king in 222 BC and he had twice been successful against Hannibal in the Second Punic War.

pari modo: 'in a similar way', i.e. by ambush.

longum est: 'it is a long task'.

unum satis erit dictum: understand *esse* – 'it will be enough that one thing has been mentioned', i.e. the one thing that Nepos will say (rather than listing details of all the battles) is that – for as long as Hannibal was in Italy – the Romans did not try to fight him in a pitched battle after their defeat at Cannae.

ex quo . . . possit: a generic *qui* clause – '[of the sort] from which it could be understood'.

in acie: 'in pitched battle'.

in campo: 'on open ground'. During Hannibal's time in Italy, there were frequent skirmishes between the Roman and Carthaginian forces, but the Romans did not attempt open battle on level ground, fearing that Hannibal would be able to repeat the devastating damage he had inflicted at the Battle of Cannae.

Chapter 6

invictus: this describes Hannibal, the subject of this sentence.

defensum: a supine to express purpose – 'called back to defend'. Under the leadership of Publius Scipio, the Romans had made the daring move to send their army on the offensive to Africa. The plan was that an attack on Carthage would force Hannibal to return – with his troops – from Italy to Africa. The Romans could then fight him in Africa, but with the advantage their earlier arrival would mean that they were better prepared for the battle than Hannibal. Scipio reasoned – correctly – that this would give them the advantage they needed to win against Hannibal.

filium eius: *eius* refers to Scipo Asina, Roman commander in the battles fought at the rivers Rhône and Po and Lake Trebia (see Chapter 4).

cum hoc: i.e. with Scipio.

impraesentiarum: Nepos' suggestion is that Hannibal did not accept that this marked a long-term surrender, but rather that he needed a truce to create time to regroup and strengthen his forces. Scipio and Hannibal, however, did not agree terms for this truce and this forced an early engagement between the two armies.

quo ... congrederetur: it is usual for a purpose clause containing a comparative (here, the adjective *valentior*) to be introduced by *quo*. English does not match this idiom and so the clause is best translated as 'so that he could ...'.

incredibili dictu: 'incredible to say'. This use of the ablative supine – to qualify an adjective – is one of its most common forms.

apud Zamam: Scipio's victory at Zama marked the turning point for the Romans. Romans are believed to have lost around 2,000 men, but the Carthaginians to have lost nearly 20,000.

biduo et duabus noctibus: the implication is that Hannibal fled without stopping for two days and two nights. The speed of this march highlights both the scale of the defeat, but also Hannibal's skill in moving a defeated army so quickly.

Numidiae: the Numidians had previously fought for the Carthaginians but after Zama they defected to the Roman sides and attacked Hannibal during his flight.

non solum . . . sed etiam: Nepos emphasizes that fact that not only did Hannibal escape the Numidians' ambush but he also managed to overpower their forces.

Hadrumeti: locative – 'at Hadrumetum'.

Chapter 7

cum . . . esset occupatus: a concessive clause – 'although …'. Nepos' point is that, although Hannibal had continued keenly to make preparations for war, the Carthaginians decide to end the conflict.

ille: the pronoun refers to Hannibal.

nihilo setius: 'all the same'. The implication is that, although Hannibal was pro war and the Carthaginians were pro peace, Hannibal continued just the same as the commander of their army.

praefuit: the natural past tense for *sum* and its compounds is the imperfect. The perfect tense is used when something took place but then stopped. Here, therefore, it is a reminder that Hannibal's time in military command would have an end point.

usque ad P. Sulpicium C. Aurelium consules: it was Roman tradition to date years by reference to the consuls. The year here is 200 BC. *usque ad* – 'right up until'.

magistratibus: *magistratus* can refer either to the political or military office held, or the office-holder. Here, the reference is to the consuls: 'with these men in office'.

qui ... agerent: *qui* + subjunctive to denote purpose – 'who were to give ...'.

quod ... fecissent: this causal clause has the subjunctive because it is sub-oblique, i.e. it represents the thoughts that were in the Carthaginians' minds.

ob eamque rem: *-que* introduces this whole phrase – 'and for that reason'.

donarent: the subjunctive shows that the purpose clause continues; idiomatic English requires us to repeat the conjunction: 'and who were to give ...'. Note that *dono* is followed by an accusative (for the recipient) and an ablative (for the gift); compare with, e.g., the English idiom 'I award you with a prize.'

peterent: the purpose clause continues; repeat in English 'and who were to ...'.

ut ... redderentur: an indirect command. The Carthaginians ask that their hostages be held by the Romans at Fregellae and that the Romans return the Carthaginian prisoners.

responsum est: an impersonal passive. The impersonal passive can be loosely translated as 'it was replied' but its most literal meaning takes the action itself as its subject ('a reply was replied'). The most idiomatic translation, therefore, typically uses a noun in order to reflect the focus on the action: 'there was a reply'.

munus ... esse: the accusative and infinitive construction shows that this is reported speech. Idiomatic English requires us to repeat a verb of saying to introduce this: '[the Romans said that] ...'.

obsides ... futuros: supply *esse* and, in English, repeat a verb of saying: 'and they said that the hostages would be ...'.

quo loco: as is often the case, the antecedent for this relative clause has been attracted into the relative clause. The meaning is 'in the location which they requested'.

captivos . . . remissuros: supply *esse* and understand the Carthaginians as the subject of this infinitive – '[but they said that] they would not return the prisoners'.

Hannibalem: object of **haberent** – 'because the Carthaginians still kept Hannibal . . .'.

susceptum . . . foret: an alternative form for *susceptum esset*.

nomini Romano: 'to the Roman name', i.e. to the Roman people.

cum imperio: 'with the right to command', i.e. Hannibal was still in a powerful position militarily.

hoc responso Carthaginienses cognito: the word order here has promoted *Carthaginienses* for emphasis. In English: 'the Carthaginians, when they had heard this answer . . .'.

huc: promoted ahead of the conjunction *ut* since it provides the connection to the previous sentence. In English, however, it is best translated after *ut*: 'when he returned there'. NB demonstrative pronouns and adverbs add emphasis; conventionally *huc* is translated as 'to here' because it is a more emphatic form than *illuc* ('to there') but sometimes English idiom requires a different translation.

rex: Nepos uses Roman political vocabulary. The Carthaginian title was *suffes*; two *suffetes* were appointed each year as the most senior non-military officials. The Carthaginians' decision reflects their wish to appease the Romans by removing Hannibal from military power while at the same time acknowledging Hannibal's importance within their community.

praetor: again, Nepos uses Roman political vocabulary but the reference is to Hannibal's appointment as commander of the Carthaginian army.

anno secundo et vicesimo: 'in the twenty-second year', i.e. twenty-two years into his time as general. The date is 196 BC.

ut . . . sic: 'for just as . . ., so too . . .'.

ut . . . consules: this clause is missing its finite verb; understand *sunt*.

Romae . . . Carthagine: both these words are in the locative case – 'in Rome . . . at Carthage'.

annui bini reges: 'two kings, each lasting for a year'. *bini* is used to mean 'two each', i.e. two each year. Nepos uses Roman political vocabulary to refer to the *suffetes*, the most senior non-military Carthaginian officials.

pari diligentia se Hannibal praebuit: very literally, 'Hannibal showed himself [to be] with equivalent care', i.e. Hannibal displayed the same diligence as *suffes* as he had as military commander. The ablatives are descriptive.

ac: 'as'

effecit . . . ut . . .: 'he brought it about that', i.e. 'he achieved the result that . . .'.

quae . . . penderetur: a purpose clause – 'which was to be paid . . .'.

ex foedere: 'in accordance with the treaty'. This refers to the peace treaty, a condition within which would have been that the Carthaginians pay an annual sum in reparation to the Romans.

quae . . . reponeretur: a generic clause – '[of the sort] which could be laid aside . . .'.

M. Claudio L. Furio consulibus: 196 BC.

hos . . . missos: understand *esse*: 'Hannibal, having thought that these men had been sent'.

sui exposcendi gratia: *sui* is the genitive of *se* – 'for the sake of him being demanded for surrender', i.e. 'to demand that the Carthaginians surrender him to them'.

senatus: here, in the sense of an official meeting – 'before a meeting was given to them'.

ad Antiochum: the text now catches up with the initial anecdote from Chapter 2 and Hannibal's alliance with King Antiochus in Syria.

hac re palam facta: 'with this thing having been made public', i.e. when everyone found out about Hannibal's flight.

quae . . . comprehenderent: purpose clause – 'which were to seize him'.

publicarunt . . . iudicarunt: these are shortened forms of the perfect indicative (*publicaverunt, iudicaverunt*).

exulem: 'an exile', i.e. an outcast from their community.

Chapter 8

L. Cornelio Q. Minucio consulibus: 193 BC.

in finibus Cyrenaeorum: Cyrene was an Egyptian province, to the east of Carthage's territory in North Africa. Hannibal has risked a return to Africa, but he does not yet risk a return to Carthaginian soil.

si forte: a type of purpose clause – 'to see if by chance . . .'.

ad bellum: 'to war against the Romans'.

Antiochi spe fiduciaque: the ablatives play a causal role – 'because of their belief and confidence in Antiochus'. Hannibal hopes that the alliance with Antiochus has created a powerful enough partner to give the Carthaginians hope of success and confidence in the alliance.

cui: this refers to Antiochus.

id: this refers to Hannibal's arrival in Cyrene and his attempt to regroup with his brother there.

Magonem eadem, qua fratrem . . . affecerunt poena: the verb *affecerunt* needs to be used with both accusatives – 'they treated Mago with the same punishment with which they treated his brother', i.e. the Carthaginians decided to punish Mago in the same way as Hannibal, even though Mago was not in Carthage at the time to defend himself.

illi: this pronoun refers to Hannibal and Mago, both of whom are now outcasts from Carthaginian society and therefore have no option but to set sail again for Syria. Hannibal makes it there but Mago dies before he arrives.

duplex memoria: 'a double account', i.e. there are two different accounts of why Mago died.

alii . . . alii . . . scriptum reliquerunt: 'some [authors] have left a written account that . . ., but others have left a written account that . . .'.

interfectum eum: supply *esse*. This indirect statement needs to be used with each *alii* clause. *eum* refers to Mago.

si . . . voluisset: 'if he had wanted . . .'.

tam . . . quam . . .: this pair of adverbs creates a correlation – 'to that extent . . . to the extent to which . . .', i.e. if Antiochus had shown the same degree of enthusiasm for waging war as he had done for initiating it. The implication was that Hannibal had been able to persuade Antiochus to sign up to the prospect of undertaking a military campaign to Italy, but not actually to follow his advice to carry out the military campaign itself.

Thermopylis: Thermopylae was in Greece and the site of the famous Spartan resistance against the Persians in the fifth century BC. Antiochus was defeated by the Romans there in 191 BC and forced to return to Syria.

de summa imperii: 'about the supremacy of command', i.e. ultimate power. The battle with the Romans was, in effect, a battle to establish which community would be the dominant power in the Mediterranean.

dimicasset: a shortened form for the pluperfect subjunctive *dimicavisset* – 'he would have fought'.

quem: connecting relative, referring to Antiochus and the subject within the accusative and infinitive indirect statement.

videbat: Hannibal is the subject. Nepos' point is that, although Hannibal could see that Antiochus was not taking the campaign seriously enough, Hannibal did everything he could to achieve success.

nulla deseruit in re: *nulla* is neuter plural and a noun needs to be understood from its number and gender – 'he abandoned no efforts in the matter', i.e. he did everything he could.

his: ablative of means – 'with these [he fought against the Rhodians' fleet]'.

quo . . . multitudine: *quo* is a connecting relative and best translated as 'by this multitude'.

cum: 'although'.

sui: understand a noun from the number and gender of this adjective – 'his men'.

quo cornu: *cornu* (the antecedent for *quo*) has been attracted into the relative clause but is best translated before it: 'on the wing in which . . .'.

Chapter 9

quod: this relative pronoun refers to the event expressed in the previous clause; idiomatic English requires us to add a noun to convey this – 'something which'.

accidisset: subjunctive to express a potential action: '[something which] would have happened'.

sui . . . potestatem: the pronoun *sui* is genitive because it is tied to another noun and, although 'of' is the preposition most frequently used in English to connect one noun with another, sometimes a different preposition is needed. Here, 'power over him', i.e. if he had given them the opportunity to capture him.

quo se conferret: an indirect question with *consideraret* – 'so that he could consider where he could take himself to'. The action is in future time, but the imperfect subjunctive is used because there is a flavour of a possible rather than a definite action.

vir omnium callidissimus: this phrase is in apposition to the subject of *vidit* (Hannibal) – 'Hannibal – the most cunning man of all –'.

nisi quid providisset: *quid* usually means 'anything' after *nisi*, but the idiomatic English equivalent here is 'unless he made some plan in advance'.

magnam . . . pecuniam: 'much money'.

tale consilium: *tale* refers forwards to the explanation that follows – 'a plan of the following sort'.

summas: this adjective requires us to understand *amphoras* – 'the tops of the amphoras'.

praesentibus principibus: 'with the leaders present', i.e. in the presence of the (local) leaders.

credere: *credo* can mean either 'I trust a person (dative)' or I entrust something (accusative) to a person (dative)'. Here, the meaning is 'entrust'.

in propatulo domi: the endings for *domus* are a mixture of second declension and fourth declension. **domi** is the genitive singular.

abicit: the verb implies a careless throwing away; Nepos' point is that Hannibal acted as if these statues were worthless.

tam . . . quam . . .: these work as a pair. Very literally, the meaning is '[not] to that extent . . . the extent to which . .', and in idiomatic English: '[not] so much [from the others] as [from Hannibal]'. Nepos' point is that the Gortynians' main objective was to prevent Hannibal returning to take back his wealth.

tolleret . . . duceret: understand *amphoras* as the object of both these verbs.

Chapter 10

suis rebus: 'with his wealth'.

Poenus: 'the Carthaginian', i.e. Hannibal.

ad Prusiam: Prusias, king of Bithynia, would ultimately betray Hannibal to the Romans.

apud quem: 'with him'.

quem: connecting relative (and so promoted ahead of *cum*) and the accusative subject of *esse* – '[when he saw] that he was ...'.

dissidebat ab eo ... Eumenes: Eumenes, king of Pergamum, does not form an alliance with Hannibal against the Romans. Notice the Latin idiom: 'be separate from' and so 'on a different side to ...'.

quo: a causal ablative; the pronoun is neuter singular, referring to the fact of Eumenes' alliance with the Romans – 'for which reason ...'.

cupiebat ... Hannibal: Hannibal is the subject, but the word order rather awkwardly separates *eum ... opprimi*.

quem si removisset: *quem* is a connecting relative and so best translated as 'him'. *removisset* is subjunctive because it is a subordinate clause in indirect speech; the pluperfect tense represents the future perfect of the original direct speech, i.e. Hannibal's thoughts ('if I remove him, everything else will be easier').

ad hunc interficiundum: *interficiundum* is an alternative spelling for the gerundive *interficiendum*.

talem ... rationem: 'the following reasoning'. *ratio* refers to a thought process, and the Latin that follows details Hannibal's plan and the reasons for it.

classe ... erant decreturi: for vividness, Nepos relays Hannibal's thought process as direct speech: 'they were about to decide [the matter] by a naval battle'. Notice that *decreturi* requires the reader to supply an object and the instrumental ablative *classe* is used to indicate a naval battle.

superabatur: this refers to previous battles – '[previously] he had been overwhelmed ...'. Notice that, although the English idiom is to use a pluperfect, Nepos uses the more vivid imperfect tense.

erat pugnandum: an impersonal gerundive of obligation – 'it had to be fought'.

par ... armis: 'equal in weapons', i.e. Eumenes' alliance with the Romans meant that he was much better resourced for this battle than Hannibal was.

imperavit ... serpentes ... colligi: unusually, *imperavit* is followed here by an infinitive rather than the more common *ut* + subjunctive construction.

venenatas: technically a ppp. ('poisoned') but in English, 'poisonous'.

harum: the pronoun provides the connection with the previous sentence, but it is best translated after *cum*.

omnes ut: the adjective has been promoted for emphasis but it is best translated after *ut*. *omnes* requires the reader to supply a noun from number and gender, i.e. 'everyone'.

in unam ... navem: the word order emphasizes *navem*. *unus* – 'one' – is often used in a way which is closer to the English adverb 'only'.

tantum satis: *tantum* – like many demonstrative words – is often used for emphasis. Here, 'entirely enough'.

habeant: the subjunctive shows that this is a reported command – 'they were to consider ...'.

id: the neuter singular pronoun refers to the act of defending themselves and, therefore, their ultimate victory.

illos ... consecuturos: the indirect speech continues. Supply *esse* and a verb to introduce the indirect statement – '[he said that] they would achieve ...'.

serpentium multitudine: *multitudine* is a causal ablative – 'because of the ...'.

rex: this noun has been promoted for emphasis but belongs inside the indirect question *in qua nave veheretur*.

se facturum: supply *esse* and a verb of saying to introduce this indirect statement. *facturum* has as its object the clause *ut scirent* which then leads into the opening indirect question: '[he said that] he would make it happen that they knew in which ship ...'.

quem: connecting relative (referring to King Eumenes) and best translated as 'him'.

cepissent ... interfecissent: subjunctives because the subordinate clause is within indirect speech; the pluperfect subjunctive represents the future perfect of the original direct speech.

magno ... praemio: a predicative dative – '[it would be] a great boon', i.e. if they captured or killed Eumenes, they would have a big reward.

iis pollicetur: *iis* is dative as the indirect object of *pollicetur*.

fore: supply *hoc* as its subject: 'he promised that this [i.e. the action of capturing/killing] would be ...'.

Chapter 11

quarum: connecting relative and best translated as 'of these fleets'.

priusquam ... daretur: the subjunctive adds a sense of purpose – 'before the signal for battle could be given'.

ut palam faceret: 'so that he could openly show ...'.

suis: supply a noun from number and gender: 'to his men'.

quo loco: ablative to show 'place where' – 'in which place'.

qui: connecting relative and best translated as 'he' or 'this man'.

nemo dubitabat, quin . . .: 'no one doubted that . . .'. *quin* + subjunctive is often used after verbs of doubting.

ducis nave declarata suis: ablative absolute. Supply a noun from the number and gender of **suis** – 'to his own men'.

quae . . . pertinerent: the clause is generic, and an antecedent needs to be supplied from the number and gender of *quae* – 'things of the sort which were relevant to . . .'.

ad irridendum eum: purpose – 'for the purpose of mocking him'. The letter contains no serious offer of peace: its purpose was to allow Hannibal's fleet to identify the king's ship but Nepos implies that Hannibal had written some insults into it as an additional, aggravating piece of strategy.

cuius: connecting relative and thus promoted ahead of its conjunction *etsi*; *cuius* is best translated 'of this letter'.

Hannibalis praecepto: *praecepto* is a causal ablative – 'because of Hannibal's instructions'.

quorum vim: *quorum* is a connecting relative and best translated as 'the force of these men'. *quorum vim* has been promoted to provide connection with the previous sentence but belongs in the *cum* clause.

quam consecutus non esset: *quam* refers to *salutem* and the pluperfect subjunctive shows that this is a past time potential statement – 'he would not have achieved this safety'.

reliquae Pergamenae naves: promoted for emphasis but best translated after *cum*.

in eas: this refers to the Pergamenian ships.

quae iacta: *quae* is a connecting relative and best translated as 'these'.

initio: ablative of time – 'at first/initially'.

concitarunt: a shortened form of the perfect indicative *concitaverunt*.

neque . . . poterat intellegi: 'nor could it be understood'. This impersonal construction with its passive infinitive creates emphasis on the action of understanding.

conspexerunt: the Pergamenian navy is the subject.

quid potissimum vitarent: a deliberative question, implying that no answer can be found to the question and offering, therefore, a tone of despair: '[since they did not see] what they were to avoid most of all'. The Pergamenian fleet does not know whether the priority is to deal with the snakes or attack Hannibal's men and – since their king has fled and they now have no leader – they lack direction.

consilio: 'by strategy'.

neque tum solum: 'and not only on that occasion'.

Chapter 12

quae: connecting relative – 'these things' – and best translated after *dum*.

accidit . . . ut . . .: 'it happened that . . .'.

Romae: locative – 'at Rome'.

id: this pronoun refers to the news that Hannibal was in Prusias' kingdom.

patres conscripti: 'conscript fathers' was a common term for the Roman senators. The name takes its root from the very first senate, set up by Romulus and comprised of the fathers of the leading families.

qui . . . existimarent: the subjunctive adds a causal flavour to this clause – 'in as much as they believed . . .'.

sine insidiis: 'without ambush', i.e. the Romans believe that they are always at risk of a surprise attack from Hannibal.

se . . . futuros: understand *esse*.

in his Flamininum: understand *miserunt* – 'and among these [they sent] Flaminius'.

qui . . . peterent: purpose clause – 'who were to ask . . .'.

sibi: this refers to the Romans.

his . . . negare: the direct object (i.e. their request) is implied and *his* is the indirect object – '[did not dare] to deny these men their request'.

illud: 'the following thing'.

ne . . . postularent: this clause explains the thing that Prusias refused to do. An idiomatic English translation requires us to supply 'and he asked': 'and he asked that they should not demand . . .'.

id a se fieri: the indirect statement acts as the object of *ne . . . postularent* – '[. . . that they should not ask] that this happen by his hands'.

quod . . . esset: the verb is subjunctive because the clause is within indirect speech.

ipsi . . . comprehenderent: the subjunctive here relays a command within extended indirect speech. English requires the reader to add a verb to introduce it: 'and he said that they should arrest him themselves'.

si possent: subjunctive because this is a subordinate clause within indirect speech.

locum . . . inventuros: supply *eos* and *esse* and – for idiomatic English – add a verb to introduce the indirect statement: 'and he said that they would find . . .'.

uno loco: ablative of place – 'in one place'.

muneri: a predicative dative – 'as a gift'.

aedificarat: a shortened form of the pluperfect *aedificaverat*. The suggestion is that Hannibal had done further construction work in order to make sure that escape routes were available to him on all sides.

exitus: accusative plural and the object of *haberet*. *aedificii* is genitive, marking its connection with *exitus* – 'escape routes from the building'.

ne usu veniret, quod accidit: understand *id* as the antecedent of *quod* and use this as the subject of *veniret* – '[fearing] that in practice the event which did take place would happen'. *venio* here has the meaning of 'come into being/arrive'.

huc: promoted for emphasis because it supplies the connection to the previous sentence, but best translated after *cum*.

plures ... armatos: supply a noun from the number and gender of this adjective – 'more armed men'.

praeter consuetudinem: 'beyond custom', i.e. 'than usual'.

qui: a connecting relative referring to Hannibal and best translated as 'Hannibal'.

puer: promoted for emphasis but best translated after *cum*.

omnes exitus occupatos: understand *esse*.

sensit: Hannibal is the subject.

id ... factum: understand *esse*.

se peti: the indirect statement continues.

neque sibi diutius vitam esse retinendam: the gerundive is a passive form of the verb, but English prefers the active voice here – '[and he realized] that he should not hold on to life any longer'. Notice that the gerundive of obligation takes a dative of agent (here, *sibi*).

quam: connecting relative, referring to *vitam* and best translated after *ne* – 'and so that he would not hand over his life ...'.

memor pristinarum virtutum: Nepos' point is that Hannibal remembers his past achievements and does not want, therefore, the degradation of whatever sort of end the Romans are intending for him.

consuerat: a shortened form of the pluperfect *consueverat*.

Chapter 13

quibus ... interierit: an indirect question; notice that the ablative *quibus consulibus* denotes time within which – 'during which consuls' tenure he died'.

non convenit: 'there is no consensus'.

Atticus ... Polybius ... Sulpicius: Nepos refers to three sources. Atticus lived in the first century BC and was a great friend of the orator Cicero; Atticus' account is now lost. Polybius lived in the second century BC and was a Greek historian who wrote an extensive account of Rome's rise to dominance in the Mediterranean. Sulpicius Blitho was Nepos' contemporary; his account is now lost. Atticus dates Hannibal's death as 183 BC, Polybius as 181 BC and Sulpicius Blitho as 182 BC.

Vocabulary

An asterisk * denotes a word in OCR's Defined Vocabulary List for AS.

* **a, ab** (+ *ablative*)	from, by
abicio, abicere, abieci, abiectum	cast away, dispose of
* **absum, abesse, afui**	be away, be distant
* **ac, atque**	and
accedo, accedere, accessi, accessum	approach
* **accido, accidere, accidi**	happen
* **accipio, accipere, accepi, acceptum**	accept
* **acer, acris, acre**	keen, sharp, fierce
* **acies -ei** *f.*	battleline
acquiesco, acquiescere, acquievi, acquietum	die
* **ad** (+ *accusative*)	to, for the purpose of
adduco, adducere, adduxi, adductum	lead to
* **adeo**	so greatly, to such an extent
adeo, adire, adii, aditum	approach
adiungo, adiungere, adiunxi, adiunctum	add
adorior, adoriri, adortus sum	attack
adversarius -i *m.*	opponent
* **adversus** (+ *accusative*)	against
* **aedificium -i** *n.*	building
* **aedifico -are**	build
aeneus -a -um	made of bronze
* **aequus -a -um**	equal

AS

aerarium -i *n.*	treasury
aetas, aetatis *f.*	age
afficio, afficere, affeci, affectum	affect, treat
Africa -ae *f.*	Africa
* **ager, agri** *m.*	territory
* **ago, agere, egi, actum**	do, carry out
alias	at another time
alienus -a -um	of another, of a stranger
* **alii . . . alii**	some . . . others
* **aliquis, aliquid**	someone, something
aliquot	some number, several
* **alius, alia, aliud**	other
Alpes, Alpium *f.*	the Alps
Alpicus -a -um	Alpine
* **alter, altera, alterum**	the other (of two)
amice	in a friendly manner
amicitia -ae *f.*	friendship
* **amicus** -i, *m.*	friend
amphora -ae *f.*	amphora (a two-handled jar)
amplius	more than
angustiae -arum *f. pl.*	narrowness
anima -ae *f.*	life, soul
* **animus** -i *m.*	mind
annalis -is *m.*	record of a year, annal
* **annus** -i *m.*	year
annuus -a -um	lasting for a year
* **ante** (+ *accusative*)	before
* **antea**	before, previously
antecedo, antecedere, antecessi, antecessum	precede, surpass
Antiochus -i *m.*	Antiochus III, king of Syria
* **appareo, apparere, apparui**	appear
apparo -are	prepare
appello -are	name
Appenninus -i *m.*	the Apennine mountain range

* **apud** (+ *accusative*)	among, at the house of, at
Apulia -ae *f.*	Apulia, a region in southern Italy
* **ara** -ae *f.*	altar
arbitrium -i *n.*	decision, judgement
arbitror -ari	think
* **argentum** -i *n.*	silver
* **arma** -orum, *n. pl.*	arms, weapons,
armo -are	arm, set to arms
* **ascendo, ascendere, ascendi, ascensum**	go on board
Asia -ae *f.*	Asia
* **at**	but
Atticus -i *m.*	Atticus (a historian and great friend to Cicero)
* **audeo, audere, ausus sum**	dare
aureus -a -um	golden
aurum -i *n.*	gold
* **aut**	or, either
* **autem**	but, however
avaritia -ae *f.*	greed
bellicosus -a -um	warlike
bello, bellare	wage war
* **bellum** -i *n.*	war
* **bene**	well
biduum -i *n.*	a two day period
bini -ae -a	two (at a time)
Bithynia -ae *f.*	Bithynia (a country in north-west Asia Minor)
Bithynii -orum *m. pl.*	Bithynians
* **bona** -orum *n. pl.*	goods, possessions
caduceus -i *m.*	herald's staff
C. Aurelius, C. Aurelii *m.*	Gaius Aurelius Cotta (consul in 200 BC)
callidus -a -um	clever, cunning
* **campus** -i *m.*	(battle) plain, field

Cannensis -e	relating to Cannae, at Cannae
* **capio, capere, cepi, captum**	take, make (a plan), capture
* **captivus -i** *m.*	captive, prisoner
Capua -ae *f.*	Capua (the chief town of Campania, now Santa Maria di Capua)
Carthaginiensis -e	Carthaginian
Carthago, Carthaginis *f.*	Carthage
castellum -i *n.*	castle, fortress
* **castra -orum** *n. pl.*	camp
casus -us *m.*	chance
* **causa -ae** *f.*	reason
celeriter	quickly
* **celo -are**	hide, conceal
ceno -are	dine
* **ceteri -ae -a**	the rest, the others
circiter	about
circumdo, circumdare, circumdedi, circumdatum	surround
circumeo, circu(m)ire, circu(m)ii, circuitum	go round
circumvenio, circumvenire, circumveni, circumventum	surround
* **civis -is** *m./f.*	citizen
* **civitas, civitatis** *f.*	state
* **clam**	secretly
clandestinus -a -um	secret
classiarii -orum *m. pl.*	naval forces
classis -is *f.*	fleet
Clastidium -i *n.*	Clastidium, a town in Gaul (now Chiasteggio)
claudo, claudere, clausi, clausum	enclose, block in
Cn. Baebius Tamphilus, Cn. Baebii Tamphili *m.*	Gnaeus Baebius Tamphilus (consul in 181 BC)
* **coepi, coepisse, coeptum**	began

Vocabulary

* **cogito -are**	think
* **cognosco, cognoscere, cognovi, cognitum**	get to know
cohortatio, cohortationis *f.*	encouragement
collega -ae *m.*	colleague
colligo, colligere, collegi, collectum	gather together
colloco -are	place
colloquium -i *n.*	conversation, conference
commemoro -are	mention
* **committo, committere, commisi, commissum**	begin (battle)
* **comparo -are**	obtain
comperio, comperire, comperi, compertum	find out
compleo, complere, complevi, completum	fill up
complures -ium	several
compono, componere, composui, compositum	settle
comprehendo, comprehendere, comprehendi, comprehensum	seize, arrest
comprobo -are	approve fully
concido, concidere, concidi, concisum	destroy, cut down
concilio -are	bring together, unite
concito -are	stir up
concurro, concurrere, concurri, concursum	charge
concursus -us *m.*	(military) charge, attack
condicio, condicionis *f.*	condition, agreement
* **confero, conferre, contuli, conlatum**	transfer
* **conficio, conficere, confeci, confectum**	complete

A S

confligo, confligere, conflixi, conflictum	come into conflict
congredior, congredi, congressus sum	meet, fight against
conicio, conicere, conieci, coniectum	throw together
* conor -ari	try
consequor, consequi, consecutus sum	catch up with, obtain
consero manum	join in hand-to-hand combat
consero, conserere, conserui, consertum	join
conservo -are	preserve
considero -are	consider
* consilium -i *n.*	council, meeting, plan
* conspicio, conspicere, conspexi, conspectum	notice
* constituo, constituere, constitui, constitutum	establish
consuesco, consuescere, consuevi, consuetum	be accustomed
consuetudo, consuetudinis *f.*	custom
* consul, consulis *m.*	consul
consularis, consulare	of consular rank
consultum -i *n.*	decree (of the senate)
contraho, contrahere, contraxi, contractum	collect
convenio, convenire, conveni, conventum	come together, agree
convoco -are	call together
* copiae -arum *f. pl.*	forces
cornu -us *n.*	horn (of an animal), wing (of an army)
corona -ae *f.*	crown

corrumpo, corrumpere, corrupi, corruptum	corrupt
* **credo, credere, credidi, creditum** (+ *dative*)	entrust
creo -are	create
Creta -ae *f.*	Crete
Cretensis -e	Cretan
* **cum**	when, since, although
* **cum** (+ *ablative*)	with
* **cunctus -a -um**	all
cupiditas, cupiditatis *f.*	desire
* **cupio, cupere, cupivi, cupitum**	desire, want
* **cura -ae** *f.*	care
* **custodio, custodire, custodivi, custoditum**	guard
Cyrenaei -orum *m. pl.*	the inhabitants of Cyrene
* **de** (+ *ablative*)	about
* **debeo, debere, debui, debitum**	ought
debilito -are	weaken
decerno, decernere, decrevi, decretum	decide, settle
declaro -are	reveal
dedo, dedere, -didi, -ditum	give up, surrender
deduco, deducere, deduxi, deductum	draw a ship down to the sea, lead to
* **defendo, defendere, defendi, defensum**	defend
defero, deferre, detuli, delatum	report
defero, deferre, detuli, delatum	hand over, refer
* **deinde**	then, next
deligo -are	tie, bind
deligo, deligere, delegi, delectum	pick, choose
depono, deponere, deposui, depositum	lay down

desero, deserere, deserui, desertum	abandon
desisto, desistere, destiti, destitum	desist, cease
* **despero -are**	despair
detrimentum -i *n.*	harm, injury
devinco, devincere, devici, devictum	conquer thoroughly
* **dexter, dextra, dextrum**	right, right-hand
Diana -ae *f.*	Diana, goddess of hunting and the moon
* **dico, dicere, dixi, dictum**	say
dictator, dictatoris *m.*	dictator
* **dies -ei** *m./f.*	day
dilectus -us *m.*	levy, recruitment of troops
diligentia -ae *f.*	carefulness, care
* **dimitto, dimittere, dimisi, dimissum**	send away
* **discedo, discedere, discessi, discessum**	depart, leave
disicio, disicere, disieci, disiectum	tear apart
dispalor -ari	wander about
dissideo, dissidere, dissedi, dissessum	be separate from, disagree with
* **diu**	for a long time
diutius	any longer
divinus -a -um	divine
* **do, dare, dedi, datum**	give
* **dolus -i** *m.*	trick
domesticus -a -um	domestic, at home
* **domus -us** *f.*	house, home
dono -are	present someone (*accusative*) with something (*ablative*)
* **dubito -are**	doubt, hesitate

dubium -i *n.*	doubt
* **dubius -a -um**	doubtful
* **duco, ducere, duxi, ductum**	lead, take
* **dum**	while
duo, duae, duo	two
duplex, duplicis	two-fold
* **dux, ducis** *m.*	leader
* **e, ex** (+ *ablative*)	from, out of
* **efficio, efficere, effeci, effectum**	carry out, accomplish, achieve
* **effugio, effugere, effugi**	escape, escape from
* **ego, mei**	I, me
* **egredior, egredi, egressus sum**	go out
elephantus -i *m./f.*	elephant
* **enim**	for
enumero -are	count up
* **eo, ire, i(v)i, itum**	go
eodem	to the same place
* **epistula -ae** *f.*	letter
equitatus -us *m.*	cavalry
* **erga** (+ *accusative*)	towards
error, erroris *m.*	mistake, deception
* **et**	and, both
* **etiam**	even
etiamnum	still, yet
Etruria -ae *f.*	Etruria, a district in north-west Italy
* **etsi**	although, even if
Eumenes, Eumenis *m.*	Eumenes, king of Pergamum
excedo, excedere, excessi, excessum	go away, leave
excio, excire, excivi, excitum	summon to help
exeo, exire, exii, exitum	get out, become known
exerceo, exercere, exercui, exercitum	make strong, train
* **exercitus -us** *m.*	army

exhaurio, exhaurire, exhausi, exhaustum	drain, finish
existimo -are	hold an opinion, believe
exitus -us *m.*	exit, way out
expedio, expedire, expedivi, expeditum	disentangle, set free
exploro -are	investigate
exposco, exposcere, expoposci	demand the surrender (of a person)
expugno -are	take by storm
* **extra** (+ *accusative*)	beyond
exul, exulis *m./f.*	an exile
* **facilis -e**	easy
* **facio, facere, feci, factum**	make, do
facultas, facultatis *f.*	resources
Falernus -a -um	Falernian (referring to an area of land to the north of the Campanian region)
* **fama -ae** *f.*	rumour
* **fero, ferre, tuli, latum**	carry
fictilis -e	made of clay
fides -ei *f.*	loyalty
* **fides -ei** *f.*	loyalty
fiducia -ae *f.*	confidence, trust
* **filius -i** *m.*	son
* **finis -is** *m.*	territory (*pl.*)
* **fio, fieri, factus sum**	happen
foederatus -a -um	allied
* **foedus, foederis** *n.*	treaty
foris, foris *f.*	door
* **forte**	by chance
* **fortis -e**	brave, strong
fortitudo, fortitudinis *f.*	physical strength, courage
fortuito	by chance
* **fortuna -ae** *f.*	fortune

* **frater, fratris** *m.*	brother
Fregellae -arum *f. pl.*	Fregellae (an Italian town, now Ceprano)
* **frustra**	in vain
frustror -ari	disappoint, frustrate, let down
* **fuga -ae** *f.*	flight, escape
fugo -are	rout, drive away
fundamentum -i *n.*	foundation
C. Centenius, C. Centenii *m.*	Gaius Centenius
C. Flaminius, C. Flaminii *m.*	Gaius Flaminius (a consul)
C. Terentius Varro, C. Terentii Varronis *m.*	Gaius Terentius Varro (a consul)
* **gens, gentis** *f.*	race, people, tribe, nation
* **genus, generis** *n.*	race, kind
* **gero, gerere, gessi, gestum**	wage war, manage, do
Cn. Servilius Geminius, Cn. Servilii Geminii *m.*	Gnaeus Servilius Geminius (consul in 217 BC)
Gortynius -a -um	Gortynian, belonging to the city of Gortyna (in Crete)
Graius -a -um	Greek
gratia (+ *genitive*)	for the sake of
* **gratias ago**	thank, give thanks
gratus -a -um	pleasing
* **gravis -e**	serious
* **habeo, habere, habui, habitum**	have, consider
Hadrumetum -i *n.*	Hadrumetum (a town on the coast of Africa)
Hamilcar, Hamilcaris *m.*	Hamilcar (Hannibal's father)
Hannibal, Hannibalis *m.*	Hannibal
Hasdrubal, Hasdrubalis *m.*	Hasdrubal (both Hannibal's brother-in-law and his brother had this name)
Hercules, Herculis *m.*	Hercules
hereditas, hereditatis *f.*	inheritance

* hic	here
* hic, haec, hoc	this, these
* hinc	from here, after this
Hispania -ae *f.*	Spain
* hodie	today
* homo, hominis *m.*	man, person
hospitium -i *n.*	hospitality
hostia -ae *f.*	sacrificial victim
* hostis -is, *m.*	enemy
* huc	here, to this place
* iacio, iacere, ieci, iactum	throw
* iam	now, already
ianua -ae *f.*	door
* ibi	there
* idem, eadem, idem	the same
* igitur	therefore, and so
* ille, illa, illud	that, those, he, she, it
illudo, illudere, illusi, illusum	mock, fool
immitto, immittere, immisi, immissum	let loose
immolo -are	sacrifice
* imperator, imperatoris *m.*	general, leader
* imperium -i *n.*	command, power
* impero -are (+ *dative*)	order
impraesentiarum	in present circumstances
imprudenter	unwisely
* in (+ *ablative*)	in
* in (+ *accusative*)	into, against
* incendo, incendere, incendi, incensum	set on fire, inflame
incola -ae *m./f.*	inhabitant
incredibilis -e	incredible
* inde	from there, next
indigeo, indigere, indigui (+ *genitive*)	be in need of

induco, inducere, induxi, inductum	lead in, lead on
ineo, inire,inii, initum	enter upon
inermis -e	unarmed
* **infero, inferre, intuli, illatum/ inlatum**	bring to
infitior -ari	deny
inicio, inicere, inieci, iniectum	throw in, cast onto
* **inimicus -i** *m.*	(personal) enemy
inimicus -a -um	hateful, hostile
* **initium -i** *n.*	beginning
* **inquam (inquit, inquiunt)**	say
insciens, inscientis	unaware
* **insidiae -arum** *f. pl.*	ambush
insidior -ari (+ *dative*)	ambush
instituo, instituere, institui, institutum	undertake
* **intellego, intellegere, intellexi, intellectum**	understand
* **inter** (+ *accusative*)	between
intereo, interire, interii, interitum	die
* **interficio, interficere, interfeci, interfectum**	kill
interior, interius	inner, private
interitus -us *m.*	death, destruction
* **intra** (+ *accusative*)	within
* **invenio, invenire, inveni, inventum**	find
invictus -a -um	unbeaten, invincible
invidia -ae *f.*	ill-will
* **ipse, ipsa, ipsum**	-self (emphatic pronoun)
irrideo, irridere, irrisi, irrisum	mock
* **is, ea, id**	he, she, it, they, that, those
* **ita**	in this way, thus

Italia -ae *f.*	Italy
* **itaque**	and so
item	likewise, similarly
* **iter, itineris** *n.*	journey
* **iterum**	again
* **iubeo, iubere, iussi, iussum**	order
iudico -are	judge
Iuppiter, Iovis *m.*	Jupiter
iuro -are	swear an oath
ius, iuris *n.*	right, rights
iuvencus -i *m.*	young cow, bullock
L. Aemilius Paulus, L. Aemilii Pauli *m.*	Lucius Aemilius Paulus (consul in 181 BC)
* **labor, laboris** *m.*	work, labour
lectica -ae *f.*	litter
* **legatus** -i *m.*	envoy
libenter	gladly, willingly
Ligures, Ligurum *m. pl.*	the Ligurians, a people living on the north-west coast of Italy
* **litus, litoris** *n.*	beach
loca -orum *n.*	places, region
* **locus** -i m.	place
* **longus** -a -um	long
Lucani -orum *m. pl.*	the Lucani, a tribe in southern Italy
L. Cornelius, L. Cornelii *m.*	Lucius Cornelius Merula (consul in 193 BC)
L. Furius, L. Furii *m.*	Lucius Furius (consul in 196 BC)
M. Baebius Tamphilus, M. Baebii Tamphili *m.*	Marcus Baebius Tamphilus (consul in 182 BC)
M. Claudius Marcellus, M. Claudii Marcelli *m.*	Marcus Claudius Marcellus (consul in 183 BC)
* **magis**	more, to a greater extent

magister equitum, magistri equitum *m.*	Master of the Horse (i.e. a dictator's second in command)
magistratus -us *m.*	magistrate, official, office
* **magnus -a -um**	great
Mago, Magonis *m.*	Mago (Hannibal's brother)
* **manus -us** *f.*	hand, band of men
Marcus Claudius Marcellus, Marci Claudii Marcelli *m.*	Marcus Claudius Marcellus
Marcus Claudius, Marci Claudii *m.*	Marcus Claudius (consul in 196 BC)
M. Minucius Rufus, M. Minucii Rufi *m.*	Marcus Minucius Rufus
* **mare, maris** *n.*	sea
maximus -a -um	greatest
memor, memoris	mindful, remembering
memoria -ae *f.*	memory, account
* **mens, mentis** *f.*	mind
mentio, mentionis *f.*	mention
* **meus -a -um**	my
* **miles, militis** *m.*	soldier
* **mille passus** (*pl.* **milia passuum**)	mile
minor, minoris	smaller, younger
minus	less, to a smaller extent
* **miror -ari**	wonder at
* **mitto, mittere, misi, missum**	send
* **modus -i** *m.*	manner, way
* **mons, montis** *m.*	mountain
* **morbus -i** *m.*	sickness, disease
* **morior, mori, mortuus sum**	die
* **moror -ari**	linger
* **multitudo, multitudinis** *f.*	multitude, large number
* **multus -a -um**	much, many
* **munio, munire, munivi, munitum**	fortify, guard
* **munus, muneris** *n.*	gift

* nam	for
* nascor, nasci, natus sum	am born
natio, nationis *f.*	nation
naufragium -i *n.*	shipwreck
nauticus -a -um	naval
navalis -e	naval
* navem solvo	cast off, set sail
* navis -is *f.*	ship
* ne	lest, that not, so that not
* -ne	(introduces question)
* nec, neque	and not, nor, neither
* nego -are	refuse
* nemo, nullius	no one, nobody
* nihil	nothing
nihilo	to no extent
* nisi	unless, if not, except
* noctu	by night
* nomen, nominis *n.*	name
* non	not
* novus -a -um	new
* nox, noctis *f.*	night
* nullus -a -um	no, none
* num	whether
Numidae -arum *m. pl.*	the Numidians
* numquam	never
* nuntio -are	report
* ob (+ *accusative*)	because of
obduco, obducere, obduxi, obductum	draw in
obicio, obicere, obieci, obiectum	put before, oppose
obitus -us *m.*	death
* obses, obsidis *m./f.*	hostage
* obsideo, obsidere, obsedi, obsessum	blockade
obtrectio, obtrectionis *f.*	disparagement

obviam (+ *dative*)	against
* **occido, occidere, occidi, occisum**	kill
* **occupo -are**	seize, occupy
* **oculus -i**, *m.*	eye
* **odium -i** *n.*	hatred
* **omitto, omittere, omisi, omissum**	make no mention of
* **omnis -e**	all, every
* **opera -ae** *f.*	work, attention
* **operam do**	give attention (to)
operio, operire, operui, opertum	cover
* **opes, opum** *f. pl.*	resources, riches
oppleo, opplere, opplevi, oppletum	fill up
* **opprimo, opprimere, oppressi, oppressum**	overwhelm, crush
optimus -a -um	best
* **orno -are**	equip
* **ostendo, ostendere, ostendi, ostentum**	show
P. Cornelius Cethegus, P. Cornelii Cethegi *m.*	Publius Cornelius Cethegus (consul in 182 BC)
Padus -i *m.*	the river Po
* **palam**	openly
Pamphylius -a -um	Pamphylian
* **par, paris**	equal
* **pareo, parere, parui** (+ *dative*)	obey
* **paro -are**	prepare
* **pars, partis** *f.*	part
patefacio, patefacere, patefeci, patefactum	open up, make accessible
* **pater, patris** *m.*	father
paternus -a -um	paternal

patres conscripti, patrum conscriptorum *m. pl.*	senators
* **patria -ae** *f.*	homeland, native land
* **pauci, paucae, pauca**	few, a few
* **pax, pacis** *f.*	peace
* **pecunia -ae** *f.*	money
pedester, pedestris, pedestre	infantry
* **pello, pellere, pepuli, pulsum**	drive, rout
pendo, pendere, pependi, pensum	pay
* **per** (+ *accusative*)	through
perfungor, perfungi, perfunctus sum (+ *ablative*)	execute, perform fully, endure
Pergamenus -a -um	of Pergamum
* **periculum -i** *n.*	danger
* **persuadeo, persuadere, persuasi, persuasum** (+ *dative*)	persuade
* **perterritus -a -um**	very frightened, terrified
pertineo, pertinere, pertinui	relate to
* **pervenio, pervenire, perveni**	reach, arrive
* **peto, petere, petivi, petitum**	seek, ask for, make for, attack
Philippus -i *m.*	Philip V, king of Macedon
plumbum -i *n.*	lead
plures, plura	more
plurimus -a -um	very great, very many
plus	to a greater extent
* **poena -ae** *f.*	punishment
Poeni -orum *m. pl.*	the Carthaginians
* **polliceor, polliceri, pollicitus sum**	promise
Polybius -i *m.*	Polybius (a Greek historian, writing in the second century BC)
* **pono, ponere, posui, positum**	put, set up (camp)

Pontus -i *m*.	the Black Sea
* **populus** -i *m*.	people, nation
* **porto** -are	carry, take
* **possum, posse, potui**	can, be able
* **post**	afterwards
* **post** (+ *accusative*)	after
* **postea**	afterwards
posterus -a -um	following, next
* **postquam**	after, when
* **postulo** -are	demand, ask
* **potens, potentis**	powerful
* **potestas, potestatis** *f*.	opportunity
potissimum	most of all
* **praebeo, praebere, praebui, praebitum**	show
praeceptum -i *n*.	order
praecipio, praecipere, praecepi, praeceptum	instruct in advance
* **praemium** -i *n*.	reward
praesens, praesentis	(being) present
* **praesidium** -i *n*.	fortification
praesto, praestare, praestiti, praestitum	stand ahead of, surpass
* **praesum, praeesse, praefui** (+ *dative*)	be in charge of
* **praeter** (+ *accusative*)	beyond, except
* **praeterea**	in addition
* **praetor, praetoris** *m*.	praetor (a senior Roman official)
premo, premere, pressi, pressum	press, weigh down
primo	at first
* **princeps, principis** *m*.	leader
pristinus -a -um	former
* **prius**	before
* **priusquam**	before
* **prodo, prodere, prodidi, proditum**	hand over

produco, producere, produxi, productum	lead forth, bring out
* **proelium -i** *n.*	battle
* **proficiscor, proficisci, profectus sum**	set out
profiteor, profiteri, professus sum	declare
profligo -are	overcome
profugio, profugere, profugi	escape, flee
prohibeo, prohibere, prohibui, prohibitum	hold back, prohibit
propatulum -i *n.*	unroofed space
* **prope** (+ *accusative*)	near
propere	rapidly
propinquus -a -um	neighbouring, near
* **propter** (+ *accusative*)	on account of
prospicio, prospicere, prospexi, prospectum	look out
provideo, providere, providi, provisum	consider in advance
* **proximus -a -um**	nearest, next
prudentia -ae *f.*	good judgement
Prusia -ae *m.*	Prusias, king of Bithynia
publico -are	confiscate, make public
* **publicus -a -um**	public
P. Cornelius Scipio, P. Cornelii Scipionis *m.*	Publius Cornelius Scipio (consul in 218 BC)
P. Scipio, P. Scipionis *m.*	Publius Scipio (son of Publius Cornelius Scipio)
P. Sulpicius, P. Sulpicii *m.*	Publius Sulpicius Galba Maximus (consul in 211 BC, dictator in 203 BC and consul in 211 BC)
* **puer, pueri** *m.*	boy
puerulus -i *m.*	little boy
* **pugna -ae** *f.*	battle
* **pugno -are**	fight

puppis, puppis *f.*	stern (of a ship)
Pyrenaeus -a -um	of the Pyrenees
Q. Fabius Labeo, Q. Fabii Labeonis *m.*	Quintus Fabius Labeo (consul in 183 BC)
quacumque	wherever
* **quaero, quaerere, quaesivi, quaesitum**	search for, ask for, ask
* **quam**	than, to the extent to which
* **quam** (+ *superlative*)	as . . . as possible
quamdiu	for as long as
quantus -a -um	the amount which
* **quantus -a -um?**	how great?
quare	for which reason, why
* **-que**	and
* **qui, quae, quod**	who, which
quidem	indeed
* **quidem**	indeed
quin (+ *subjunctive*)	that
quinque	five
quinquies	five times
Q. Fabius Maximus, Q. Fabii Maximi *m.*	Quintus Fabius Maximus (dictator in Rome in 217 BC)
Q. Minucius, Q. Minucii *m.*	Quintus Minucius Thermus (consul in 193 BC)
* **quis? quid?**	who? what? any
* **quisquam, quicquam**	anyone, anything
* **quo?**	where to? to where?
* **quod**	because
* **quoque**	also
quotannis	every year
quotienscumque	whenever
* **ratio, rationis** *f.*	reasoning
* **recipio, recipere, recepi, receptum**	take back; *me recipio* – return
recuso -are	object to, refuse

* reddo, reddere, reddidi, redditum	give back, make
* redeo, redire, redii, reditum	return
* refero, referre, rettuli, relatum	take back
* regnum -i *n.*	kingdom
* relinquo, relinquere, reliqui, relictum	leave, leave behind
* reliquus -a -um	the rest of, remaining
remitto, remittere, remisi, remissum	send back, give up
removeo, removere, removi, remotum	remove, move away
renuntio -are	report back
reor, reri, ratus sum	think
* repente	suddenly
repentinus -a -um	sudden, unexpected
reperio, reperire, repperi, repertum	discover
repo, repere, repsi, reptum	crawl
repono, reponere, reposui, repositum	put aside
* res -ei *f.*	thing, matter
rescisco, resciscere, rescivi, rescitum	find out
* resisto, resistere, restiti (+ *dative*)	resist, oppose
* respondeo, respondere, respondi, responsum	answer, reply
* responsum -i *n.*	answer, reply
* retineo, retinere, retinui, retentum	keep
reverto, revertere, reverti, reversum	return
revoco -are	call back
* rex, regis *m.*	king

Rhodanus -i *m.*	the river Rhône
Rhodii -orum *m. pl.*	the people of Rhodes (an island off the south coast of Asia Minor)
risus -us *m.*	laughter
robustus -a -um	strong, powerful
* **rogo -are**	ask, ask for
Roma -ae *f.*	Rome
Romanus -a -um	Roman
ruber, rubra, rubrum	red
sacrifico -are	conduct a sacrifice
* **saepe**	often
Saguntum -i *n.*	Saguntum (a town on the coast of Spain)
saltus -us *m.*	mountain pass
* **salus, salutis** *f.*	safety
sarmentum -i *n.*	small twig, brushwood
* **satis**	enough
saucius -a -um	wounded
scapha -ae *f.*	small boat
scilicet	doubtless, no doubt
* **scio, scire, scivi, scitum**	know
* **scribo, scribere, scripsi, scriptum**	write
* **se, sui**	himself, herself, itself, themselves (reflexive pronoun)
secum	with him/her/them
* **secundus -a -um**	second
* **sed**	but
segrego -are	separate
seiungo, seiungere, seiunxi, seiunctum	separate
* **semper**	always
* **senatus -us** *m.*	senate
* **sentio, sentire, sensi, sensum**	feel, realize

septuagesimus -a -um	seventieth
serpens, serpentis *m./f.*	snake
servolus -i *m.*	a young slave
setius	differently
* **si**	if
* **sic**	thus, in this way
* **signum -i** *n.*	signal
* **simul**	at the same time
simulo -are	pretend
* **sine** (+ *ablative*)	without
societas, societatis *f.*	alliance
* **solum**	only
* **solvo, solvere, solvi, solutum**	loose, open (a letter)
* **spes -ei** *f.*	hope
* **statim**	at once, immediately
statua -ae *f.*	statue
* **stultus -a -um**	stupid, foolish
subigo, subigere, subegi, subactum	subdue, conquer
sufficio, sufficere, suffeci, suffectum	substitute
Sulpicius Blitho, Sulpicii Blithonis *m.*	Sulpicius Blitho (a historian and contemporary of Nepos)
* **sum, esse, fui**	be
summa -ae *f.*	entirety, total amount
* **summus -a -um**	greatest, top (of)
* **sumo, sumere, sumpsi, sumptum**	take
superior, superius	earlier, previous, superior
* **supero -are**	overcome, overpower
* **supersum, superesse, superfui**	be left (over)
* **superus -a -um**	superior
supra	above, previously
* **suscipio, suscipere, suscepi, susceptum**	undertake

Vocabulary

suspicio, suspicionis *f.*	suspicion
sustineo, sustinere, sustinui, sustentum	withstand
* **suus -a -um**	his (own), her (own), its (own), their (own)
Syria -ae *f.*	Syria
T. Quintius Flaminius, T. Quintium Flaminium *m.*	Titus Quintius Flaminius
tabellarius -i *m.*	letter-carrier
* **talis -e**	such, of this sort
* **tam**	so, to that extent
* **tamen**	nevertheless
tamquam	as if
* **tantum**	only, to this extent
* **tantus -a- um**	so much, that amount
* **templum -i** *n.*	temple
* **tempus, temporis** *n.*	time
* **teneo, tenere, tenui, tentum**	hold, keep
* **terra -ae** *f.*	land
* **terror, terroris** *m.*	terror, panic
tertio	for the third time
tertius -a -um	third
Thermopylae -arum *f. pl.*	Thermopylae (a famous mountain pass on the boarders of Thessaly)
Tiberis, Tiberis *m.*	the river Tiber
Tiberius Longus, Tiberii Longi *m.*	Tiberius Longus
Tiberius Sempronius Gracchus, Tiberii Sempronii Gracchi *m.*	Tiberius Sempronius Gracchus (consul in 216 BC and in 213 BC)
* **tollo, tollere, sustuli, sublatum**	remove, destroy
traduco, traducere, traduxi, traductum	lead across
transeo, transire, transii, transitum	cross

transitus -us *m.*	crossing
Trasumenus -i *m.*	Lake Trasimene (now Lago de Perugia)
Trebia -ae *m.*	the river Trebbia
trecenti -ae -a	three hundred
tres, tria	three
triennium -i *n.*	three-year period
* **tu, tui**	you (*sg.*)
* **tum**	then
* **ubi**	where, when
* **ullus -a -um**	any
umquam	ever
* **unde**	from where
* **undique**	on all sides
universi -ae -a	all together
unus -a -um	one
* **urbs, urbis** *f.*	city
* **usque**	all the way, continuously
* **usus -us** *m.*	practice
* **ut** (+ *indicative*)	just as, when
* **ut** (+ *subjunctive*)	that, so that, to
* **uterque, utraque, utrumque**	each (of two), both
* **utor, uti, usus sum** (+ *ablative*)	use
utpote	inasmuch as
utrobique	in both places
valens, valentis	strong, powerful
* **valeo, valere, valui**	be strong
valetudo, valetudinis *f.*	state of health
vallum -i *n.*	defensive palisade, barrier
varius -a -um	various, manifold
vas, vasis *n.*	receptacle, vessel
vectigal, vectigalis *n.*	revenue, tax
* **veho, vehere, vexi, vectum**	carry
velum -i *n.*	sail
* **velut**	as if

veneno -are	poison
venenum -i *n.*	drug, poison
* **venio, venire, veni, ventum**	come
* **ventus -i** *m.*	wind
Venusia -ae *f.*	Venusia, a town on the borders of Lucania
* **verbum -i,** *n.*	word
* **vereor, vereri, veritus sum**	fear, be afraid
* **verto, vertere, verti, versum**	turn
* **verus -a -um**	true
vicesimus -a -um	twentieth
* **video, videre, vidi, visum**	see
* **videor, videri, visus sum**	seem
* **vinco, vincere, vici, victum**	defeat
* **vir, viri** *m.*	man
* **virtus, virtutis** *f.*	courage, virtue
* **vis, vim** (*accusative sg.*), **vires** (*nominative pl.*) *f.*	force
visus -us *m.*	sight
* **vita -ae** *f.*	life
* **vito -are**	avoid
* **vivus -a -um**	alive
* **vix**	hardly, scarcely, with difficulty
* **volo, velle, volui**	want
voluntas, voluntatis *f.*	wish, inclination
Zama -ae *f.*	Zama (a town in Numidia, Africa, and the location of Scipio's famous victory over Hannibal)

Tacitus

Annals XIV.29–37 and 59
(...*et posito metu*)–65

Introduction

The emperor Nero

The emperor Nero continues to fascinate readers. The two most important literary sources for this period are the historical works written by Tacitus and Suetonius. Both writers paint a lurid picture of Nero's rule, characterized by an unrestrained pursuit of fame and a savage readiness to remove any potential threat to his power. The beginning and end of his rule were no less dramatic than many of the events in between: he came to power in AD 54 after his mother, Agrippina, murdered her husband, the emperor Claudius, and his rule ended with a humiliating night-time escape from Rome in AD 68.

It is conventional to divide Nero's rule into two phases. The first five years of Nero's rule were seen as a golden age, perhaps because of the restraining influence of his mother, Agrippina, and the positive influence of Seneca, his tutor, and Burrus, the commander of the Praetorian Guard. By AD 59, however, Nero had grown to find his mother's influence burdensome and he resented her opposition to his affair with Poppaea. He enlisted the help of Anicetus, the commander of the Roman fleet at Misenum, and arranged for her death. After his mother's murder, Nero became increasingly unrestrained in his decisions; contrary to the Roman tradition that it was unseemly for a noble to be seen performing on stage, he craved public adulation and decided to sing publicly and take part in chariot racing. He instituted a series of lavish public games for this purpose, much to the dismay of Rome's traditionalists.

The real turning point in his rule, however, is seen by Tacitus to be AD 62. Burrus died and Seneca took a step back from public life; in the absence of these two men, other advisors took their place. Tacitus characterizes the most important of these men – Faenius Rufus and Tigellinus – as dark characters, responsible for much of the brutality

A Level

that began to take place towards members of the senate. Nervous of potential challenges to his position as emperor, Nero started to use accusations of crimes against his *maiestas* as a way to remove his political rivals. *Maiestas* trials had been used by previous emperors and provided the precedent for prominent nobles to be put to death on the grounds of disrespect for the dignity of the emperor. Within this structure, any disagreement with the emperor or lack of adulation for him could be seen as an act of treason, punishable by death.

Over time, the Roman nobles increasingly resented what had become a rule of terror. With Gaius Calpurnius Piso as their figurehead, a major conspiracy unfolded in AD 65 which aimed to assassinate Nero and make Piso the emperor. Nero discovered the conspiracy and a bloodbath ensued. Seneca, Nero's former tutor, was among those killed. The murders, however, did not quell the tide of opposition and a series of military uprisings followed in Gaul, Spain and Africa. In AD 68 the senate turned against him and declared Nero a public enemy. Nero fled from Rome, disguised by a cloak and crawling through thickets and ditches for safety. He took refuge in a house belonging to one of his freedmen and committed suicide.

Tacitus

Tacitus is arguably the greatest of Rome's historians. His fame rests on the bitingly sharp and innovative quality of his Latin and his piercing analysis of the faults of the emperors. Nero is believed by many modern-day historians to have been popular with the Roman people who enjoyed his largesse towards them and his lavish public entertainments. Tacitus, however, characterizes his rule with bitter criticism, centred upon the abuses of power which took place and lamenting the reduced freedom for senators, Rome's traditional ruling class.

Tacitus was born in AD 56 and reached high-ranking political office under the emperors Vespasian, Titus and Domitian. The *Annals* are

Tacitus' most famous work and within them Tacitus provides an account of the early emperors, analysing their rule through contrast with political life in the Roman Republic. This contrast is set up by the annalistic (and therefore Republican) structure of the work, grouping his material by year and dating each year by reference to the consuls, even though the emperors' time in office was defined by lifespan. At the start of the *Annals*, Tacitus states that he will write about emperors who predate him and, for this reason, he will write *sine ira et studio*. It would be a misinterpretation, however, to think that this means that Tacitus writes without bias: judgement pulses through every sentence of the text. Tacitus' point is that writing about earlier emperors means that he has no personal axe to grind (*sine ira*), nor is he trying to win favour and secure political advancement (*sine studio*); this gives him the liberty to expose the details of the imperial political structure that he finds so distasteful.

Tacitus' analysis of Nero's rule

Tacitus' criticisms of the principate were no doubt shared by many of Rome's traditional elite. Rome's dominant political structure had been the Republic, a power-sharing structure which had lasted for nearly 500 years until the civil wars of the late first century BC caused it to fracture. The Republic had achieved a delicate power balance, enfranchizing the wider Roman people into government through their right to vote for the holders of political offices and to ratify laws. There was no doubt, however, that Rome's social elite – the senators – were the engine room of government. Senators met to debate key issues: decision by open discussion and consensus was integral to the ideology of the Republic.

The move to a principate was, in effect, a move to one-man rule. Inevitably, therefore, the raw power held by senators within government decreased. The political offices of the Republic continued, but the power that came with them was increasingly superficial: senators had to look to the princeps' wishes first. In addition, the risk that offending the princeps could lead to the death penalty (see *maiestas* trials above) meant that open debate was inevitably stifled. Tacitus' central criticism of the principate is the farce of an ostensibly consultative, decision-making process in the context of a widening gap between what people believed and what they felt able to say publicly.

In the extracts explored by this edition, Tacitus' nostalgia for the political freedoms of the Republic is to the fore: underpinning this nostalgia is the idea that these freedoms brought with them accountability and self-restraint and thus acted as a safeguard against abuses of power. Tacitus' critical judgement, therefore, homes in on examples that demonstrate a lack of accountability and the excesses that could take place. In Chapters 14 to 15 and 20 to 21, Tacitus' focus is on Nero's desire to perform on stage: Tacitus highlights that Nero courts mass popularity and has no concern to limit his desires by observing traditional Roman patterns of behaviour. In Chapters 29 to 39, Tacitus implies that the British rebellion is the result of Roman greed; his characterization of Boudicca emphasizes the value she puts on her own political freedoms and the securities these bring. In Chapters 51 to 58, Tacitus focuses on Nero's relationship with prominent nobles. The conversation between Seneca and Nero highlights that even Nero's closest advisor is guarded in what he can say to Nero and that he cannot question openly Nero's decisions. The deaths of Sulla and Plautus are indicative of Nero's readiness to murder potential threats to his power. In Chapters 59 to 65, Poppaea's influence overrides the respect due to Octavia as daughter of the previous emperor.

Undertanding Tacitus: Key people

Jumping into a section of a larger historical text can be challenging. To understand what is happening in each section, it is helpful to have a clear understanding of who the main people are.

A Level

The imperial family

- **Agrippina**, wife of the emperor Claudius and Nero's mother. Agrippina is believed to have been responsible for Nero's rise to power: she persuaded Claudius to adopt him into the imperial family and then murdered Claudius (AD 54) and his son (AD 55), clearing the obstacles in Nero's way.
- **Nero**, born in AD 37 and emperor from AD 54–68.
- **Octavia**, daughter of the emperor Claudius; Agrippina persuaded Claudius that Octavia should be betrothed to Nero. Nero and Octavia were married in AD 53.
- **Poppaea**, Nero's mistress; their affair started in AD 58 and in AD 62 she persuaded Nero to divorce (and later murder) Octavia.

Boudicca's rebellion

- **Paulinus Suetonius**, appointed governor of Britain in AD 58 and commander of the Roman legions there.
- **Decianus Catus**, imperial procurator of Britain during Boudicca's rebellion. As imperial procurator, Catus was responsible for administrative matters such as tax collection.
- **Prasutagus**, king of the Iceni (a tribe based in modern-day Norfolk). His death in AD 61 led to the rebellion by the Britons.
- **Boudicca**, Prasutagus' wife and queen of the Iceni. She led the Iceni and the Trinovantes' rebellion against the Romans, achieving victories in Camulodunum, Londinium and Verulamium before losing in a pitched battle against Paulinus Suetonius.

Prominent Romans in Rome

- **Seneca**, a famous writer and philosopher. He was Nero's tutor when he was a young boy and his close advisor during the early years of Nero's rule. Seneca died in AD 65 in the aftermath of the Pisonian conspiracy.

A Level

- **Burrus**, commander of the Praetorian Guard and a close advisor to Nero in the early years of his rule.
- **Tigellinus**, a close advisor to Nero in the later years of his rule. He is characterized by Tacitus as a ruthless and brutal man who was instrumental in plotting the deaths of many of Rome's elite.
- **Faenius Rufus**, commander of the Praetorian Guard after Burrus' death.
- **Plautus**, a Roman noble murdered by Nero in AD 62. His grandfather was Drusus, son of the emperor Tiberius, and this connection to the imperial family made him a potential rival for the position of emperor.
- **Sulla**, a Roman noble murdered by Nero in AD 62. He had been consul in AD 51 and he was connected to the imperial family because he was married to Antonia, daughter of the emperor Claudius.
- **Anicetus**, commander of the Roman fleet at Misenum. He had helped Nero murder his mother and in AD 62 he was persuaded by Nero to confess (falsely) to an affair with Octavia, thus giving Nero the justification he needed to divorce and execute her.
- **Gaius Calpurnius Piso**, a popular Roman noble who lived a lavish lifestyle and who was famous for his oratorical skill. He was the figurehead for the conspiracy against Nero, discovered in AD 65.

Understanding Tacitus: Chapter summaries

Tacitus' terse literary style means that he moves quickly through material, often with limited overt explanation. Before reading the Latin, therefore, it is helpful to be familiar with the core content within each chapter.

Chapter 14 (English)	AD 59: **Nero** wishes to take part in the chariot racing and to sing to the lyre on stage. His advisors – **Seneca** and **Burrus** – are unable to dissuade him and chariot races are arranged. The Roman people are delighted; Tacitus is appalled. Nero offers large cash payments to prominent senators and equestrians if they compete as well.

A Level

Chapter 15 (English)	**Nero** institutes the Youth Games, an extravagant festival to celebrate the coming of age of Rome's youth. He gives cash-handouts to the Roman people as spending money for the festival. Nobles, women and Nero perform on stage. Tacitus laments the days of excess and debauchery that take place. All praise Nero lavishly; some mourn the disgraceful behaviour.
Chapter 20 (English)	**AD 60**: **Nero** establishes the Neronia, a public quinquennial festival in his honour, innovatively combining chariot racing, musical competitions and gymnastics. Tacitus reports the public reaction to this: some mourn the decline in Rome's moral standards, reflecting on the change from the tough military character of old to soft and indulgent pastimes such as singing on stage and night-time debauchery. There is criticism of the changed character of the festival and the innovation that Roman nobles perform at them.
Chapter 21 (English)	Tacitus' account of public reaction continues: some Romans were in favour of the games, arguing that the permanent buildings set up for them would be cost-efficient in the long run and that the festival offered fun not vice.
Chapter 29 (Latin)	**AD 61**: Tacitus moves to events in Britain and signals that he will report on the major defeat suffered by the Romans there. **Paulinus Suetonius** – governor of Britain – has decided to extend Roman control and attacks the island of Mona (modern-day Anglesey), an important refuge for opponents to Roman rule.
Chapter 30 (Latin)	Tacitus reports the attack on Mona, offering a dramatic account of the unnervingly wild battleline of Britons which face the Roman troops when they land. The Romans regain their nerve, win a decisive victory and destroy groves which are sacred to the druids.
Chapter 31 (Latin)	While Suetonius is away, **Prasutagus**, king of the Iceni, dies. His kingdom is looted by the Romans and his wife, **Boudicca**, and their daughters are beaten and sexually abused. The Iceni persuade a nearby tribe, the Trinovantes, to join them in fighting back and they attack the Roman colony at Camulodunum (modern-day Colchester).

A Level

Chapter 32 (Latin)	The Britons are confident of success, interpreting various omens as signs of support from the gods. The Roman soldiers at Camulodunum take refuge in the temple of Claudius there. The Britons lay siege to the temple and take it within two days. The Ninth Legion arrives in support but the Britons rout the legion and kill all the infantry. The imperial procurator, **Decianus Catus**, flees in fear to Gaul.
Chapter 33 (Latin)	**Suetonius** marches back from North Wales to Londinium (modern-day London) but decides to abandon the town and amass a larger army before fighting the Britons. **Boudicca**'s troops ravage Londinium and Verulamium (modern-day St Albans), looting and killing as they go. Tacitus' reports that 70,000 inhabitants died in these two towns.
Chapter 34 (Latin)	**Suetonius** gathers a fighting force of 10,000 men, made up of the Fourteenth Legion, reinforcements from the Twentieth Legion and local auxiliaries. He decides to fight the Britons and chooses an advantageous location for this. He picks an enclosed and narrow battleground, reducing the impact of the Britons' greater numbers. As the armies get into position for battle, Tacitus contrasts the ordered control of the Romans with the Britons' chaotic battlelines. The Britons gather their wives as spectators on wagons, stationed around the battlefield.
Chapter 35 (Latin)	**Boudicca** addresses her army, and highlights that she – like all of them – is fighting for her freedom and the right to avoid sexual abuse. She reflects on their success so far and asserts that the choice is victory or death. She says that she – as a woman – refuses to live enslaved to the Romans.
Chapter 36 (Latin)	In contrast, **Suetonius** encourages his troops by referring to their superior skill and experience. He says that the Britons will be no match for them and he reminds his army that great glory awaits them if they, as a small fighting force, achieve a victory equal in significance to victories won by much larger armies. Suetonius' soldiers are fired up and ready for battle; Suetonius gives the signal for attack, confident that he will win.

A Level

Introduction

Chapter 37 (Latin)	The Roman legion hold their ground and then charge forwards, using a wedge-formation to break through the British battleline. The cavalry charge with outstretched spears, smashing through anything in their way. The Britons turn to flee but find their escape routes are blocked by the wagons and spectators. The Romans slaughter opponents, spectators and animals alike. Tacitus gives an estimated death toll of 80,000 Britons but only 400 Romans. Boudicca ends her life with poison. **Poenius Postumus**, commander of the Second Legion and a man who had disobeyed Suetonius' summons to come and join him, commits suicide when he hears of the Roman victory.
Chapter 38 (English)	Nero sends reinforcements to help **Suetonius** finish the war and all troops in Britain are held ready to fight. Fierce resistance continues from some tribes, exacerbated by the new imperial procurator, **Julius Classicianus**, who urges them not to surrender until Suetonius is replaced. Classicianus writes to Nero to say that there will not be peace while Suetonius is in office.
Chapter 39 (English)	Nero sends one of his freedmen, **Polyclitus**, to establish concord between Classicianus and Suetonius. The rebellious Britons treat Polyclitus with contempt, finding it hard to believe that an ex-slave could hold so much power. Suetonius continues in office as governor but he is told to hand over the control of the army to **Petronius Turpilianus**. Tacitus comments acerbically that Turpilianus achieves peace through inertia.
Chapter 51 (English)	**AD 62**: After several chapters reporting the death/murder of prominent Romans, Tacitus focuses on the death of **Burrus**. Opinion is divided as to whether he died from ill-health or whether he was poisoned by Nero. Romans mourn Burrus' death and the loss of his virtuous influence upon Nero. Nero replaces Burrus as commander of the Praetorian Guard with two men: **Faenius Rufus** and **Ofonius Tigellinus**. Faenius Rufus is popular with the people because he has overseen the grain supply without corruption; Tigellinus' shamelessness wins him greater influence and favour with Nero.

A Level

Chapter 52 (English)	Burrus' death weakens **Seneca**'s position and his opponents start to turn Nero against him, claiming that Seneca's wealth is excessive, his popularity with the people too great, and that Seneca is jealous of Nero's literary success. Seneca's opponents claim that Nero has no need now of his boyhood tutor.
Chapter 53 (English)	**Seneca** – aware of the increasing enmity towards him – requests a meeting with **Nero**. Tacitus reports Seneca's speech to Nero, in which he asks to be allowed to retire. Seneca says that he has been in Nero's service for fourteen years and that the great Augustus had allowed those loyal to him to retire. Seneca thanks Nero for his great generosity and says that he now has more wealth than he could ever have wished for.
Chapter 54 (English)	**Seneca**'s speech continues: he says that, now he is an old man, he needs relief from his wealth and he asks that Nero take back his property and administer it through his own staff. Seneca asks that he be allowed to redirect the time spent on overseeing his huge wealth and focus instead on matters of the soul.
Chapter 55 (English)	Tacitus presents **Nero**'s response: Nero says that his ready reply is proof of the fine oratorical training he has received from Seneca. Nero says that Augustus granted leisure to his trusted advisors, Agrippa and Maecenas, but he did not strip them of their possessions. Nero highlights the enduring nature of Seneca's gifts to him and says that the material rewards he has given Seneca are transient in comparison. He says that many men – including freedman – are wealthier than Seneca.
Chapter 56 (English)	**Nero**'s speech continues: Seneca is not yet an old man and Nero is still in the early years of his rule; there is much that each man can still do for the other. If he lets Seneca retire and return his wealth, then others will accuse Nero of cruelty and greed. Seneca should not wish to do something which would cause criticism of Nero. Tacitus suggests that Nero's charming affection towards Seneca is only a veneer, disguising his hatred. Seneca maintains the facade and offers thanks to Nero. Even so, Seneca withdraws from Rome, claiming as an excuse ill-health or philosophical pursuits.

Chapter 57 (English)	After Seneca withdraws from Rome, **Tigellinus** moves against **Faenius Rufus** and uses Rufus' friendship with Agrippina against him. Tacitus claims that Rufus decides to increase his influence over Nero by making him complicit in crimes and persuades him to remove **Sulla** and **Plautus**, men whom Nero fears are growing too powerful. Rufus argues that Plautus is in Asia, close to the Roman legions in the East and that Sulla is close to the legions in Germany. Either man could lead these legions against Nero. Nero takes action: Sulla is murdered and his head is brought back to Nero who mocks his grey hair.
Chapter 59 (Latin)	After describing Plautus' murder, Tacitus moves to **Poppaea**, Nero's mistress, and Nero's wish to divorce **Octavia** and marry Poppaea instead. Tacitus suggests that Nero's reasons are partly his love for Poppaea, and partly that he sees Octavia as a threat because of her imperial lineage and popularity with the people. Nero writes to the senate saying that Sulla and Plautus were dangerous and that Nero had to give careful attention to the security of the state; the senate sanction their removal and offer thanks.
Chapter 60 (Latin)	After the senate's reaction to Sulla and Plautus' death, Nero is emboldened. He casts **Octavia** out, claiming that she is unable to have children, and marries **Poppaea**. Poppaea compels one of Octavia's attendants to allege that Octavia had an affair with an Alexandrian flute-player. Octavia's slaves are interrogated under torture. Some of the slaves offer false confirmation of the allegation; others maintain Octavia's innocence. Octavia is first granted Burrus' house and Plautus' estates but then banished under military guard to Campania. The Roman people protest and a rumour arises that Nero has reinstated Octavia as his wife.
Chapter 61 (Latin)	The **Roman people** celebrate by offering thanks to the gods on the Capitoline Hill. Poppaea's statues are toppled and Octavia's statues placed in the temples and forum. Soldiers are sent to disperse the crowd, beating them and threatening them with swords. Honour is restored to Poppaea. **Poppaea** urges Nero to take action against Octavia, arguing that the Roman people's support for Octavia shows that they are ready to favour her over him, making her a threat to his power.

A Level

Chapter 62 (Latin)	**Nero** is persuaded but knows that he needs a better pretext than Poppaea's disproven allegation of adultery. He summons **Anicetus**, commander of the fleet at Misenum and the man who devised Agrippina's murder. Nero asks Anicetus to confess to adultery with Octavia and promises lavish rewards if he agrees but instant death if he refuses. Anicetus agrees, confesses adultery in front of many witnesses. He is exiled to Sardinia where he enjoys a wealthy retirement.
Chapter 63 (Latin)	**Nero** announces publicly that Octavia seduced Anicetus in an attempt to gain control over the fleet and that she had an abortion to disguise the evidence of their affair. **Octavia** is imprisoned on Pandateria (an island off the west coast of Italy). The Roman people feel great pity for her, reflecting on her unhappy marriage as a young girl, the murder of her father and brother, and Nero's love affair first with a former slave and then with Poppaea.
Chapter 64 (Latin)	**Octavia** – aged twenty – is murdered. Soldiers tie her down, open her veins and use a sauna to hasten her death. Her head is cut off and taken to Rome for Poppaea to look at. Gifts are offered to the gods in thanksgiving.
Chapter 65 (Latin)	Tacitus details that **Nero** poisoned the most important of his **freedmen**: Doryphorus, for opposing Nero's marriage to Poppaea, and Pallas, for his immense wealth. Some Romans in secret accuse Seneca and Piso of plotting against Nero. Tacitus suggests that this was the trigger for **Piso** – in fear for his life – to begin his famous conspiracy against Nero, a conspiracy leading to Seneca's death in AD 65.

Understanding Tacitus: Literary style

Writers of Classical Latin, such as Caesar and Cicero, established Latin as a language built around smooth rhetorical groupings of pairs or triplets within sentences with a careful clause structure. Tacitus, however, is writing in the first century AD and he displays a literary style which is very different. Concision (*brevitas*), variation (*variatio*), vividness and a fondness for the dramatic punch of nouns rather than verbs are the hallmarks of his style. The effect is Latin which is bristling

A Level

with energy, pointed in its judgement but sometimes jagged in its structure and much harder to translate into English.

The most important differences for the reader arise from Tacitus' fondness for nouns. This brings with it many consequences:

- **Converting nouns into verbs**: Tacitus often uses a noun to convey information which is more naturally expressed in English with a finite verb. This is particularly true when the noun used is a cognate of a verb, e.g. *repentina defectio provinciae* (XIV.30) – 'the sudden defection of the province' is more idiomatically translated into English as 'the province had rebelled'.
- **Prevalence of adjectives and participles**: the preference for nouns means that additional information is often conveyed via adjectives and participles. Tacitus' natural brevity means that the noun described by these adjectives/participles is often left out, requiring the reader to infer it from context and the number/gender of the adjective/participle. In addition, information subordinated by a participle is often better expressed in English with a finite verb, e.g. *receptae ... Armeniae decus ... cupiens* (XIV.29) – 'desiring the glory of having-been-taken-back Armenia' is much better expressed as 'because he desired the glory which had arisen when Armenia had been recaptured'.
- **The ablative case**: the ablative case is the most adverbial of Latin's cases. Tacitus' inclination to use noun phrases rather than clauses means that he often uses an ablative noun phrase in place of a temporal or causal clause, e.g. *multa in Neronem adulatione* (XIV.29) might be best translated as 'after he praised Nero greatly'.
- **The genitive case**: the genitive case is used to tie one noun to another. In Classical Latin the most common relationship is one of possession and it becomes very natural therefore to equate the genitive case with the English preposition 'of'. In reality, however, a much wider range of prepositions can be needed to translate a genitive case and it is important to think about what the relationship between the two nouns is before they are translated; for example, *Octaviae adulterium* (XIV.62) means 'adultery with Octavia'.

- **Prepositional phrases**: Tacitus' fondness for nouns means that prepositional phrases often do the work of Classical Latin's clauses and great flexibility is needed over the meaning of prepositions, especially *in* and *ad*. Both of these can carry a sense of purpose, e.g. *in spem sociandae classis* (XIV.63) means '[aiming] towards the hope of the fleet being allied' but a more idiomatic English translation would be 'because she hoped that she would win the fleet over to her side'.

Tacitus has often been described as the greatest painter of antiquity and his ability to create vivid scenes is superb. This partly rests in his skill in creating a vignette which conveys something broader (e.g. the image of the druids standing on the shores of Mona highlights the chaotic and wild nature of their army in contrast with the regimented order of the Roman legions). It is helpful to think about Tacitus' history as a series of freeze frames and to ask what can be seen at any one moment and how this colours our understanding of characters and events.

The vivid nature of Tacitus' writing is helped by the following dramatic techniques:

- **the historic present**: like many other Roman authors, Tacitus often conveys the most dramatic moments of his text via the present tense (e.g. *nuntiatur*, XIV.30). This encourages the reader to imagine the action as if it is happening right now. English, however, does not use this idiom so much, and historic present tense verbs are often best translated as a past tense.
- **the historic infinitive**: sometimes Tacitus uses an infinitive instead of a finite verb as the main verb in a sentence. This adds drama because the infinitive encourages the reader to focus on the action itself.
- **the impersonal passive construction**: an action can be rendered via the 3rd sg. neuter form of the verb. This formation allows the action itself to be subject, rather than a separate person – e.g. *itur* (XIV.61), 'a going is gone'. This dramatic focus on the action itself often means that the best translation for it is a noun in English, e.g. 'There is a move …'.

- **demonstrative pronouns** such as *hic, ille, is* add vigour to a text by emphasizing a detail (compare with English 'this here pen').
- **primary sequence verbs**: in a technique similar to the historic present, Tacitus often treats his subordinate clauses as if they were primary sequence, using the present and perfect subjunctive rather than the imperfect and pluperfect. This technique is particularly common in his extended indirect speech (*oratio obliqua*) where the move to primary sequence allows the tenses to be closer to the tense of the original direct speech, adding vividness accordingly.

Tacitus' terse *brevitas* adds tremendous punch to his literary style, but it means there is much more work for the reader to do in unpicking his meaning. Latin is a naturally concise language but Tacitus takes this to a new level and routinely leaves out words which are integral to the sentence's meaning. The most frequent omissions are as follows: the finite verb for a clause; the verb *to be* as an auxiliary to the perfect or future participle; the subject for a verb; the object for a verb; the noun described by an adjective or participle. The commentary to the text notes these omissions. In addition, the meaning of a sentence often rests upon an inference from a previous section and it is often the case that far more words are needed in English to explain Tacitus' meaning than just to translate his Latin.

Finally, some elements of Tacitus' syntax are different from the conventions of Classical Latin. For example, Tacitus uses the dative of agent more widely than would be typical in Caesar or Cicero and he uses a subjunctive more often in subordinate clauses (e.g. after *quamquam*) than might be the case in Classical Latin. These differences are detailed in the commentary.

Suggested further reading

Ash, Rhiannon (2006), *Tacitus*, Ancients in Action, London: Bristol Classical Press.

Cassell's Latin Dictionary (1982), London: Cassell Ltd.

Hornblower, Simon, Antony Spawforth and Esther Eidinow, eds (2012), *The Oxford Classical Dictionary*, 4th edn, Oxford: Oxford University Press.

Johnson, Marguerite (2012), *Boudicca*, Ancients in Action, London: Bristol Classical Press.

Morwood, James, ed. (1999), *A Latin Grammar*, Oxford: Oxford University Press.

Opper, Thorsten (2012), *Nero: The Man behind the Myth*, London: British Museum Press.

Suetonius (2007), *The Twelve Caesars*, trans. Robert Graves, London: Penguin Classics.

Tacitus (2012), *Annals*, trans. Cynthia Damon, London: Penguin Classics.

Tacitus (2013), *Annals Book XIV*, ed. E. C. Woodcock, London: Bristol Classical Press.

Woodman, A. J., ed. (2010), *The Cambridge Companion to Tacitus*, Cambridge: Cambridge University Press.

A Level

Text

Book XIV, Chapters 1 to 28: Nero decides to kill his mother, Agrippina. He hosts lavish chariot races and sings at public festivals. Tacitus describes military activity in Armenia.

[**29**] Caesennio Paeto et Petronio Turpiliano consulibus gravis clades in Britannia accepta; in qua neque A. Didius legatus, ut memoravi, nisi parta retinuerat, at successor Veranius, modicis excursibus Siluras populatus, quin ultra bellum proferret, morte prohibitus est. magna, dum vixit, severitatis fama, supremis testamenti verbis ambitionis manifestus: quippe multa in Neronem adulatione addidit subiecturum ei provinciam fuisse, si biennio proximo vixisset. sed tum Paulinus Suetonius obtinebat Britannos, scientia militiae et rumore populi, qui neminem sine aemulo sinit, Corbulonis concertator, receptaeque Armeniae decus aequare domitis perduellibus cupiens. igitur Monam insulam, incolis validam et receptaculum perfugarum, adgredi parat, navesque fabricatur plano alveo adversus breve et incertum. sic pedes; equites vado secuti aut altiores inter undas adnantes equis tramisere.

[**30**] stabat pro litore diversa acies, densa armis virisque, intercursantibus feminis; in modum Furiarum veste ferali, crinibus disiectis faces praeferebant; Druidaeque circum, preces diras sublatis ad caelum manibus fundentes, novitate adspectus perculere militem, ut quasi haerentibus membris immobile corpus vulneribus praeberent. dein cohortationibus ducis et se ipsi stimulantes, ne muliebre et fanaticum agmen pavescerent, inferunt signa sternuntque obvios et igni suo involvunt. praesidium posthac impositum victis excisique luci saevis superstitionibus sacri: nam cruore captivo adolere aras et hominum fibris consulere deos fas habebant. haec agenti Suetonio repentina defectio provinciae nuntiatur.

[**31**] rex Icenorum Prasutagus, longa opulentia clarus, Caesarem heredem duasque filias scripserat, tali obsequio ratus regnumque et

domum suam procul iniuria fore. quod contra vertit, adeo ut regnum per centuriones, domus per servos velut capta vastarentur. iam primum uxor eius Boudicca verberibus adfecta et filiae stupro violatae sunt; praecipui quique Icenorum, quasi cunctam regionem muneri accepissent, avitis bonis exuuntur, et propinqui regis inter mancipia habebantur. qua contumelia et metu graviorum, quando in formam provinciae cesserant, rapiunt arma, commotis ad rebellationem Trinovantibus et qui alii nondum servitio fracti resumere libertatem occultis coniurationibus pepigerant, acerrimo in veteranos odio. quippe in coloniam Camulodunum recens deducti pellebant domibus, exturbabant agris, captivos, servos appellando, foventibus impotentiam veteranorum militibus similitudine vitae et spe eiusdem licentiae. ad hoc templum divo Claudio constitutum quasi arx aeternae dominationis adspiciebatur, delectique sacerdotes specie religionis omnes fortunas effundebant. nec arduum videbatur exscindere coloniam nullis munimentis saeptam; quod ducibus nostris parum provisum erat, dum amoenitati prius quam usui consulitur.

[32] inter quae nulla palam causa delapsum Camuloduni simulacrum Victoriae ac retro conversum, quasi cederet hostibus. et feminae in furorem turbatae adesse exitium canebant, externosque fremitus in curia eorum auditos, consonuisse ululatibus theatrum visamque speciem in aestuario Tamesae subversae coloniae; iam Oceanus cruento adspectu, ac labente aestu humanorum corporum effigies relictae, ut Britannis ad spem, ita veteranis ad metum trahebantur. sed quia procul Suetonius aberat, petivere a Cato Deciano procuratore auxilium. ille haud amplius quam ducentos sine iustis armis misit; et inerat modica militum manus. tutela templi freti, et impedientibus qui occulti rebellionis conscii consilia turbabant, neque fossam aut vallum praeduxerunt, neque motis senibus et feminis iuventus sola restitit: quasi media pace incauti multitudine barbarorum circumveniuntur. et cetera quidem impetu direpta aut incensa sunt: templum, in quo se miles conglobaverat, biduo obsessum expugnatumque. et victor Britannus, Petilio Ceriali, legato legionis nonae, in subsidium adventanti

obvius, fudit legionem, et quod peditum interfecit: Cerialis cum equitibus evasit in castra et munimentis defensus est. qua clade et odiis provinciae, quam avaritia eius in bellum egerat, trepidus procurator Catus in Galliam transiit.

[**33**] at Suetonius mira constantia medios inter hostes Londinium perrexit, cognomento quidem coloniae non insigne, sed copia negotiatorum et commeatuum maxime celebre. ibi ambiguus, an illam sedem bello deligeret, circumspecta infrequentia militis, satisque magnis documentis temeritatem Petilii coercitam, unius oppidi damno servare universa statuit. neque fletu et lacrimis auxilium eius orantium flexus est, quin daret profectionis signum et comitantes in partem agminis acciperet: si quos imbellis sexus aut fessa aetas vel loci dulcedo attinuerat, ab hoste oppressi sunt. eadem clades municipio Verulamio fuit, quia barbari omissis castellis praesidiisque militarium, quod uberrimum spolianti et defendentibus intutum, laeti praeda et laborum segnes petebant. ad septuaginta milia civium et sociorum iis, quae memoravi, locis cecidisse constitit. neque enim capere aut venundare aliudve quod belli commercium, sed caedes patibula ignes cruces. tamquam reddituri supplicium, at praerepta interim ultione, festinabant.

[**34**] iam Suetonio quarta decima legio cum vexillariis vicesimanis et e proximis auxiliares, decem ferme milia armatorum, erant, cum omittere cunctationem et congredi acie parat. deligitque locum artis faucibus et a tergo silva clausum, satis cognito nihil hostium nisi in fronte et apertam planitiem esse, sine metu insidiarum. igitur legionarius frequens ordinibus, levis circum armatura, conglobatus pro cornibus eques astitit. at Britannorum copiae passim per catervas et turmas exultabant, quanta non alias multitudo, et animo adeo feroci, ut coniuges quoque testes victoriae secum traherent plaustrisque imponerent, quae super extremum ambitum campi posuerant.

[**35**] Boudicca curru filias prae se vehens, ut quamque nationem accesserat, solitum quidem Britannis feminarum ductu bellare testabatur, sed tunc non ut tantis maioribus ortam regnum et opes,

verum ut unam e vulgo libertatem amissam, confectum verberibus corpus, contrectatam filiarum pudicitiam ulcisci. eo provectas Romanorum cupidines, ut non corpora, ne senectam quidem aut virginitatem impollutam relinquant. adesse tamen deos iustae vindictae; cecidisse legionem, quae proelium ausa sit; ceteros castris occultari aut fugam circumspicere. ne strepitum quidem et clamorem tot milium, nedum impetus et manus perlaturos. si copias armatorum, si causas belli secum expenderent, vincendum illa acie vel cadendum esse. id mulieri destinatum: viverent viri et servirent.

[36] ne Suetonius quidem in tanto discrimine silebat. quamquam confideret virtuti, tamen exhortationes et preces miscebat, ut spernerent sonores barbarorum et inanes minas: plus illic feminarum quam iuventutis adspici. imbelles inermes cessuros statim ubi ferrum virtutemque vincentium totiens fusi agnovissent. etiam in multis legionibus paucos qui proelia profligarent; gloriaeque eorum accessurum, quod modica manus universi exercitus famam adipiscerentur. conferti tantum et pilis emissis post umbonibus et gladiis stragem caedemque continuarent, praedae immemores: parta victoria cuncta ipsis cessura. is ardor verba ducis sequebatur, ita se ad intorquenda pila expedierat vetus miles et multa proeliorum experientia, ut certus eventus Suetonius daret pugnae signum.

[37] ac primum legio gradu immota et angustias loci pro munimento retinens, postquam in propius suggressos hostes certo iactu tela exhauserat, velut cuneo erupit. idem auxiliarium impetus; et eques protentis hastis perfringit quod obvium et validum erat. ceteri terga praebuere, difficili effugio, quia circumiecta vehicula saepserant abitus. et miles ne mulierum quidem neci temperabat, confixaque telis etiam iumenta corporum cumulum auxerant. clara et antiquis victoriis par ea die laus parta: quippe sunt qui paulo minus quam octoginta milia Britannorum cecidisse tradant, militum quadringentis ferme interfectis nec multo amplius vulneratis. Boudicca vitam veneno finivit. et Poenius Postumus, praefectus castrorum secundae legionis, cognitis quartadecimanorum vicesimanorumque prosperis rebus, quia pari

gloria legionem suam fraudaverat abnueratque contra ritum militiae iussa ducis, se ipse gladio transegit.

Chapters 38 to 58: Tacitus finishes his account of the Britons' rebellion and then the focus returns to Rome. Tacitus describes the appalling crimes taking place there and laments the end of Burrus and Seneca's good influence on Nero.

[**59**] ... et posito metu nuptias Poppaeae ob eius modi terrores dilatas maturare parat Octaviamque coniugem amoliri, quamvis modeste ageret, nomine patris et studiis populi gravem. sed ad senatum litteras misit de caede Sullae Plautique haud confessus, verum utriusque turbidum ingenium esse, et sibi incolumitatem rei publicae magna cura haberi. decretae eo nomine supplicationes, utque Sulla et Plautus senatu moverentur, gravioribus iam ludibriis quam malis.

[**60**] igitur accepto patrum consulto, postquam cuncta scelerum suorum pro egregiis accipi videt, exturbat Octaviam, sterilem dictitans; exim Poppaeae coniungitur. ea diu paelex et adulteri Neronis, mox mariti potens, quendam ex ministris Octaviae impulit servilem ei amorem obicere. destinaturque reus cognomento Eucaerus, natione Alexandrinus, canere per tibias doctus. actae ob id de ancillis quaestiones, et vi tormentorum victis quibusdam, ut falsa adnuerent, plures perstitere sanctitatem dominae tueri; ex quibus una instanti Tigellino castiora esse muliebria Octaviae respondit quam os eius. movetur tamen primo civilis discidii specie domumque Burri, praedia Plauti infausta dona accipit; mox in Campaniam pulsa est addita militari custodia. inde crebri questus nec occulti per vulgum, cui minor sapientia et ex mediocritate fortunae pauciora pericula sunt. his ... tamquam Nero paenitentia flagitii coniugem revocarit Octaviam.

[**61**] exim laeti Capitolium scandunt deosque tandem venerantur. effigies Poppaeae proruunt, Octaviae imagines gestant umeris, spargunt floribus foroque ac templis statuunt. itur etiam in principis laudes, strepitu venerantium. iamque et Palatium multitudine et clamoribus

A Level

complebant, cum emissi militum globi verberibus et intento ferro turbatos disiecere. mutataque quae per seditionem verterant, et Poppaeae honos repositus est. quae semper odio, tum et metu atrox, ne aut vulgi acrior vis ingrueret aut Nero inclinatione populi mutaretur, provoluta genibus eius: non eo loci res suas agi, ut de matrimonio certet, quamquam id sibi vita potius, sed vitam ipsam in extremum adductam a clientelis et servitiis Octaviae, quae plebis sibi nomen indiderint, ea in pace ausi, quae vix bello evenirent. arma illa adversus principem sumpta; ducem tantum defuisse, qui motis rebus facile reperiretur: omitteret modo Campaniam et in urbem ipsa pergeret, ad cuius nutum absentis tumultus cierentur. quod alioquin suum delictum? quam cuiusquam offensionem? an quia veram progeniem penatibus Caesarum datura sit? malle populum Romanum tibicinis Aegyptii subolem imperatorio fastigio induci? denique, si id rebus conducat, libens quam coactus acciret dominam, vel consuleret securitati. iusta ultione et modicis remediis primos motus consedisse: at si desperent uxorem Neronis fore Octaviam, illi maritum daturos.

[62] varius sermo et ad metum atque iram adcommodatus terruit simul audientem et accendit. sed parum valebat suspicio in servo, et quaestionibus ancillarum elusa erat. ergo confessionem alicuius quaeri placet, cui rerum quoque novarum crimen adfingeretur. et visus idoneus maternae necis patrator Anicetus, classi apud Misenum, ut memoravi, praefectus, levi post admissum scelus gratia, dein graviore odio, quia malorum facinorum ministri quasi exprobrantes adspiciuntur. igitur accitum eum Caesar operae prioris admonet: solum incolumitati principis adversus insidiantem matrem subvenisse; locum haud minoris gratiae instare, si coniugem infensam depelleret. nec manu aut telo opus: fateretur Octaviae adulterium. occulta quidem ad praesens, sed magna ei praemia et secessus amoenos promittit, vel, si negavisset, necem intentat. ille, insita vaecordia et facilitate priorum flagitiorum, plura etiam quam iussum erat fingit fateturque apud amicos, quos velut consilio adhibuerat princeps. tum in Sardiniam pellitur, ubi non inops exilium toleravit et fato obiit.

[63] at Nero praefectum in spem sociandae classis corruptum, et incusatae paulo ante sterilitatis oblitus, abactos partus conscientia libidinum, eaque sibi comperta edicto memorat insulaque Pandateria Octaviam claudit. non alia exul visentium oculos maiore misericordia adfecit. meminerant adhuc quidam Agrippinae a Tiberio, recentior Iuliae memoria obversabatur a Claudio pulsae; sed illis robur aetatis adfuerat; laeta aliqua viderant et praesentem saevitiam melioris olim fortunae recordatione adlevabant: huic primum nuptiarum dies loco funeris fuit, deductae in domum, in qua nihil nisi luctuosum haberet, erepto per venenum patre et statim fratre; tum ancilla domina validior et Poppaea non nisi in perniciem uxoris nupta; postremo crimen omni exitio gravius.

[64] ac puella vicesimo aetatis anno inter centuriones et milites, praesagio malorum iam vitae exempta, nondum tamen morte adquiescebat. paucis dehinc interiectis diebus mori iubetur, cum iam viduam se et tantum sororem testaretur communesque Germanicos et postremo Agrippinae nomen cieret, qua incolumi infelix quidem matrimonium, sed sine exitio pertulisset. restringitur vinclis venaeque eius per omnes artus exsolvuntur; et quia pressus pavore sanguis tardius labebatur, praefervidi balnei vapore enecatur. additurque atrocior saevitia, quod caput amputatum latumque in urbem Poppaea vidit. dona ob haec templis decreta; quem ad finem memorabimus? quicumque casus temporum illorum nobis vel aliis auctoribus noscent, praesumptum habeant, quotiens fugas et caedes iussit princeps, totiens grates deis actas, quaeque rerum secundarum olim, tum publicae cladis insignia fuisse. neque tamen silebimus, si quod senatus consultum adulatione novum aut patientia postremum fuit.

[65] eodem anno libertorum potissimos veneno interfecisse creditus, Doryphorum quasi adversatum nuptiis Poppaeae, Pallantem, quod immensam pecuniam longa senecta detineret. Romanus secretis criminationibus incusaverat Senecam ut C. Pisonis socium, sed validius a Seneca eodem crimine perculsus est. unde Pisoni timor, et orta insidiarum in Neronem magna moles et improspera.

A
Level

Commentary Notes

Book XIV, Chapters 1 to 28: Spurred on by his lover, Poppaea, Nero decides to kill his mother, Agrippina. He tries to feign an accidental death at sea but, after Agrippina swims to safety, Nero dispatches his freedman, Anicetus, to murder her. To disguise his guilt, Nero claims that Agrippina had sent her own freedman to kill Nero; leading Roman nobles congratulate Nero on his escape and public celebrations take place.

Nero returns to Rome and decides to host lavish chariot races. The Roman people rejoice at his generosity but Tacitus highlights the shameful nature of Nero's actions. Nero forces other Roman nobles to compete. Nero's lust for attention motivates him to sing on the public stage.

Tacitus describes military activity in Armenia.

Chapter 29

Caesannio Paeto et Petronio Turpiliano consulibus: Tacitus preserves the annalistic tradition of dividing his history by years and dating each by reference to the consuls for that year. Caesannius Paetus and Petronius Turpilianus were consuls in AD 61.

gravis clades: Tacitus signals the focus of this section – the serious defeats inflicted on the Roman army by Boudicca before Paulinus Suetonius mustered enough troops to defeat her (see Chapters 34 to 37 for Suetonius' victory).

accepta: supply *est*.

in qua: as is so often the case, idiomatic English requires the reader to restate the antecedent for this. *qua* refers back to *Britannia* and so it is best translated as 'a province in which …'.

A Level

neque: used at the start of a section like this, *neque* refers forwards and implies that this is the first detail in a list (compare with the English idiom 'neither ... nor ...'). Tacitus, however, often avoids smoothly balanced pairings and the reference to A. Didius' time as governor of Britain is followed by the contrasting example of Veranius. Idiomatic English, therefore, will avoid translating *neque* as 'and ... not ...'; instead, it is best translated as a simple negative – 'a province in which A. Didius ... did *not* hold on to ...'.

legatus: *legatus* means a man appointed to do a task on behalf of another and so it carries a wide range of meanings in different contexts. Here, the task is to govern Britain on behalf of the Roman emperor and it is best translated, therefore, as 'governor'. The noun is in apposition to *A. Didius* and so 'A. Didius, as governor, ...'.

ut memoravi: Tacitus refers the reader back to his previous account of Roman Britain in *Annals* XII.40.

nisi parta retinuerat: supply an object for *retinuerat* from context – '... had [not] held on to anything except the territory already acquired'. *parta* requires the reader to understand a noun from its number and gender; the neuter pl. form can have a wide reference – 'the things, the areas' and so 'the territory'.

quin ... proferret: *quin* + subjunctive is often used after a verb of prevention to explain the action that someone was able to do: '... [was prevented] from extending ...'.

morte: a causal ablative – he was prevented *by death*. Veranius died in his first year as governor of Britain (AD 58).

magna ... fama: supply *erat* – 'his reputation for strictness was great'. *severitas* as an abstract noun refers to the qualities of self-restraint and self-discipline and the will to develop these in others. It was seen, therefore, as a virtue and conducive to good order in the army and a readiness to put the needs of Rome ahead of individual desire or self-interest.

A Level

supremis ... verbis: a causal ablative – 'because of his last words'.

ambitionis manifestus: supply *erat* – 'he was manifestly ambitious'. The Latin idiom uses an adjective and a genitive noun, a use of the genitive known as the objective genitive (compare with *cupidus* + genitive – 'desirous of ...'). The objective genitive takes its name from the idea that the genitive noun supplies something close to the object of a verb. *ambitio* refers to personal ambition and the lengths that a Roman might go to for their own self-advancement. It was not seen, therefore, as a virtue, since it implied that a Roman was willing to put their own interests ahead of the principle of serving the interests of the Roman state. The statement is a typically Tacitean sting in the tail: previous praise for Veranius has been undercut by the idea that – despite outward appearances – he lusted after personal glory.

addidit subiecturum ei provinciam fuisse: Tacitus' implication is that despite Veranius' flattery towards Nero, the final detail of his will served to praise himself with the claim that he would have offered up to him all of Britain as a province. *subiecturum ... fuisse*: the future participle + *fuisse* represents a past-time potential statement – 'he would have offered up to his control ...'. *provinciam* is fairly loose in its reference; the implication is that he would have extended Roman control across the whole island.

si ... vixisset: the subjunctive verb is used for a conditional clause in indirect speech – 'if he had lived ...'.

biennio proximo: Tacitus uses the ablative case much more widely than earlier authors; here it denotes time *throughout which*, i.e. if Veranius had lived 'for the next two years'.

Paulinus Suetonius: Paulinus Suetonius took over as governor of Britain in AD 58.

scientia militiae et rumore populi: this appears to be a balanced pair of ablatives but Tacitus' *variatio* is at play all the same since the ablative case carries a different function for each. *scientia militiae* explains

Suetonius' fine reputation as the result of his own knowledge of military matters; *rumore populi* locates his reputation within general popular opinion. Idiomatic English would naturally, therefore, separate this pair: 'As a result of his military skill, he was believed by popular opinion to be a rival for Corbulo'.

qui neminem sine aemulo sinit: Tacitus makes frequent reference to general opinion (*rumor*), often with an overtone of criticism. In the backdrop to his analysis of the Roman principate is that it lacked the high-quality open debate of the Republic (see further, pp. 89–90). Instead, matters were discussed more privately and less robustly. Tacitus' barbed comment here implies that popular opinion always compares one man with another, whether or not the comparison is valid. In this case, *rumor* has inflated the skills of Suetonius in order to compare him with Corbulo, the Roman general who won a major victory for Rome against the Armenians.

Corbulonis concertator: understand 'he was' or 'he was believed to be'. Note that the genitive case ties one noun to another; English uses a range of prepositions to achieve this function. Here, 'a rival for Corbulo'.

receptae Armeniae decus: *decus* is accusative and the object of *aequare*. Tacitus' preference for nouns means that he often uses a noun-phrase ('the glory of a having-been-recaptured Armenia') where English would convey the same information via a clause: '[he wished] to equal the glory which Corbulo had won when he recaptured Armenia'.

cupiens: Tacitus' fast-paced style often favours participles over finite verbs, but English idiom does not, and so this participle is best translated as 'and he wished'.

domitis perduellibus: *perduellibus* refers to rebels, i.e. the tribes within Britain who were resisting Roman rule. *domitis* incorporates the metaphor of taming a wild animal.

incolis validam: *incolis* is a causal ablative – 'strong in its inhabitants', i.e. the island of Mona could resist Roman attack strongly because of its fierce inhabitants.

receptaculum perfugarum: this supplies the reason why it was strategically important to gain control of the island. Mona offered a safe haven for deserters, i.e. anyone who had fled from Roman rule or who had escaped from battle. This was problematic for the Romans because a safe haven like this allowed for opponents to Roman rule to regroup there.

adversus breve et incertum: both these adjectives require the reader to supply a noun from their number and gender. The neuter sg. endings and the context of a sea-crossing indicate that the noun to be supplied is *mare*. *adversus* here carries the sense of 'ready to contend with', i.e. 'suitable for the shallow and dangerous sea'. *incertus* – 'uncertain' – has the meaning 'dangerous' in this context because it refers to the danger caused by water of uncertain depth.

sic pedes: supply a finite verb – 'in this way he transported the infantry'.

equites vado secuti: supply *sunt*. *vado* – 'in the shallow water'.

altiores inter undas: take these words together – 'in the deeper waters'.

adnantes equis tramisere: *tramisere* is a shortened form of *transmiserunt* – 'the Romans sent them across, swimming beside their horses'.

Chapter 30

diversa acies: *diversus* means that the battleline was made up of diverse elements, i.e. it lacked the uniformity of the Roman army.

in modum Furiarum: 'in the manner of the Furies'. The Furies were Greek mythological spirits of revenge, often depicted as winged female creatures who would swoop down upon anyone who had committed a crime against their own family. The image is designed to convey the terror felt by the Roman army when the soldiers looked at the women in the battleline opposite.

A Level

crinibus disiectis: 'with their hair torn down', i.e. loose and in disarray. The contrast is with the carefully arranged hairstyle typical of a Roman woman.

novitate adspectus perculere militem: *perculere* is a shortened form of *perculerunt*. 'The druids struck fear into the army because of the strangeness of the sight'. *militem* is used in the singular to refer to the whole army. Notice Tacitus' fondness for nouns: *novitate adspectus* uses two nouns rather than, e.g., a noun and an adjective.

ut ... praeberent: a result clause. The Roman army is terrified so that they [the soldiers] stand – motionless – offering up their bodies for injury.

quasi haerentibus membris: 'as if with their limbs stuck fast'.

cohortationibus ducis et se ipsi stimulantes: Tacitean *variatio*. *et* joins the two reasons why the Roman army began to advance, but a different grammatical structure is used for each of these reasons: 'because of the encouragements from their leader and because the soldiers themselves were urging each other on'. Notice that the Latin participle – *stimulantes* – is best translated as a finite verb in English.

ne ... pavescerent: an indirect command. Verbs ending in -*esco* often refer to an increasing action, i.e. 'they should not become afraid'. The implication is that the fear was not there at first and they should not let it build just because they have seen an unusual battleline against them.

inferunt ... sternunt ... involvunt: dramatic historic present verbs, best translated as a past tense in English. Tacitus compresses the stages of the attack into a fast-paced sentence: the Roman army moves forwards, cuts down anyone in their way and then throws the women's fire-brands onto their opponents.

impositum: understand *est*.

victis: understand a noun with this participle – 'for/over the conquered inhabitants'.

excisi: understand *sunt*.

saevis superstitionibus: '[sacred] to their savage superstitions'. Both words are critical in tone: *saevus* implies that the druids' beliefs were uncivilized; *superstitio* implies a religious belief or practice which lacks sound foundations or reasons for it.

nam … habebant: Tacitus tells us that the Druids practised human sacrifice. *fas habebant* – 'they considered it right …'. *cruore captivo adolere aras* – 'to make their altars smoke with the blood of prisoners', i.e. the Druids poured human blood onto the altars and burned it as a sacrifice to their gods. *hominum fibris* – 'with the entrails of humans'. The process of consulting the gods via animal entrails was a familiar one to the Romans and their sacrifices routinely involved inspecting the inner organs of an animal for signs of divine approval or disapproval. Tacitus presents the shocking detail here that the Druids used human entrails for the same purpose.

repentina defectio provinciae: this detail takes us back to the *gravis clades*, mentioned at the start of Chapter 29. Suetonius' decision to attack the island of Mona is relevant context: he was far away on the Welsh coast when Boudicca led the revolt in the eastern parts of Britain, an area already under Roman rule. The Roman legions who encountered her troops were not able to defeat her until they were joined by Suetonius and his legions.

nuntiatur: a dramatic historic present; the English idiom is to translate as a past tense instead.

Chapter 31

rex Icenorum Prasutagus: Roman control over Britain was maintained by a mixture of direct governorship and partnership with local kings. These kings were known as client kings, and they promised loyalty to the Romans in return for comparative autonomy in ruling their tribes. Prasutagus was one of these client kings. He had hoped to preserve this relationship after his death by leaving sufficient wealth in his will to

Nero to buy his support. Unfortunately, the scale of his remaining wealth proved too strong a temptation for the local Roman troops who chose to rape and pillage after his death in a way which resembled the actions of a conquering army.

longa opulentia: causal ablative – 'because of his long-lasting wealth'.

Caesarem: *Caesar* was used as an honorific name for the emperors; here it refers to the emperor Nero.

scripserat: '[he] had named in his will'.

tali obsequio: causal ablative – 'because of such obsequiousness'. The idea is that the choice to leave so much money to Nero is an act of such deference that the Romans will feel no need to prove their authority by requiring a greater degree of control over the Iceni than before.

regnumque et domum suam: 'both his kingdom and his household'. Prasutagus is aiming to protect his family's right to rule and also the safety of his household, i.e. his material possessions and the people who live there. The risk was a real one: enslaving members of the ruling family was an excellent way for the Romans to demonstrate their power and intimidate other powerful families into submission.

fore: an alternative form for the future infinitive of *sum*.

quod: the relative pronoun can be used at the start of a sentence to create a smooth connection with something in the previous sentence. This use is known as the connecting relative. The connecting relative is best translated as 'he', 'she', 'this' etc. Here, the neuter sg. form of the pronoun shows that it is referring to Prasutagus' plan for the future: 'This scenario turned out in the opposite way', i.e. the reverse of what Prasutagus had intended took place.

per centuriones: 'at the hands of …'.

domus: probably plural, suggesting that looting took place not just across the public areas of the kingdom but also in the private houses of the inhabitants.

per servos: the Roman presence in Britain had two strands, military and civic. The military governor was in charge of the Roman legions but a separate official – the imperial procurator – was in charge of civic administration and taxation. The slaves referred to here are probably the public slaves who were part of the imperial procurator's administrative staff. Tacitus' point, therefore, is that men from each of these strands took the opportunity to loot.

velut capta: 'as if it had been captured'. The slaves and Roman troops are treating the kingdom as conquered territory and acting as if its inhabitants no longer have any rights of ownership to their own property.

iam primum: *iam* adds emphasis to the adverb *primum* – 'the very first thing to take place was …'.

adfecta: understand *est*.

praecipui quique: *quique* is the nominative pl. form of *quisque*. *praecipui* requires the reader to understand a noun from its number and gender: 'all the leading men'.

quasi … accepissent: supply 'the Romans' as the subject.

muneri: a predicative dative – 'as a gift'.

propinqui: this adjective is working as noun – 'the people near to [the king]', i.e. his relations.

qua contumelia: connecting relative – 'Because of this insult'.

graviorum: supply a noun for this adjective from its number and gender – '[fear of] worse things'.

quando in formam provinciae cesserant: 'since they had been reduced to the appearance of a province'. *cedo* means 'yield' or 'give way' and it is a verb commonly used to denote military defeat. The local troops are treating the Iceni as if they are now a Roman province, i.e. under full Roman control, rather than respecting their rights as a client kingdom.

rapiunt: understand 'the Iceni' as the subject.

Trinovantibus: the Trinovantes were a nearby tribe in the east of England who were persuaded to join the Iceni in their rebellion. Camulodunum (see below) was their capital.

et qui alii: 'and those others who …'.

pepigerant: from *pango*.

acerrimo in veteranos odio: Tacitus likes to use the ablative case as a way to include detail which is broadly relevant to the rest of the sentence. This use of the ablative is very similar to the way the ablative case works in an ablative absolute construction, but Tacitus extends its use to noun phrases that do not include a participle. Like an ablative absolute, this type of adverbial ablative is often best translated as a clause with a finite verb, and so, too, here: 'their hatred was fiercest against the veterans'.

in veteranos: Roman soldiers were promised pay and land at the end of a fixed term of military service. These veterans, therefore, are former soldiers who had been given land in the Roman colony at Camulodunum.

recens: a neuter sg. adjective can be used as an adverb (compare with *primum* above) – 'recently'.

deducti: supply a noun for this participle – 'the men [recently] settled …'.

pellebant: supply an object from context – '[they] were driving the local inhabitants'.

captivos, servos appellando: 'by calling them captives, slaves', i.e. by referring to the inhabitants as prisoners and slaves, the veterans were claiming that these inhabitants had no rights of ownership over their houses and lands.

foventibus … militibus: the situation was made worse because the soldiers still in military service were encouraging the veterans.

impotentiam veteranorum - 'the veterans' lack of self-restraint', i.e. their greed in taking land and possessions from the local inhabitants.

similitudine vitae et spe eiusdem licentiae: the ablative nouns supply the reason for the soldiers' encouragement. The soldiers still in military service knew that life as a veteran awaited them also and, therefore, they hoped that the veterans' behaviour would set a precedent for equal lawlessness when they became veterans themselves.

ad hoc: 'in addition to this', i.e. 'furthermore'.

templum: this section gives a further reason as to why the Iceni and Trinovantes decided to focus their first attack on the Roman colony at Camulodunum. In addition to their hatred of the veterans who had been settled there, they saw the temple to Claudius as a symbol of Roman rule and they resented the fact that the priests had been requiring donations from them under the pretext of religious devotion.

arx: this word is used metaphorically. Its literal meaning – 'citadel' – refers to the most important area within town and containing the buildings and wealth which cemented local rule. As a metaphor here, the implication is that the temple to Claudius is seen as the pinnacle, bastion or symbol of Roman power.

dominationis: Tacitus' sharp analysis often rests in his choice of words. *dominatio* is a noun that conveys strong criticism because it presents Roman rule over the Britons as similar to the relationship between a master (*dominus*) and a slave.

delecti sacerdotes: the priests were chosen from among the Britons. Enfranchizing local people into Roman structures in this way helped embed Roman rule and customs.

omnes fortunas: 'everyone's wealth'.

coloniam nullis munimentis saeptam: 'a colony not protected by any defences'. Camulodunum lacked defensive infrastructure, such as a city wall.

A Level

quod: 'this was something which …'. The neuter sg. pronoun refers back to the idea of suitable defences.

ducibus nostris: the dative case is sometimes used to express agent (e.g. after a gerundive of obligation). Tacitus extends this use, and so here: 'by our leaders'.

amoenitati prius quam usui consulitur: an example of the impersonal passive construction much favoured by Tacitus (see further, p. 100) – 'since thought had been given to charm ahead of practicalities'. *usus* refers to use or experience, i.e. the practicalities of actually living in the colony. Tacitus' claim is that the Romans had been more interested in building aesthetically pleasing representations of their power (such as the temple to Claudius) than in making sure there was sufficient infrastructure to maintain the security of the colony.

Chapter 32

inter quae: *quae* is a connecting relative and best translated as 'among these things'. Tacitus now provides a list of portents which confirmed the Britons' belief that they would win against the Romans. The list of portents creates a sinister atmosphere but it is also in keeping with the Roman tradition of recording signs from the gods. The Romans believed that the gods sent signs in many different ways (e.g. unusual weather conditions, strange happenings in nature and so on) and these signs were notoriously difficult to interpret. The Roman interest in recording these signs was no doubt partly an attempt to aid subsequent interpretation by recording previous portents.

nulla palam causa: the adverb *palam* is working adjectivally here – 'and without any obvious cause'.

delapsum … conversum: understand *est* with each of these participles.

Camuloduni: locative – 'at Camulodunum'.

Victoriae: the capital letter shows that this is the name of the deity *Victoria*, the personification of victory.

quasi cederet: *quasi* can be followed by a subjunctive in a way which is similar to an 'if' clause – 'as if it were yielding ...'.

in furorem turbatae: the literal translation 'having been thrown into confusion into madness' needs some recasting in idiomatic English: 'in frenzied disarray'.

externosque fremitus ... auditos: the accusatives show that the indirect statement (introduced by *canebant*) is continuing. Supply *esse* with *auditos*. Idiomatic English requires the reader to repeat an introductory verb with each new section of indirect speech: 'and they were saying that ...'.

visamque: understand *esse*.

speciem ... subversae coloniae: 'an image of the overthrown colony'. Tacitus gives no further details about how such an image would appear, but the idea is that the inhabitants believed they had seen a sign that the Roman colony would be overthrown.

iam Oceanus: this sentence is very compressed. Understand *erat* – 'now there was the Ocean, with a bloodied appearance' – and the idea that this is the next example in the list of a sign from the gods.

labente aestu: 'with the tiding falling', i.e. as the waters receded from the shoreline, likenesses of human bodies were left behind.

ut ... ita ...: these words signal a correlation between the two clauses and indicate that the verb *trahebantur* needs to be taken with each section. The subject of *trahebantur* are all the portents previously described: 'and – just as these things were interpreted by the Britons as a sign for hope, in the same way they were interpreted by the veterans as a reason to be afraid'. The prepositional phrases – *ad spem* and *ad metum* – mark the direction of the interpretation, leading to hope/fear. As is often the case, idiomatic English requires some expansion in order to make the meaning

A Level

clear. The Britons hope that their rebellion will be successful; the veterans fear that they now face divine punishment for their greed.

petivere: the subject are the Romans based in Camulodunum.

a Cato Deciano procuratore: Catus Decianus was the imperial procurator at the time and responsible therefore for the administration of the province and the tax revenue. He is able to provide only a small amount of help.

sine iustis armis: 'without suitable weapons'.

et inerat modica militum manus: 'and there was in addition a small group of soldiers present in the area'. Catus sends men from his staff but there is also some help from the army.

tutela templi: *tutela* is ablative, after the adjective *freti* ('relying on + ablative'). Temples were believed to provide safety because they were the homes of the gods; an attack on a temple, therefore, was an attack on the gods and brought the risk of divine anger.

impedientibus qui: understand *eis* as the noun for the participle and the antecedent for *qui* – 'and with men hindering them who ...'.

consilia turbabant: the idea is that the Britons who know about the secret rebellion kept disrupting the plans of the Roman reinforcements (presumably by, for example, tearing down attempts at defensive structures).

neque fossam aut vallum praeduxerunt: the *fossa* and *vallum* were the two main defences for a military base. The combination of a *fossa* – ditch – and *vallum* – fence/rampart – was designed to slow down the speed of an attacking force.

neque ... iuventus sola restitit: this introduces another reason why the Romans were not able to defeat the Britons in Camulodunum: not only had they failed to build sufficient defences but – because they did not remove the old men and women – it was 'not the case that the youth alone took the stand' (unimpeded by those incapable of fighting getting in their way).

quasi media pace: Tacitus' point is that the Romans underestimate the threat posed by the Britons and are taken off guard, acting as they would in the middle of peace.

circumveniuntur: the Romans are the subject.

et cetera: the reference is to other public buildings (i.e. the Britons do not just attack the temple to Claudius).

direpta: understand *sunt*.

miles: the singular noun is used to represent the troops as a whole.

biduo: another example of Tacitus' use of the ablative to show duration – 'for two whole days'.

obsessum expugnatumque: understand *est* with each of these: '[the temple] was besieged and then taken by storm'.

et victor Britannus: in an idiom similar to use of *miles* to denote a whole fighting force, the singular noun here represents the British soldiers.

Petilii Ceriali: Petilius Cerialis, commander of the ninth legion, brings this legion to help the Romans, but the victorious British forces meet him as he approaches, rout the legion and kill all the infantry.

in subsidium: the prepositional phrase denotes purpose – 'for protection', i.e. 'in order to help them'.

adventanti obvius: *obvius* describes *victor Britannus*, i.e. the Britons block his path as his legion approaches.

quod peditum interfecit: a very compressed expression – understand *id* and *aderat* – '[they] killed that [part] of the infantry which was there', i.e. the Britons kill all the foot soldiers who are in their way and are unable to escape.

qua clade: connection relative – 'because of this defeat'.

A
Level

avaritia eius: *eius* refers to the procurator, Catus. His greed in looting the households of the Britons (and allowing his staff to do the same) had driven the province into war.

Chapter 33

mira constantia: Suetonius holds his nerve and Tacitus highlights this as a contrast with Catus' decision to flee to Gaul.

medios inter hostes: not quite literally true, but Suetonius had been in Wales and therefore his march to London took him through territory which was now in the control of the rebellious Britons.

Londinium: this was believed to be the oldest known reference to London until the Bloomberg Tablets were discovered between 2010 and 2014, establishing a reference which predates Tacitus by approximately fifty years.

cognomento ... coloniae non insigne: *insigne* agrees with *Londinium*, a town which was not distinguished by the name (i.e. status) of a Roman colony, but it was a centre for trade and therefore a busy and wealthy town. Tacitus is reflecting on the reasons why Londinium would or would not have been a priority for the Romans to defend: it lacked the status of one of their colonies but it did contain significant wealth.

copia: causal ablative – 'because of the abundance ...'.

ibi ambiguus: Suetonius is the subject; understand *erat*. 'There he was undecided as to whether ...'.

an: introduces an indirect question in the way that *num* would in Classical Latin.

illam sedem ... deligeret: '... he should choose that base ...', but in idiomatic English, '... he should choose that city as a base for the war'.

circumspecta infrequentia ... magnis documentis: these ablatives provide the reasons for Suetonius' decision to abandon London rather than risk a total defeat there which would cause the loss of the whole province. The causal ablatives are best translated as a causal clause in English: 'Since he had considered the low numbers of soldiers and since he had sufficiently large proof that Petilius' rashness had been his downfall ...'.

temeritatem ... coercitam: understand *esse*. The phrase is very compressed: 'the rashness had been enclosed/cut back', i.e., Petilius' rashness in fighting the Britons with an insufficient number of troops and without sufficient attention to defence had meant that he was surrounded by them and beaten.

unius oppidi damno: *damno* is an ablative of instrument – 'by the loss of one town'.

universa: understand *oppida* – i.e. Suetonius decided that if he abandoned London he would be able to muster more troops or find a better location to fight and thus achieve the victory against the Britons which would regain control of the whole province.

orantium: participle requires the reader to supply a noun/pronoun – 'of those begging for ...'.

neque ... flexus est, quin daret: *quin* + subjunctive follows verbs of prevention/hindering and *flexus est* is used metaphorically – 'he was not dissuaded from giving ...'.

profectionis signum: the genitive case joins one noun to another. In English a range of different prepositions fulfil this function; here, 'the signal for departure'.

comitantes: the participle requires the reader to supply a noun (and also an object) – 'people accompanying him'.

agminis: the *agmen* was the formation used for travelling ('marching column') and should not be confused with *acies*, the formation used for fighting ('battleline').

A Level

si quos: *quis, quid* means 'anyone', 'anything' when it is used after *si*. Tacitus implies there was total destruction for anyone who stayed behind in London.

fuit: 'happened'.

omissis castellis praesidiisque militarium: the Britons had no interest in attacking the military fortifications and focused their attention instead on looting. The genitive pl. adjective here is used as a noun – 'of the soldiers'.

quod uberrimum spolianti et defendentibus intutum: *quod* requires the reader to understand *id* as its antecedent – 'that which', i.e. 'whatever'. Supply *erat*. *defendentibus* is an example of a dative of agent; the participle requires the reader to understand its noun/pronoun and its object – 'unguarded by those defending the town'.

laeti praeda et laborum segnes: Tacitean *variatio* is at play in this phrase since *laeti* is qualified by a causal ablative noun, but *segnes* by a genitive noun. The soldiers were 'happy from plunder and lazy in their labours', i.e. they were uninterested in the hard work of attacking military fortifications and they were focused instead on the quick gains of looting.

ad septuaginta milia . . . cecidisse: 'roughly 70,000'. *milia* is followed by two genitive nouns and is the accusative subject of *cecidisse*.

iis . . . locis: these should be taken together; the ablative shows place where – 'in those places'.

quae memoravi: i.e. London and Verulamium.

constitit: this verb can be used to denote general agreement because its most literal meaning ('it has stood firm') implies an established fact. In English, 'it is agreed that'.

neque . . . capere aut venundare aliudve quod . . .: the infinitive is a verbal noun and so *capere* and *venundare* are both subjects in this sentence, along with *aliud*. Understand *erat*: 'there was neither taking nor selling nor anything else which . . .'. Tacitus is referring to the trading which was a standard part of warfare (e.g. the capturing of people and the selling of them as slaves); the Britons were looting for their own enjoyment but they were not slowing down to enter into trading.

quod belli commercium: understand *est*.

caedes patibula ignes cruces: the list is brutal and implies savage destruction or punishment of the people Boudicca's army found in the town. *patibula* (fork-shaped yokes) and *cruces* (crosses) were both used in the torture or execution of criminals and slaves.

reddituri supplicium: Tacitus implies that the Britons knew that they were likely to be beaten and punished but they were in a rush to cause as much destruction as vengeance first.

festinabant: 'they were in a rush'.

Chapter 34

Suetonio: possessive dative – 'for Suetonius now there were …', i.e. 'Suetonius now had …'.

quarta decima legio … auxiliares: Tacitus lists Suetonius' troops. With him now were the fourteenth legion, some veteran reservists from the twentieth legion and the auxiliary soldiers from the nearest legions, nearly 10,000 men in total.

e proximis: understand *legionibus* with this adjective.

cum … parat: an example of an inverted *cum* clause, i.e. a *cum* clause which presents what is – in meaning – the main event of the sentence. English idiom means that it is best to convert to a main clause and subordinate the previous clause instead: 'When Suetonius had …, he prepared …'. It is common for an inverted *cum* clause to have its verb in the present indicative, increasing the dramatic vividness.

deligitque locum: Tacitus explains Suetonius' skilful choice of location. He chose a place with only one narrow entrance; this meant that there

A Level

was no risk of ambush. No doubt Suetonius was confident that the superior fighting skills and discipline of his men meant that in a pitched battle in a contained location, the Romans were likely to win.

satis cognito: 'sufficient for him when he realized', i.e. when Suetonius realized that there was no risk of an attack from the rear or ambush, he knew that he had found a sufficiently suitable location.

nihil hostium: understand *futurum esse*. *nihil hostium* is equivalent in meaning to *nullos hostes*.

igitur legionarius frequens ordinibus . . . astitit: *legionarius* is singular but represents the legionary soldiers as a whole. Suetonius packed his legionaries into a tight mass; this would prevent the Britons gaining much advantage from their superior numbers because they would be unlikely to be able to break through the solid battleline of the Romans.

legionarius . . . armatura . . . eques: these are all subjects of *astitit* – 'the legionary soldiers took up their position … the light-armed troops stood … and the cavalry were stationed …'. Idiomatic English requires a verb with each subject and favours variety of choice of verb rather than straight repetition.

at: Tacitus marks the contrast between the tightly ordered Roman army and the chaotic and loosely assembled Britons. In what was essentially an infantry battle, tightness of battleline was an important tactic, since it reduced the likelihood that the other side would be able to break through, surround their opposition and win.

quanta . . . multitudo: in English, *multitudo* is best taken before *quanta* – 'a crowd of a size which had existed at no other time' (understand *fuerat*).

ut . . . imponerent: the decision to surround the edge of the battlefield with the wagons of spectators proved a fatal mistake for the Britons. When the Roman battleline proved superior, the Britons found themselves trapped in the battlefield with no escape route open to them because their wagons were in the way.

quae: neuter pl., referring to the *plaustra*.

Chapter 35

Boudicca: speeches are a major part of the Roman historiographical tradition (see further, p. 11) and Tacitus now moves to a focus on the two leaders – Boudicca and Suetonius – and their speeches before the battle. These speeches are likely to be an imagined recreation of what might have been said; they allow Tacitus to deepen his characterization and increase the emotional intensity of the battle. Boudicca's speech focuses on the sexual violation and physical abuse that the Britons have suffered and the Roman military cowardice and failure so far.

ut quamque nationem accesserat: 'as she approached each tribe'. The pluperfect indicative is a natural pairing with a main clause imperfect (*testabatur*) when the writer is referring to a repeated action. Here, Boudicca goes to each section of her army and gives the same speech each time.

solitum . . . bellare: understand *esse* to complete this indirect statement – 'that it was usual [for the Britons] to wage war'.

feminarum ductu: an ablative of instrument – 'by means of/under the leadership of women'. The plural is suitable for a general statement like this, but it resonates with the image of Boudicca and her daughters, working together to lead their rebellion.

testabatur: 'she kept bearing witness', i.e. stating as a truth.

sed tunc: Tacitus moves to *oratio obliqua* (see further, p. 14–15), shown by the accusative and infinitive constructions and subjunctive verbs. English idiom requires the reader to supply an introductory verb for each new sentence: 'She said that on this occasion, however, . . .'.

A Level

non ut ... ortam ... verum ut unam ... ulcisci: Latin oratory favoured balance, and contrasting pairs like this are typical of an elevated style; Latin's natural concision means that words which are needed in each section often only appear once, but English idiom requires more explicit repetition. Here, *ortam* and *unam* both refer to Boudicca and both require *ulcisci* as their verb: '[she said that] she was taking vengeance not for her kingdom and wealth, as one born from great ancestors, but – as one from the crowd – she was taking vengeance for their lost freedom, ...'. Her point is that she is fighting for reasons that are shared with her troops.

libertatem ... corpus ... pudicitiam: all three of these nouns are objects for *ulcisci*.

eo: a demonstrative adverb and – like demonstrative adjectives such as *tantus, talis, tot* – it often adds emphasis: 'to such a point/degree'.

provectas ... cupidines: understand *esse* with *provectas* and add an introductory verb in English: 'and she said that ...'.

ut ... relinquant: the result clause has a present subjunctive. This creates drama by suggesting that this is an ongoing situation. It also makes the speech more vivid because the tense represents directly the tense of the original direct speech (e.g. 'The Romans' greed has grown so great that they do not leave ...') rather than respecting the rules of sequence for *oratio obliqua* (see further, p. 14–15 and p. 101).

adesse ... deos: supply an introductory verb in English – 'and she said that ...'.

quae ... ausa sit: again, a vivid primary sequence subjunctive, echoing the tense of the original direct speech.

ceteros: supply a noun for this adjective – 'the other soldiers'.

strepitum ... clamorem ... impetus ... manus: a list of accusatives, all working as the object of *perlaturos*. The list builds in intensity as Boudicca details the things that the Romans are not brave enough to put before the Britons, moving from a mere shout to a battle-charge and then hand-to-hand combat.

perlaturos: understand *esse*. The subject is an understood *Romanos*: '[and she said that] the Romans would bring forth not even a rumbling, the shouting of so many thousands, far less their attacks and their hands'.

si ... expenderent: the Britons are the subject. The imperfect subjunctive represents what would have been a present subjunctive in the original direct speech, denoting a future time, remote conditional clause – 'if they were to consider ...'.

vincendum ... vel cadendum esse: a compressed accusative and infinitive construction which requires the reader to supply 'she said that they would realize that ...'. The gerundives of obligation are both impersonal (see further, p. 100): '... either they must win ... or they must die'.

id: a neuter pronoun can refer to a statement, idea or event. Here it refers to the necessity either to win or to die.

destinatum: understand *esse*.

viverent viri et servirent: the main clause subjunctives show that this is a command within *oratio obliqua* – 'Let the men live and be slaves'. Boudicca's point is that living – in effect as slaves – under Roman control brought with it for the women such risk of sexual violation that it was an option only tolerable for men.

Chapter 36

Suetonius: Suetonius' speech focuses on the Roman army's superior military skill and the glory available to them if they win.

in tanto discrimine: Tacitus' presents this battle as a major turning point. Up until this point Boudicca had fought against only sections of the Roman army. Now she faces the governor, Suetonius, with the greatest number of troops he could muster. Defeat in this battle would, in effect, represent loss of control over the whole province.

quamquam confideret: Tacitus uses the subjunctive much more liberally in subordinate clauses than is typical in Classical Latin. The meaning here is equivalent to *quamquam confidebat*.

ut spernerent: this indirect command marks the beginning of the *oratio obliqua*. Supply an introductory verb: '... saying that ...'.

plus ... adspici: an indirect statement; supply an introductory verb in English: 'and he said that ...'. *plus* often functions as a noun and so here it is the subject of the infinitive and followed by a dependent genitive (*feminarum*). The passive infinitive *adspici* is awkward in English and best translated as '[more women] were in view ...'.

imbelles inermes cessuros: supply *eos* and *esse* to complete this indirect statement, as well as an introductory verb in English – 'and he said that they were ...'. As is often the case, the future participle carries a sense of 'likely to ...'.

statim ubi: 'immediately when', i.e. 'as soon as'.

vincentium: supply a noun with this participle – 'of men who had won'. The present participle creates the sense that the men have won in the past and are continuing to do so.

fusi: this nominative participle describes the Britons, the subject of *agnovissent*.

in multis legionibus: 'in the midst of large armies'.

paucos qui proelia profligarent: *qui* + subjunctive here conveys a generic result, describing *paucos* as 'men of the sort who could ...'. As a whole statement, therefore, the meaning is: '[and he said that] even in the midst of large armies, a few men could all but finish the fighting'. Suetonius is urging his men not to be daunted by the Britons' greater

accessurum: supply *esse* to complete this future infinitive. The infinitive's subject is the content expressed in the *quod* clause: 'and [he said that] the fact that ... would add to their glory'.

modica manus ... adipiscerentur: the subject – *modica manus* – is technically singular, but refers to multiple men, hence the plural verb.

universi exercitus famam: 'the glory of a whole army'. Suetonius' fighting force is much smaller than a large Roman army, but he encourages the men to believe that they are capable of a victory equal in importance to that achieved by much larger forces.

conferti ... continuarent: Suetonius makes his battle strategy clear. The Romans are to maintain tight-packed ranks (designed to prevent the Britons breaking through their battleline and gaining any advantage from their greater numbers). They should throw their spears and then continue the fighting at close quarters, using swords and their shield bosses. The main clause subjunctive shows that this is a command within *oratio obliqua*.

praedae immemores: 'paying no attention to plunder', i.e. the Roman soldiers should not be distracted by the opportunity to loot valuable armour from the bodies of the dead Britons, but press on with their attack.

parta victoria: ablative absolute.

cuncta: supply a noun for this adjective – 'all things'.

cessura: supply *esse* to complete this future infinitive. The idea is that, once the soldiers have won, then everything is theirs.

is ardor ... ita ...: demonstrative pronouns and adverbs add emphasis and *is* is used here in a way that is parallel to *ita*: 'such enthusiasm ... in such a way ...'.

A Level

vetus miles: *vetus* means 'old', but here the idea is 'experienced'. Suetonius has a seasoned army at his disposal and he knows that this will work to his advantage. The singular noun is used to represent the soldiers in general.

expedierat: a shortened form of *expediverat*.

multa ... experientia: this nominative noun supplies the third ingredient that makes Suetonius confident of victory, but significant recasting is needed in English to achieve a smooth flow into the result clause: '... and their sizeable experience from previous battles achieved the result that Suetonius ...'.

certus eventus: *eventus* is an objective genitive (see Chapter 29 above, **ambitionis manifestus**) – 'sure of the outcome'.

Chapter 37

legio ... immota et ... retinens: understand *erat*.

angustias loci pro munimento: the legion made use of the narrowness of the location in place of defence. The Britons had much greater numbers and – on a larger battlefield – there would have been significant risk that the Romans ended up surrounded and beaten (hence the need for defence). The narrow location, however, meant that only a small section of the British forces could gain access to the Roman fighting line; this removed the advantage of their superior numbers, provided the Romans held their line.

in propius suggressos hostes: this prepositional phrase is best expanded with a relative clause in English: '... at the enemy who had moved closer'.

velut cuneo erupit: when the Roman army had run out of missiles to throw, it advanced in a wedge formation. This allowed the men to focus their pressure on a smaller section of the Britons' battleline and achieve the impact needed to break their line.

idem: the neuter pronoun is used adverbially here: 'in the same way'.

auxiliarum impetus: supply a verb from context – 'the auxiliaries' charge took place in the same way'.

eques protentis hastis perfringit quod . . .: the cavalry could move much faster than the infantry; the extra momentum increased the force of its attack and therefore it did not need to use the wedge formation. *eques* is singular but represents the cavalry as a whole. The object of *perfringit* is the missing antecedent for *quod*: 'that which', i.e. 'whatever . . .'.

validum: 'strong' in the sense of strong enough to resist the cavalry charge. The cavalry dealt with this by using the horsemen's outstretched spears.

praebuere: a shortened form of *praebuerunt*.

abitus: accusative pl. and the object of *saepserant*.

miles: singular but representing the soldiers in general.

ne . . . quidem; these words emphasize the word they surround. The shocking detail emphasized here is that the soldiers killed even the women and probably refers to the women watching the battle, who – as bystanders – should have been spared.

clara et . . . par . . . laus: the adjectives *clara* and *par* both describe *laus*. The adjectives have been promoted for emphasis.

parta: understand *est*.

sunt qui: the reader needs to supply a pronoun as the antecedent for *qui* – 'there are those who . . .'.

qui . . . tradant: the subjunctive indicates a generic clause – 'of the sort who record that . .', but this nuance is lost in the most idiomatic English translation: 'indeed, some authors record that . . .'.

militum quadringentis: the genitive is partitive, i.e. 'four hundred of the soldiers'. *militum* refers to the Roman soldiers.

A Level

abnueratque contra ritum militiae iussa ducis: Tacitus claims that Poenius Postumus had been ordered to bring his legion to join Suetonius but he had refused to do so.

se ... transegit: no doubt Poenius Postumus knew that he would be punished for disobeying Suetonius' orders and he had lost the respect of his soldiers in denying them their chance to be part of such a significant victory.

Chapters 38 to 58: Tacitus finishes his account of the Britons' rebellion: Suetonius' attempts to subdue the British forces are thwarted by the imperial procurator's attempts to get him replaced. Nero sends his freedman Polyclitus to mediate between them.

The focus of Tacitus' account returns to Rome and Tacitus describes shocking crimes that took place. In the midst of increasing public scandal, Tacitus mourns the decline of Burrus and Seneca's good influence on Nero. Burrus dies; Tacitus reports that it remains unclear whether he died from natural causes or was murdered by Nero. Seneca decides to withdraw from public life and asks Nero to let him hand back some of his huge wealth. Nero refuses; Seneca leaves Rome, claiming ill-health. Further murders take place to remove potential rivals to Nero.

Chapter 59

positu metu: the senate's reaction to Plautus' death has emboldened Nero and he believes that it will approve any action, no matter how shameful.

ob eius modi terrores: the reference is to Nero's fear that the senate would disapprove. A recurring theme in Tacitus' characterization of Nero is that, although he was capable of appalling actions, he was a man who craved public approval all the same. Poppaea was a former slave and Octavia the daughter of the previous emperor, Claudius. Nero's legitimacy as an heir to Claudius rested partly on his mother's marriage to the emperor and also on his own marriage into the family, via Octavia. To divorce Octavia and marry Poppaea, therefore, was not just a move to a wife of much lower social status but also removed the direct link to the bloodline of the imperial family.

quamvis modeste ageret: Octavia is the subject. Tacitus often uses a subjunctive in a concessive clause; its meaning here is no different from an indicative. *modeste* implies that Octavia acted with the self-restraint appropriate for a Roman noble, a pointed contrast with the power-hungry excesses of unrestrained Romans such as Nero.

nomine patris et studiis populi gravem: *gravem* describes Octavia. The phrase is probably best converted into a clause in English – 'Octavia was burdensome to him because of . . .'. The ablative nouns *nomine* and *studiis* supply the reasons: Nero resents Octavia's status as the direct descendent of the emperor Claudius and he is threatened by her popularity.

haud confessus: Nero does not confess that he is responsible for Sulla and Plautus' death; presumably his hope was that the senate would confirm that they had to be removed and thus create an *ex post facto* justification for their murder.

verum . . . esse: the accusative *ingenium* and its infinitive *esse* indicate a move to indirect statement. In English, supply an introductory verb: 'but he said that the character of each was deranged'.

sibi: dative of agent – 'by him'.

incolumitatem . . . magna cura haberi: *habeo* often has a meaning of 'think/consider'. The passive is awkward in English and so this indirect statement is best rendered in the active voice: '[and he said that] he thought about the safety of the state with great care'.

decretae: understand *sunt*.

eo nomine: 'under this name', i.e. the murders of Sulla and Plautus were labelled as actions to preserve the safety of the state.

utque ... moverentur: supply the main verb needed to introduce this indirect command: 'and the senate decreed that [Sulla and Plautus] should be removed ...'.

gravioribus iam ludibriis quam malis: Tacitus often ends a sentence with a barbed judgement. The idea here is that the senate's decision to expel Sulla and Plautus is risible since they are already dead. The mockery referred to by *ludibrium* applies both to Sulla and Plautus (who suffer the degradation of this formal edict) but also to the senate, since the seriousness of a senatorial decree is now trivialized by the farce of expelling dead men from its ranks.

Chapter 60

accepto ... consulto: i.e. the senate's ratification of Sulla's and Plautus' removal.

cuncta scelerum suorum: the genitives show that *cuncta* is working as a noun – 'the totality of his own crimes'.

pro egregiis: the adjective *egregiis* requires the reader to supply a noun: Nero's crimes are received by the senate 'in place of outstanding actions', i.e. the senate offers thanks for Nero's crimes as if they were the glorious victories achieved by Rome's most eminent leaders.

sterilem: understand *eam* and *esse* to complete this indirect statement. An inability to have children was seen as legitimate grounds for divorce since the wife's role was partly to provide an heir.

adulteri Neronis, mox mariti: *potens* (meaning 'powerful over somebody else') can be followed by a genitive noun. Tacitus emphasizes Poppaea's move from mistress to wife by labelling Nero as 'her lover, then her husband'.

servilem ei amorem obicere: *obicere* means 'to put forward as an allegation against someone' (dative). The crime alleged here is an affair with a slave; if true, the mismatch in social status would have been scandalous and the risk of polluting the imperial bloodline with servile blood was a crime punishable by exile or death.

canere . . . doctus: the infinitive explains the scope of *doctus* – 'learned/ skilled in making music . . .'.

actae: understand *sunt*.

ob id: 'about this', i.e. the alleged affair.

de ancillis: Octavia's slaves would have had intimate knowledge of her private life and so were interrogated about the truth of the allegation.

vi tormentorum: slaves were expected to be loyal to their masters at all costs and – on this assumption – it was usual to question them under torture. The rationale was that only thus could they be expected to speak the truth.

ut . . . adnuerent: a result clause. For some of the slaves, the torture was so great that they lied (no doubt in the hope of stopping the torture).

perstitere . . . tueri: a shortened form of *perstiterunt*. The infinitive *tueri* supplies the object for this verb: 'they stood firm in defending . . .'.

ex quibus: as a connecting relative this is best translated with a demonstrative – '[one] of these slaves'.

instanti Tigellino: the participle phrase is best translated as a clause: 'when Tigellinus pressed her'. Tacitus characterizes Tigellinus as one of the main villains of Nero's rule. The implication here is that Tigellinus is trying to further Nero's wishes by pushing Octavia's slaves to accuse her falsely.

muliebria: supply a noun for this adjective – 'the female parts', i.e. her genitals.

quam os eius: the suggestion is that Tigellinus' mouth has been closer to another man's penis than Octavia has.

movetur: Octavia is the subject.

A Level

civilis discidii specie: 'under the pretext of a citizen's divorce', i.e. in the absence of sufficient proof for the allegation of an affair with a slave (a crime punishable by exile or death), Octavia was divorced but maintained her status as a citizen.

infausta dona: Octavia is given property which belonged once to Burrus and Plautus. Both of these men had been murdered by Nero, hence Tacitus' barbed comment that these were 'ill-omened gifts'.

in Campaniam ... addita militari custodia: Octavia's status as Claudius' daughter and her popularity with the people made her a threat to Nero. The fear was that a potential rival could use marriage to Octavia to legitimize a coup. For this reason Nero moved her further from Rome and added a military guard.

inde crebri questus: understand *erant*. The Roman people object to Octavia's removal from Rome.

vulgum: an alternative accusative sg. form for the neuter noun *vulgus*.

cui: possessive dative, referring to *vulgum*.

pauciora pericula: in an age where Roman emperors took increasingly brutal measures to protect their power, the higher a Roman's social status and the greater his wealth, the greater the threat posed to the emperor's power. This is why Tacitus equates lower social status and wealth with fewer risks for the individual concerned: speaking out against the emperor was less dangerous if it came from someone who posed no direct threat to him. As evidenced by the murders of Sulla and Plautus, Nero wasted no time in getting rid of potential rivals.

his ... Octaviam: the text is damaged here and words are missing, but the overall sense must be that in response to the people's complaints, Nero acted as if he regretted his actions and had recalled Octavia as his wife or there was a rumour that this had happened.

revocarit: a shortened form of the perfect subjunctive, *revocaverit*. Tacitus often follows *tamquam* with a subjunctive; the perfect tense belongs to primary sequence and so adds vividness to the text.

Chapter 61

exim ... venerantur: the Roman people are the subject; mistakenly believing that Octavia has been reinstated, they rejoice and give thanks to the gods.

spargunt ... statuunt: understand *imagines* as the object of both these verbs.

itur: Tacitus favours the impersonal passive as a way to emphasize the action. This is because the impersonal passive uses the action itself as the subject: 'a going is gone'. In English, the best way to convey this focus on the action is to use a noun: 'there was a move [towards ...]'.

strepitu venerantium: 'with noise arising from those honouring him', i.e. different people are shouting out praise for Nero, creating a loud hubbub. Note that Nero is the object of *venerantium*; this participle requires us to understand 'people' as its noun.

cum ... disiecere: an inverted *cum* clause, i.e. a clause that is technically subordinate but conveys the main information within the sentence. It is usual for *cum* to be followed by an indicative in this instance. *disiecere* is a shortened form of *disiecerunt*.

verberibus et intento ferro: *ferro* is singular as a generalized comment, but it is more idiomatic as a plural noun in English: 'with beatings and outstretched swords'.

turbatos: understand a noun for this participle – 'the citizens thrown into confusion'. In idiomatic English, however, the participle is best converted to a finite verb: 'the groups of soldiers ... threw the crowds into confusion and dispersed them'.

mutataque: understand *sunt*. The subject of this verb is the missing antecedent for *quae*; supply *ea*: 'those things were changed which ...'.

per seditionem: *seditio* refers to violent uprisings on the streets, and therefore represents something which would have no place in a stable and well-governed society.

quae semper: understand *erat*.

odio ... metu: causal ablatives: Poppaea is cruel 'because of her hatred ... because of her fear'. Her hatred is directed at Octavia, and her fear is that she will lose her position as Nero's wife.

ne aut ... ingrueret aut ... mutaretur: the fear clause explains what Poppaea fears.

provoluta: understand *est*. Like many verbs of movement (such as *verto* or *moveo*), *provolvo* is a transitive verb. Its passive voice, therefore, has a meaning similar to an English intransitive verb such as 'she fell at/she grovelled at'.

genibus: dative as an indirect object after the passive *provoluta [est]*: 'she grovelled at his knees'.

eo loci ... ut ... certet: *eo loci* means 'to that/to such a state of affairs' and its reference is then explained by the *ut* clause.

res suas agi: the accusative and infinitive indicate that this is indirect speech. English requires the reader to supply an introductory verb: 'Poppaea said that her situation was not being driven to such a state of affairs that she was competing for her marriage'.

id: the pronoun refers back to *matrimonium*. Supply *erat*.

vita: ablative of comparison after *potius*.

vitam ipsam ... adductam: supply *esse*.

in extremum: 'to the brink'.

a clientelis: *clientela* refers to the client-patron relationship, i.e. the loyalty expected by a patron from his clients. This relationship operated at all levels of Roman society: wealthier Romans could act as patrons to less wealthy or influential Romans (their clients). These clients often included slaves who had been freed. A patron would offer financial or practical support to their clients in return for political or practical help.

The reference, therefore, to Octavia's clients and slaves is to a group of people whom Octavia could count on to carry out her wishes.

quae: the gender of pronouns is sometimes driven by the actual gender of the noun referred to, rather than the technical gender of the piece of vocabulary. Here, the pronoun is feminine because it refers back to Octavia's female slaves and clients. It would be implausible to believe that Octavia's supporters were exclusively female, but Poppaea's presentation of them in this way goads Nero into anger that a group of women is achieving public power in opposition to his wishes.

quae plebis sibi nomen indiderint: the suggestion is that Octavia's supporters are claiming to represent the Roman people in general. Note that the perfect subjunctive gives the indirect speech the vividness of primary sequence (see further, p. 101).

ea in pace ausi, quae vix bello evenirent: Poppaea's speech is a gross exaggeration; her implication is that the public support for Octavia resembles a coup, i.e. the Roman people are attempting to overthrow Nero, thus daring things which are achieved with difficulty in full-blown war.

sumpta: understand *esse* and add an introductory verb in English: 'Poppaea said that ...'.

qui ... reperiretur: a type of idealized result clause, where the subjunctive indicates a probable action: 'who could be found'.

motis rebus: 'since the rebellion was underway'.

omitteret ... pergeret: the main clause subjunctives indicate a suggested action: 'Just let her leave Campania and set foot in the city in person!' Poppaea's point is that, if Octavia has been able to achieve so much while under guard in Campania, then she is capable of creating a far greater threat to Nero's power.

ad cuius nutum absentis: take all these words as part of the prepositional phrase; idiomatic English, however, leans towards expanding the participle into a clause: 'at whose nod – when she was not even present – uprisings …'.

quod … delictum: the adjectival form of *quis*, *quid* has slightly different endings; *quod* is in agreement with *delictum*; supply *esse* (since a rhetorical question within indirect speech takes the accusative + infinitive construction): 'What was her wrong-doing?' Poppaea has moved to considering what possible reason there could be for the uprisings if not some sort of political opposition: her point here is that she – Poppaea – has done no wrong and there is no justification of this sort for Octavia's actions.

quam cuiusquam offensionem: understand *esse*. Tacitus uses a noun, but idiomatic English favours a verb: 'Had she offended anyone?'

an quia …: the causal clause offers another possible reason for the uprising. The tone is scornful: 'or was it because …'.

veram progeniem … datura sit: 'a true offspring'; Poppaea reasserts her allegation that Octavia had been unfaithful; any children of hers, therefore, would be illegitimate. Poppaea, however, can be trusted to bear only Nero's children. Note that the present subjunctive carries the vividness of primary sequence (see further, p. 101).

malle populum Romanum: the accusative and infinitive signals another rhetorical question.

imperatorio fastigio: 'to the heights of the imperial family'. *fastigium* refers to highest point of a roof and therefore is used metaphorically to represent that the imperial family has the highest social status of all.

si id rebus conducat: the subjunctive shows that the indirect speech continues: '[Poppaea said that] that benefitted the situation', i.e. if Nero really thought it appropriate to reinstate a wife who would pollute the imperial bloodline.

libens quam coactus acciret dominam: the subjunctive shows that this is a main clause command – 'he should summon …'. The vocabulary is

inflammatory: *dominam* suggests that the power balance between Nero and Octavia equates to that of a slave and his master. *quam*: 'rather than'.

vel consuleret securitati: the command continues – 'or he should take thought for his safety'. The implication is that Octavia's next step will be to plot Nero's death.

primos motus consedisse: the indirect speech continues – '[Poppaea said that] the first uprisings had settled down'.

si desperent ... daturos: supply *esse* to complete the main clause. The Roman people are the subject.

illi: this pronoun refers to Octavia. Poppaea's point is that, if Octavia is not reinstated as Nero's wife, then the Roman people will find her a different husband. The implication is that this new husband will seize power and take Nero's place as emperor.

Chapter 62

in servo: 'against the slave', i.e. the allegation of an affair between Octavia and the Alexandrian flute-player, Eucaerus.

quaestionibus ancillarum elusa erat: i.e. too few of Octavia's slaves had supplied corroborating evidence for the allegation to be convincing.

cui ... adfingeretur: another result clause indicating probability – 'on whom [the accusation ...] could be pinned'.

rerum ... novarum: 'political revolution'.

visus: understand *est*.

maternae necis: Nero had murdered his mother, Agrippina, in AD 59 with Anicetus' help.

classi: dative – Anicetus was prefect 'for the fleet', i.e. he was in charge of the fleet. Anicetus' military responsibilities, therefore, make him an excellent candidate: if he confessed to an affair with Octavia, it would be plausible that she had seduced him in order to secure his – and the Roman fleet's – support in a political coup.

levi ... gratia ... graviore odio: the descriptive ablatives are best converted into a clause: 'Anicetus had only a small degree of favour after the crime had been committed, and soon an increasing degree of hatred ...'.

quia ... adspiciuntur: Tacitus' point is that the men who carry out a crime for someone else often then incur their hatred because their knowledge of the crime means that it can seem as if they are judgemental or critical about their instructor's guilt.

Caesar: i.e. Nero; *Caesar* was used as an honorific title for the princeps.

solum ... subvenisse: the accusative and infinitive shows that Tacitus is reporting Nero's speech. English requires an introductory verb: 'Nero said that he alone had come to the aid of ...'.

adversus insidiantem matrem: Nero's retrospective justification is that Agrippina had been plotting against him in an attempt to seize power.

locum: 'opportunity'.

nec manu aut telo opus: supply *esse*. Note that *opus* is followed by an ablative. The reference to no need for 'a hand or a weapon' means that Nero is not asking him to kill Octavia in person (as Anicetus had done to Agrippina).

fateretur: the subjunctive denotes a main clause command in indirect speech. English requires an introductory verb: 'Nero said that he should confess ...'.

Octaviae adulterium: the genitive case links one noun to another and a variety of prepositions can be needed in English to achieve this; here, 'adultery with Octavia'.

occulta ... magna: both these adjectives agree with *praemia*.

ad praesens: the participle requires us to understand a noun: 'for the present moment'.

successus amoenos: Ancietus would, of course, lose his military office if implicated in a power coup with Octavia, but Nero promises a pleasant retirement for him.

promittit ... intentat: both historic present tenses, creating vividness but better translated as a past tense in English.

si negavisset: the pluperfect subjunctive is awkward in English and is the result of Tacitus' compressed style. Embedded within *necem intentat* is a virtual indirect statement, since 'he threatened death' is broadly equivalent to 'he threatened that he would kill him if ...'. Thus the *si* clause is constructed as a subordinate clause in indirect speech, and the pluperfect subjunctive represents the future perfect indicative of the direct speech. Idiomatic English works better without this compression: 'and Nero threatened death if Anicetus refused'.

vaecordia et facilitate: causal ablatives – 'because of ...'.

Chapter 63

praefectum ... corruptum: supply *esse*. The indirect statement is introduced by *memorat*.

in spem sociandae classis: a compressed prepositional phrase that is translated best as a clause in English: 'because Octavia hoped to have the fleet on her side'.

incusatae paulo ante sterilitatis oblitus: the genitive participle phrase is best translated as a clause: 'forgetting that he had accused her of sterility just a little earlier'.

abactos partus: supply *esse*.

conscientia libidinum: a causal ablative – 'because they were proof of their passion'.

A Level

ea: this pronoun refers to the information provided in the previous indirect statements.

insula Pandateria: the island of Pandateria was in the Tyrrhenian sea and used for Roman exiles.

visentium: understand a noun for this participle – 'of those visiting'.

meminerant: *memini* is perfect in form but present in meaning and so its pluperfect form equates to a simple past tense – '[some] remembered'.

Agrippinae: this refers not to Nero's mother, Agrippina, but to his grandmother. She was banished to Pandateria in AD 33 by the emperor Tiberius.

a Tiberio ... a Claudio pulsae: the participle *pulsae* applies in both these phrases.

Iuliae: Julia was Agrippina's daughter; she was banished in AD 41 under the emperor Claudius.

robur aetatis: 'the toughness of age'; in contrast, Octavia is only twenty.

laeta aliqua: neuter in gender and so 'other things that were happy'.

huic: i.e. Octavia. The dative case marks possession.

primum: 'first/first of all' – this introduces the first detail in the list.

loco funeris: 'in the place of a funeral', i.e. her wedding day was, in effect, her funeral.

deductae: the participle describes Octavia and it is dative in agreement with *huic*. The participle is best translated as a finite verb in English: 'she had been led'.

in qua ... haberet: generic *qui* clause – 'a house of the sort in which she had nothing ...'.

luctuosum: the adjective is best translated as a noun – 'pain'.

et statim: the adverb denotes speed – 'and very shortly afterwards'.

tum: understand *fuit*.

ancilla: the reference is to Claudia Acte, a slave who had an affair with Nero.

non nisi: 'for no reason other than'.

in perniciem uxoris: *in* denotes purpose. Tacitus has used a noun but idiomatic English favours a verb: 'to destroy his wife'.

nupta: supply *est*.

crimen: i.e. the accusation that she and Anicetus had been plotting to seize power from Nero.

Chapter 64

praesagio malorum iam vitae exempta: 'now finished with life in her awareness of her troubles'. *vitae* is an objective genitive after *exempta*. Tacitus' point is that Octavia knows that life holds nothing for her now.

cum . . . testaretur: *cum* here means 'although'. Octavia has nothing to live for but she is not yet ready to die and she pleads with the soldiers, arguing that she poses no threat to Nero.

viduam se: understand *esse*.

sororem: the emperor Claudius (Octavia's father) had adopted Nero.

Germanicos: the reference is to members of the imperial family who had had this name (i.e. her grandfather Drusus and her uncle Germanicus. Octavia is arguing that their shared family connections mean that her loyalty can be trusted.

Agrippina: Nero's mother. Agrippina had married the previous emperor Claudius and engineered Nero's rise to power through adoption into the imperial family.

pertulisset: subjunctive because it is a subordinate clause within indirect speech.

A Level

quod ... vidit: this clause explains *saevitia*: 'worse cruelty is added, i.e. the fact that Poppaea looked at her head ...'.

decreta: understand *sunt*.

quem ad finem: 'for what purpose'.

memorabimus: supply *dona* as its object.

nobis vel aliis auctoribus: 'either from me or from other authors'.

praesumptum habeant: the subjunctive is exhortative – 'they should take it as an assumption that ...'.

grates ... actas: supply *esse* to complete the indirect statement.

quaeque: 'and those things which'.

quod: the adjectival form of *quis, quid* and in agreement with *consultum*. After *si* the meaning is 'any'.

adulatione novum aut patientia postremum: 'novel in its flattery or extreme in its endurance'. The phrase sums up Tacitus' characterization of Nero's rule: the Romans had to praise Nero in increasingly lavish ways or for increasingly bizarre reasons and they had to suffer increasing humiliations.

Chapter 65

eodem anno: AD 62.

libertorum: under the emperors, freedmen held important administrative positions. The emperor Claudius set the precedent for this: freedmen, because they lacked the social status of Rome's noble elite, did not pose the same risk as potential political rivals and their loyalty, therefore, was more likely.

creditus: supply *est*; Nero is the subject.

Romanus: probably the name of one of Nero's freedmen.

C. Piso: Gaius Calpurnius Piso had been consul under the emperor Claudius. He lived a magnificent lifestyle and his oratorical skill made him popular with the Roman people. This popularity made him suspicious to Nero and his advisors, who feared that a Roman noble with enough popular support might be able to get rid of Nero and take power for himself.

sed ... perculsus est: Romanus is the subject. Tacitus' point is that Seneca made the same accusation against Romanus (i.e. that he was Piso's ally in a plot against Nero) and had greater impact.

unde ... timor: understand *erat*. Piso's fear is because he realizes that others are making accusations against him and there is a risk, therefore, that Nero will take pre-emptive action to remove him.

orta: understand *est*.

magna moles: *moles* is used to refer to a large mass or rock. It is used metaphorically here to suggest the scale of the Pisonian conspiracy.

magna ... et improspera: The Pisonian conspiracy planned to assassinate Nero and make C. Piso emperor in his place. It was large in scale but did not end well: it was discovered in AD 65 and led to many deaths, including those of Seneca and Faenius Rufus.

A Level

Vocabulary

While there is no Defined Vocabulary List for A-level, words in the OCR Defined Vocabulary List for AS-level are marked with * so that students can quickly see the vocabulary with which they should be particularly familiar.

* **a, ab** (+ *ablative*)	from, by
A. Didius, A. Didii *m.*	A. Didius, governor of Britain from AD 50 to AD 58
abigo, abigere, abegi, abactum	remove
abitus -us *m.*	way out
abnuo, abnuere, abnui, abnutum	deny, refuse
* **absum, abesse, afui**	be absent, be away
* **ac, atque**	and
accedo, accedere, accessi, accessum	approach, join, be added to
accendo, accendere, accendi, accensum	inflame
accio, accire, accivi, accitum	summon
* **accipio, accipere, accepi, acceptum**	accept, receive
* **acer, acris, acre**	sharp, fierce
* **acies -ei** *f.*	battleline
* **ad** (+ *accusative*)	to, for the purpose of, towards, at, about
adcommodatus -a -um	adapted, adjusted
* **addo, addere, addidi, additum**	add
adduco, adducere, adduxi, adductum	lead to, bring to
* **adeo**	to such an extent

A Level

adficio, adficere, adfeci, adfectum	affect, treat, afflict with
adfingo, adfingere, adfinxi, adfictum	invent in addition
adhibeo, adhibere, adhibui, adhibitum	employ, call on a person
* **adhuc**	still
* **adipiscor, adipisci, adeptus sum**	obtain
adlevo, adlevare	lighten
admitto, admittere, admisi, admissum	commit
admoneo, admonere, admonui, admonitum	remind
adno, adnare	swim beside, swim towards
adnuo, adnuere, adnui, adnutum	agree to
adoleo, adolere, adolevi	make to smoke, worship at
adquiesco, adquiescere, adquievi, adquietum	take comfort in, be pleased with
adspectus -us *m.*	sight, appearance
adspicio, adspicere, adspexi, adspectum	look at, consider
* **adsum, adesse, adfui**	be present
adulatio, adulationis *f.*	flattery
adulter, adulteri *m.*	adulterer
adulterium -i *n.*	adultery
advento -are	approach
adversor, adversari (+ *dative*)	oppose
* **adversus** (+ *accusative*)	against
Aegyptius -a -um	Egyptian
aemulus -i *m.*	rival
aequo -are	equal
aestuarium -i *n.*	estuary
aestus -us *m.*	tide

aetas, aetatis *f.*	age, lifetime
aeternus -a -um	eternal
* **ager, agri** *m.*	land
* **aggredior, aggredi, aggressus sum**	attack
* **agmen, agminis** *n.*	column of men, marching column, army
agnosco, agnoscere, agnovi, agnotum	understand
* **ago, agere, egi, actum**	do, carry out, act, drive
Agrippina -ae *f.*	Agrippina, wife of Germanicus and grandmother of Nero
Alexandrinus -a -um	Alexandrian, from Alexandria
alias	at another time
alioquin	otherwise
* **aliquis, aliquid**	someone, something
* **alius, alia, aliud**	other
* **altus -a -um**	deep
alveus -i *m.*	hull
ambiguus -a -um	uncertain
ambitio, ambitionis *f.*	ambition
ambitus -us *m.*	circumference
* **amicus -i** *m.*	friend
* **amitto, amittere, amisi, amissum**	lose
amoenitas, amoenitatis *f.*	charm, pleasantness
amoenus -a -um	charming
amolior, amoliri, amolitus sum	remove
* **amor, amoris** *m.*	love
amplius	more (than)
amputo -are	cut off
* **an**	or, whether
* **ancilla -ae** *f.*	slave-girl, slave-woman
angustiae -arum *f. pl.*	narrowness

A Level

Anicetus -i *m.*	Anicetus, commander of the Roman fleet
* **animus -i** *m.*	spirit, soul
* **annus -i** *m.*	year
* **antea, ante**	before, previously
antiquus -a -um	ancient
apertus -a -um	open
appello, appellare, appellavi, appellatum	name
* **apud** (+ *accusative*)	among, in the presence of, at
* **ara -ae** *f.*	altar
ardor, ardoris *m.*	eagerness
arduus -a -um	steep, difficult
* **arma -orum** *n. pl.*	weapons
armatura -ae *f.*	armed troops
armatus -a -um	armed
Armenia -ae *f.*	Armenia (a country in Asia)
artus -a -um	narrow
artus -uum *m. pl.*	limbs
arx, arcis *f.*	citadel
asto, astare, astiti	stand by
* **at**	but
atrox, atrocis	cruel
attineo, attinere, attinui, attentum	hold fast, detain
auctor, auctoris *m.*	author
* **audeo, audere, ausus sum**	dare
* **audio, audire, audivi, auditum**	hear, listen to
* **augeo, augere, auxi, auctum**	increase
* **aut**	or, either
auxiliaris, auxiliaris *m.*	auxiliary soldier
* **auxilium -i** *n.*	help
avaritia -ae *f.*	greed
avitus -a -um	ancestral
balneum -i *n.*	bath

barbari -orum *m. pl.*	barbarians
bello, bellare	wage war
* bellum -i *n.*	war
biduum -i *n.*	a two-day period
biennium -i *n.*	a two-year period
* bona -orum *n. pl.*	goods, possessions
Boudicca -ae *f.*	Boudicca, queen of the Iceni
* brevis -e	shallow
Britanni -orum *m. pl.*	the Britons
Britannia -ae *f.*	Britain
Burrus -i *m.*	Burrus, commander of the Praetorian Guard (murdered by Nero)
C. Piso, C. Pisonis *m.*	Gaius Piso, the Roman noble who led the conspiracy against Nero in AD 65
* cado, cadere, cecidi, casum	fall, perish
* caedes, caedis *f.*	slaughter, murder
* caelum -i *n.*	sky, heaven
Caesar, Caesaris *m.*	Caesar (an honorific title used for the Roman emperor)
Caesennius Paetus, Caesennii Paeti *m.*	Caesannius Paetus, consul in AD 61
Campania -ae *f.*	Campania, a district in central Italy
* campus -i *m.*	(battle) plain
Camulodunum -i *n.*	Camulodunum, a Roman colony on the site of modern-day Colchester
* cano, canere, cecini, cantum	sing, make music
* capio, capere, cepi, captum	take, capture
Capitolium -i *n.*	the Capitoline Hill, the location of Rome's most important temples
captivus -a -um	belonging to a prisoner
* captivus -i *m.*	captive

A Level

* **caput, capitis** *n.*	head
castellum -i *n.*	fortress
* **castra -orum** *n. pl.*	camp
castus -a -um	pure, chaste
casus -us *m.*	chance, happening
caterva -ae *f.*	troop
Catus Decianus, Cati Deciani *m.*	Catus Decianus, imperial procurator of Britain in AD 61
* **causa -ae** *f.*	cause, reason
* **cedo, cedere, cessi, cessum**	give way, yield
celeber, celebris, celebre	much frequented, crowded
* **centurio, centurionis** *m.*	centurion
certo, certare	compete
* **certus, certa, certum**	certain, sure
* **ceteri -ae -a**	the others
cieo, ciere, civi, citum	rouse, summon
circum	all around
circumicio, circumicere, circumieci, circumiectum	place around
circumspicio, circumspicere, circumspexi, circumspectum	consider
circumvenio, circumvenire, circumveni, circumventum	surround
civilis -e	belonging to a citizen, civil
* **civis -is** *m./f.*	citizen
* **clades, cladis** *f.*	disaster, defeat
* **clamor, clamoris** *m.*	shout
* **clarus -a -um**	famous
classis -is *f.*	fleet
Claudius -i *m.*	Claudius, emperor of Rome from AD 41 to AD 54
claudo, claudere, clausi, clausum	enclose, imprison

clientela -ae *f.*	group of dependents, clients
coerceo, coercere, coercui, coercitum	restrain, enclose
cognomentum -i *n.*	name
* **cognosco, cognoscere, cognovi, cognitum**	find out
* **cogo, cogere, coegi, coactum**	force
cohortatio, cohortationis *f.*	encouragement
colonia -ae *f.*	colony
comitor -ari	accompany
commeatus -us *m.*	trading, provisions
commercium -i *n.*	trade
commoveo, commovere, commovi, commotum	move, stir
communis -e	shared, in common
comperio, comperire, comperi, compertum	find out
compleo, complere, complevi, completum	fill up
concertor, concertoris *m.*	rival, competitor
conducit, conducere, conduxit (+ *dative*)	(it) profits
confertus -a -um	packed tight
confessio, confessionis *f.*	confession
* **conficio, conficere, confeci, confectum**	wear out
* **confido, confidere, confisus sum** (+ *dative*)	have confidence (in)
configo, configere, confixi, confixum	pierce through
confiteor, confiteri, confessus sum	confess
conglobo -are	bunch together
congredior, congredi, congressus sum	meet, fight against

A Level

coniungo, coniungere, coniunxi, coniunctum	join in marriage, marry
* **coniunx, coniugis** *m./f.*	husband, wife, spouse
coniuratio, coniurationis *f.*	conspiracy
conscientia -ae *f.*	consciousness
conscius -a -um	knowing, aware of
consido, considere, consedi, consessum	settle down
* **consilium -i** *n.*	meeting, plan
* **consisto, consistere, constiti, constitum**	stand firm
consono, consonare, consonui	resound
constantia -ae *f.*	courage, firmness
constitit	it is agreed
* **constituo, constituere, constitui, constitutum**	establish
* **consul, consulis** *m.*	consul
* **consulo, consulere, consului, consultum**	consult, consider
consultum -i *n.*	decree (of the senate)
continuo -are	continue
contra	in the opposite way
* **contra** (+ *accusative*)	against
contrecto -are	manhandle, defile
contumelia -ae *f.*	insult
converto, convertere, converti, conversum	turn around
copia -ae *f.*	abundance
* **copiae -arum** *f. pl.*	troops
Corbulo, Corbulonis *m.*	Corbulo, a famous Roman general who had subdued the Armenians in AD 58
cornu -us *n.*	wing (of an army)
* **corpus, corporis** *n.*	body

corrumpo, corrumpere, corrupi, corruptum	corrupt
creber, crebra, crebrum	frequent, numerous
* **credo, credere, credidi, creditum** (+ *dative*)	believe
* **crimen, criminis** *n.*	accusation, crime
criminatio, criminationis *f.*	accusation
crinis, crinis *m.*	hair
cruentus -a -um	bloodied
cruor, cruoris *m.*	blood
crux, crucis *f.*	cross, crucifix
* **cum**	when, although
* **cum** (+ *ablative*)	with
cumulus -i *m.*	heap, pile
cunctatio, cunctationis *f.*	hesitation, delay
* **cunctus -a -um**	all, whole
cuneus -i *m.*	wedge formation
cupido, cupidinis *f.*	desire, lust, greed
* **cupio, cupere, cupivi, cupitum**	desire
* **cura -ae** *f.*	care
curia -ae *f.*	senate house
currus -us *m.*	chariot
custodia -ae *f.*	guard
damnum -i *n.*	loss
* **de** (+ *ablative*)	about, from
decem	ten
decerno, decernere, decrevi, decretum	decide, decree
decus, decoris *n.*	glory
deduco, ducere, deduxi, deductum	lead to
defectio, defectionis *f.*	rebellion
* **defendo, defendere, defendi, defensum**	defend
dehinc	from here

A Level

* deinde, dein	then
delabor, delabi, delapsus sum	fall down
delictum -i *n.*	wrongdoing
deligo, deligere, delegi, delectum	choose
* denique	in short
densus -a -um	thick, closely packed
depello, depellere, depuli, depulsum	drive off
* despero, desperare, desperavi, desperatum	despair, lose hope
destino -are	choose, mark out
desum, deesse, defui	be lacking
detineo, detinere, detinui, detentum	hold on to
* deus -i *m.*	god
dictito -are	say repeatedly
* dies -ei *m./f.*	day
difero, diferre, distuli, dilatum	delay
* difficilis -e	difficult
diripio, diripere, diripui, direptum	tear apart, plunder
* dirus -a -um	dreadful
discidium -i *n.*	divorce
discrimen, discriminis *n.*	turning point, danger
disicio, disicere, disieci, disiectum	tear apart, tear down, scatter
* diu	for a long time
diversus -a -um	diverse
divus -a -um	divine
* do, dare, dedi, datum	give
* doceo, docere, docui, doctum	teach, inform
documentum -i *n.*	proof
* domina -ae *f.*	mistress
dominatio, dominationis *f.*	domination

A Level

domo, domare, domui, domitum	tame, subdue
*** domus -us** *f.*	house, home
*** donum -i** *n.*	gift
Doryphorus -i *m.*	Doryphorus, one of Nero's imperial freedmen
Druidae -arum *m. pl.*	the Druids
ducenti -ae -a	two hundred
ductus -us *m.*	leadership
dulcedo, dulcedinis *f.*	charm
*** dum**	while
duo, duae, duo	two
*** dux, ducis** *m.*	leader
*** e, ex** (+ *ablative*)	from
edictum -i *n.*	edict
effigies -ei *f.*	likeness, effigy
effugium -i *n.*	escape
effundo, effundere, effudi, effusum	pour forth, squander
egregius -a -um	distinguished, outstanding
eludo, eludere, elusi, elusum	ward off
emitto, emittere, emisi, emissum	hurl, send forth
eneco -are	kill off
*** enim**	for
*** eo**	to that point, to such a point
*** eo, ire, i(v)i, itum**	go
*** eques, equitis** *m.*	horseman, cavalry
*** equus -i** *m.*	horse
*** ergo**	therefore
eripio, eripere, eripui, ereptum	seize, snatch away
erumpo, erumpere, erupi, eruptum	break through
*** et**	and
*** etiam**	even

A Level

Eucaerus -i *m.*	Eucaerus, an Alexandrian flute-player
evado, evadere, evasi, evasum	escape
evenio, evenire, eveni, eventum	happen
eventus -us *m.*	outcome
excido, excidere, excidi, excisum	cut down
excursus -us *m.*	excursion, attack
* **exercitus -us** *m.*	army
exhaurio, exhaurire, exhausi, exhaustum	finish, use up
exhortatio, exhortationis *f.*	encouragement
* **exilium -i** *n.*	exile
exim	then
eximo, eximere, exemi, exemptum	take out, remove
* **exitium -i** *n.*	ruin, destruction
expedio, expedire, expedivi, expeditum	make ready
expendo, expendere, expendi, expensum	consider
experientia -ae *f.*	experience
exprobro -are	reproach with, bring up against
expugno, expugnare, expugnavi, expugnatum	take by storm
exscindo, exscindere, exscidi, exscissum	destroy utterly
exsolvo, exsolvere, exsolvi, exsolutum	open
externus -a -um	external
extremus -a -um	outermost
exturbo -are	drive out
exul, exulis *m./f.*	an exile
exulto -are	jump about

exuo, exuere, exui, exutum	deprive someone (*accusative*) of something (*ablative*)
fabricor -ari	construct
* **facilis -e**	easy
facilitas, facilitatis *f.*	ease
* **facinus, facinoris** *n.*	crime
falsum -i *n.*	falsehood, lie
* **fama -ae** *f.*	fame, reputation, glory
fanaticus -a -um	mad, fanatical
fas *n.*	right
fastigium -i *n.*	high rank, summit
fateor, fateri, fassus sum	confess
fatum -i *n.*	fate, death
fauces, faucium *f. pl.*	narrow gorge, defile
fax, facis *f.*	torch, fire-brand
* **femina -ae** *f.*	woman
feralis -e	funereal
ferme	about
* **fero, ferre, tuli, latum**	bring
* **ferox, ferocis**	fierce
* **ferrum -i** *n.*	iron, sword
fessus -a -um	tired
* **festino -are**	hurry
fibra -ae *f.*	fibre, entrails
* **filia -ae** *f.*	daughter
fingo, fingere, finxi, fictum	invent
finio, finire, finivi, finitum	end
* **finis -is** *m.*	end
flagitium -i *n.*	disgrace, shameful act
flecto, flectere, flexi, flexum	bend
fletus -us *m.*	weeping
flos, floris *m.*	flower
forma -ae *f.*	appearance
* **fortuna -ae** *f.*	fortune
* **forum -i** *n.*	forum

A Level

fossa -ae *f.*	ditch
foveo, fovere, fovi, fotum	encourage
* **frango, frangere, fregi, fractum**	break
* **frater, fratris** *m.*	brother
fraudo -are	cheat of
fremitus -us *m.*	howling, roaring
frequens, frequentis	numerous, crowded
fretus -a -um (+ *ablative*)	relying on
frons, frontis *f.*	front
* **fuga -ae** *f.*	flight, escape
* **fundo, fundere, fudi, fusum**	pour, rout
funus, funeris *n.*	funeral
Furiae -arum *f. pl.*	the Furies (ancient spirits of revenge)
* **furor, furoris** *m.*	rage, madness
Gallia -ae *f.*	Gaul (territory in modern-day France)
genu, genus *n.*	knee
Germanici -orum *m. pl.*	the Germanici
gesto -are	carry
* **gladius -i** *m.*	sword
globus -i *m.*	bunch, crowd
gloria -ae *f.*	glory
gradus -us *m.*	step
grates (*nominative/accusative only*) *f. pl.*	thanks
* **gratia -ae** *f.*	favour
* **gravis -e**	heavy, serious, painful, important
* **habeo, habere, habui, habitum**	have, hold, consider
haereo, haerere, haesi, haesum	stick
* **hasta -ae** *f.*	spear
* **haud**	not
heres, heredis *m./f.*	heir

* hic, haec, hoc	this, these
* homo, hominis *m*.	man, person
honos, honoris *m*.	honour
* hostis -is *m*.	enemy
humanus -a -um	human
iactus -us *m*.	throw, aim
* iam	now, already
* ibi	there
Iceni -orum *m. pl.*	the Iceni, a tribe based in modern-day Norfolk
* idem, eadem, idem	the same
* idoneus -a -um	suitable
* igitur	therefore
* ignis, ignis *m*.	fire
* ille, illa, illud	that, those, he, she, it, they
* illic	there
imago, imaginis *f*.	statue
imbellis -e	unwarlike
immemor, immemoris	paying no attention to
immensus -a -um	vast
immobilis -e	immobile, immoveable
immotus -a -um	motionless
* impedio, impedire, impedivi, impeditum	hinder
impello, impellere, impuli, impulsum	urge on, impel
imperatorius -a -um	imperial
* impetus -us *m*.	attack
impollutus -a -um	undefiled
impono, imponere, imposui, impositum	put in place
impotentia -ae *f*.	lack of self-control
improsper, improspera, improsperum	unfortunate
* in (+ *ablative*)	in, in the midst of

A Level

* **in** (+ *accusative*)	into, against, towards, for the purpose of
inanis -e	empty, meaningless
incautus -a -um	careless
* **incendo, incendere, incendi, incensum**	burn
incertus -a -um	uncertain
inclinatio, inclinationis *f.*	inclination
incola -ae *m./f.*	inhabitant
incolumis -e	unharmed
incolumitas, incolumitatis *f.*	safety
incuso -are	accuse
* **inde**	thereupon, next
indo, indere, indidi, inditum	put on
induco, inducere, induxi, inductum	lead in, bring in
inermis -e	unarmed
infaustus -a -um	unlucky
infelix, infelicis	unhappy
infensus -a -um	hostile
* **infero, inferre, intuli, illatum/ inlatum**	carry against
infrequentia -ae *f.*	lack of numbers, sparseness
* **ingenium -i** *n.*	character
ingruo, ingruere, ingrui	attack
* **iniuria -ae** *f.*	injury
inops, inopis	destitute
* **insidiae -arum** *f. pl.*	ambush, surprise attack
insidior -ari (+ *dative*)	ambush, plot against
insigne, insignis *n.*	marker, indicator
* **insignis -e**	distinguished
insitus -a -um	innate
insto, instare, institi	press upon
* **insula -ae** *f.*	island
insum, inesse, infui	be in, be there
intento -are	threaten with

A Level

intentus -a -um	ready, outstretched
* **inter** (+ *accusative*)	between, among
intercurso -are	dash amongst
* **interim**	in the meantime
* **interficio, interficere, interfeci, interfectum**	kill
intericio, intericiere, interieci, interiectum	place in between, intervene
intorqueo, intorquere, intorsi, intortum	hurl
intutus -a -um	unguarded
involvo, involvere, involvi, involutum	surround
* **ipse, ipsa, ipsum**	-self (emphatic pronoun)
* **ira -ae** *f.*	anger
* **is, ea, id**	he, she, it, they, that, those
* **ita**	in this way, in such a way
* **iubeo, iubere, iussi, iussum**	order
Iulia -ae *f.*	Julia, daughter of Germanicus and Agrippina
iumentum -i *n.*	pack animal
iussum -i *n.*	order
* **iustus -a -um**	right, just, lawful, complete
iuventus, iuventutis *f.*	youth
* **labor, labi, lapsus sum**	fall, flow
* **labor, laboris** *m.*	work, labour
lacrima -ae *f.*	tear
* **laetus -a -um**	happy
* **laus, laudis** *f.*	praise, honour
* **legatus -i** *m.*	commander
* **legio, legionis** *f.*	legion
legionarius -i *m.*	legionary soldier
* **levis -e**	light, slight
* **libens, libentis**	willing
* **libertas, libertatis** *f.*	freedom
* **libertus -i** *m.*	freedman, ex-slave

A Level

libido, libidinis *f.*	passion, lust
licentia -ae *f.*	lawlessness
* **litterae -arum** *f. pl.*	letter
* **litus, litoris** *n.*	seashore, beach
* **locus -i** *m.*	place, situation, opportunity
Londinium -i *n.*	London
* **longus -a -um**	long, long-lasting
luctuosus -a -um	pitiable
lucus -i *m.*	grove, wood
ludibrium -i *n.*	mockery
* **magnus -a -um**	big, great
maior, maioris	greater
maiores -um *m. pl.*	ancestors
* **malo, malle, malui**	prefer
* **malus -a -um**	bad
mancipium -i *n.*	slave, household possession
manifestus -a -um	evident, clear
* **manus -us** *f.*	hand, band of men
* **maritus -i** *m.*	husband
* **mater, matris** *f.*	mother
maternus -a -um	of a mother
matrimonium -i *n.*	marriage
maturo -are	hasten
maximus -a -um	greatest
mediocritas, mediocritatis *f.*	mediocrity, insignificance
* **medius -a -um**	middle (of)
melior, melioris	better
membrum -i *n.*	limb
memini, meminisse (+ *genitive*)	remember
memoria -ae *f.*	memory
memoro -are	mention
* **metus -us** *m.*	fear
* **miles, militis** *m.*	soldier
milia, milium *n. pl.*	thousands
militaris -e	of a soldier, military

militia -ae *f.*	warfare
mina -ae *f.*	threat
minister, ministri *m.*	attendant, servant, agent
minor, minoris	less
minus	less
mirus -a -um	wonderful
misceo, miscere, miscui, mixtum	mix together
Misenum -i *n.*	Misenum, a Roman port
misericordia -ae *f.*	pity
* **mitto, mittere, misi, missum**	send
modeste	with restraint
modicus -a -um	moderate
* **modo**	only
* **modus -i** *m.*	manner, kind
moles -is *f.*	huge mass
Mona -ae *f.*	the island of Mona (modern-day Anglesey)
* **morior, mori, mortuus sum**	die
* **mors, mortis** *f.*	death
motus -us *m.*	movement, rebellion
* **moveo, movere, movi, motum**	move
* **mox**	soon
muliebris -e	female
* **mulier, mulieris** *f.*	woman
* **multitudo, multitudinis** *f.*	crowd, multitude
* **multus -a -um**	much, many
municipium -i *n.*	town, municipality
munimentum -i *n.*	fortification, defence
* **munus, muneris** *n.*	gift
* **muto, mutare, mutavi, mutatum**	change
* **nam**	for
natio, nationis *f.*	nation, tribe
* **navis, navis** *f.*	ship
* **ne … quidem**	not even

A Level

* **ne** (+ *subjunctive*)	lest, that not, so that not
* **nec, neque**	and not, nor, neither
nedum	still less
* **nego, negare, negavi, negatum**	refuse
negotiator, negotiatoris *m.*	trader, banker
* **nemo, nullius**	no one, nobody
Nero, Neronis *m.*	Nero, emperor of Rome from AD 54 to AD 68
nex, necis *f.*	murder, death
* **nihil**	nothing
* **nisi**	if not, except
* **nomen, nominis** *n.*	name, label
* **non**	not
* **nondum**	not yet
nonus -a -um	ninth
* **nos, nostrum/nostri**	we, us
nosco, noscere, novi, notum	get to know
* **noster, nostra, nostrum**	our
novitas, novitatis *f.*	novelty, strangeness
* **novus -a -um**	new
nubo, nubere, nupsi, nuptum	marry
* **nullus -a -um**	no, not any
* **nuntio, nuntiare, nuntiavi, nuntiatum**	report
nuptiae -arum *f. pl.*	marriage
nutus -us *m.*	nod, command
* **ob** (+ *accusative*)	because of, on account of
obeo, obire, obii, obitum (+ *dative*)	meet
obicio, obicere, obieci, obiectum	put before, allege against
* **obliviscor, oblivisci, oblitus sum** (+ *genitive*)	forget
obsequium -i *n.*	obedience, obsequiousness
* **obsideo, obsidere, obsedi, obsessum**	besiege

obtineo, obtinere, obtinui, obtentum	hold
obversor -ari	present itself
obvius -a -um (+ *dative*)	in the way
occulto -are	hide
occultus -a -um	hidden, secret
Oceanus -i *m.*	the ocean
Octavia -ae *f.*	Octavia, Nero's wife; daughter of the emperor Claudius
octoginta	eighty
* **oculus -i** *m.*	eye
* **odium -i** *n.*	hatred
offensio, offensionis *f.*	offence, annoyance
* **olim**	once, formerly
* **omitto, omittere, omisi, omissum**	neglect, disregard, lay aside
* **omnis -e**	all, every
* **opera -ae** *f.*	work, effort
* **opes, opum** *f.*	riches
* **oppidum -i** *n.*	town
* **opprimo, opprimere, oppressi, oppressum**	overwhelm, crush
opulentia -ae *f.*	wealth
* **opus est, esse, fuit** (+ *ablative*)	there is need (for)
* **opus, operis** *n.*	work
* **ordo, ordinis** *m.*	rank, line
* **orior, oriri, ortus sum**	originate
* **oro, orare, oravi, oratum**	beg
* **os, oris** *n.*	mouth
paelex, paelicis *f.*	mistress
* **palam**	openly
Palatium -i *n.*	Palatine Hill, the location of Nero's palace
Pallas, Pallantis *m.*	Pallas, one of Nero's imperial freedmen

A Level

Pandateria -ae *f.*	Pandateria, an island in the Tyrrhenian sea
pango, pangere, pepigi, pactum	agree
* **par, paris**	equal
* **pario, parere, peperi, partum**	win, acquire
* **paro, parare, paravi, paratum**	prepare
* **pars, partis** *f.*	part
partus -us *m.*	offspring
parum	too little
* **passim**	everywhere
* **pater, patris** *m.*	father
patibulum -i *n.*	a fork-shaped yoke (used to punish slaves and criminals)
patientia -ae *f.*	endurance
patrator, patratoris *m.*	perpetrator
* **pauci, paucae, pauca**	a few
Paulinus Suetonius, Paulini Suetonii *m.*	Paulinus Suetonius, governor of Britain in AD 58
* **paulum, paulo**	a little, somewhat
pavesco, pavescere	grow fearful, become alarmed at
pavor, pavoris *m.*	fear, panic
* **pax, pacis** *f.*	peace
* **pecunia -ae** *f.*	money, wealth
* **pedes, peditis** *m.*	foot soldier, infantry
* **pello, pellere, pepuli, pulsum**	push out, drive
penates, penatium *m. pl.*	household gods, family
* **per** (+ *accusative*)	through, throughout
percello, percellere, perculi, perculsum	discourage, strike fear into, strike
perduellis, perduellis *m.*	rebel
perfero, perferre, pertuli, perlatum	bring through to the end
perfringo, perfringere, perfregi, perfractum	break through
perfuga -ae *m.*	deserter

pergo, pergere, perrexi, perrectum	proceed
* **periculum** -i *n.*	danger
pernicies -ei *f.*	destruction, ruin
persto, perstare, perstiti	stand firm
Petilius Cerialis, Petilii Cerialis *m.*	Petilius Cerialis, a distinguished military officer and future governor of Britain
* **peto, petere, petivi, petitum**	ask for, attack
Petronius Turpilianus, Petronii Turpiliani *m.*	Petronius Turpilianus, consul in AD 61
pilum -i *n.*	javelin
* **placet, placere, placuit** (+ *dative*)	it pleases
planities -ei *f.*	plain, level ground
planus -a -um	flat, level
plaustrum -i *n.*	wagon
Plautus -i *m.*	Plautus, great-grandson of the emperor Tiberius
* **plebs, plebis** *f.*	the people
plures, plura	more
plus	more
Poenius Postumus, Poenii Postumi *m.*	Poenius Postumus, a Roman officer
* **pono, ponere, posui, positum**	put, put aside
Poppaea -ae *f.*	Poppaea, Nero's mistress and then wife
populor -ari	ravage, lay waste
* **populus** -i *m.*	people
* **post**	afterwards
* **post** (+ *accusative*)	after
posthac	afterwards
* **postquam**	after
postremo	finally

* **postremus -a -um**	last
potens, potentis	powerful, influential
potior, potius	preferable
potissimus -a -um	most powerful
prae (+ *ablative*)	before
* **praebeo, praebere, praebui, praebitum**	offer
praecipuus -a -um	chief
* **praeda -ae** *f.*	plunder
praedium -i *n.*	estate, farm
praeduco, praeducere, praeduxi, praeductum	set up in front
praefectus -i *m.*	prefect, commander
praefero, praeferre, praetuli, praelatum	carry in front
praefervidus -a -um	very hot
* **praemium -i** *n.*	reward
praeripio, praeripere, praeripui, praereptum	take beforehand
praesagium -i *n.*	foreboding
praesens, praesentis	present
* **praesidium -i** *n.*	garrison, fortification
praesumptum -i *n.*	assumption
Prasutagus -i *m.*	Prasutagus, king of the Iceni
preces, precum *f. pl.*	prayers
premo, premere, pressi, pressum	weigh down
primo	at first
primum	at first
* **primus -a -um**	first
* **princeps, principis** *m.*	emperor
* **prior, prioris**	previous
* **priusquam, prius quam**	before
* **pro** (+ *ablative*)	in front of, for, in place of
* **procul**	far away

procul (+ *ablative*)	far from
procurator, procuratoris *m.*	procurator (i.e. the official who managed the tax revenue)
* **proelium -i** *n.*	battle
profectio, profectionis *f.*	departure
profero, proferre, protuli, prolatum	carry forth, extend
profligo, profligare, profligavi, profligatum	overcome, all but finish
progenies -ei *f.*	offspring
prohibeo, prohibere, prohibui, prohibitum	prevent
* **promitto, promittere, promisi, promissum**	promise
propinquus -a -um	near
propius	nearer
proruo, proruere, prorui, prorutum	fall down, hurl down
prosperus -a -um	successful
protentus -a -um	stretched out
proveho, prevehere, provexi, provectum	advance
provideo, providere, providi, provisum	consider in advance
* **provincia -ae** *f.*	province
provolvo, provolvere, provolvi, provolutum	roll forward
* **proximus -a -um**	nearest, next
* **publicus -a -um**	public
pudicitia -ae *f.*	chastity
* **puella -ae** *f.*	girl
* **pugna -ae** *f.*	battle
quadringenti -ae -a	four hundred
* **quaero, quaerere, quaesivi, quaesitum**	search for, ask for

A Level

quaestio, quaestionis *f.*	investigation, questioning under torture
* **quam**	than
* **quamquam**	although
quamvis	although
quando	since
quantus -a -um	the amount/size which
quartadecimani -orum *m. pl.*	soldiers of the fourteenth legion
quartus decimus, quarta decima, quartum decimum	fourteenth
* **quasi**	as if
* **-que**	and
questus -us *m.*	complaint, lament
* **qui, quae, quod**	who, which
* **quia**	because
quicumque, quaecumque, quodcumque	whoever, whichever, whatever
* **quidam, quaedam, quoddam**	one, a certain, some
* **quidem**	indeed
quin (+ *subjunctive*)	from (doing something)
quippe	indeed
* **quis?, quid?**	who? what? any
* **quisquam, quicquam**	anyone, anything
* **quisque, quaeque, quidque**	each, every
* **quod**	because, the fact that
* **quoque**	also, too
* **quotiens**	as often as, whenever
* **rapio, rapere, rapui, raptum**	seize
rebellio, rebellionis *f.*	rebellion
* **recens, recentis**	recent
receptaculum -i *n.*	refuge
* **recipio, recipere, recepi, receptum**	regain, take back
recordatio, recordationis *f.*	recollection, memory

* **reddo, reddere, reddidi, redditum**	give back, hand over
regio, regionis *f.*	region
* **regnum -i** *n.*	kingdom
religio, religionis *f.*	religion
* **relinquo, relinquere, reliqui, relictum**	leave, leave behind
remedium -i *n.*	remedy
reor, reri, ratus sum	think
reperio, reperire, repperi, repertum	discover
repentinus -a -um	sudden
repono, reponere, reposui, repositum	put back, restore
* **res -ei** *f.*	thing, affair, matter
* **res publica, rei publicae** *f.*	state, republic
* **resisto, resistere, restiti** (+ *dative*)	oppose
* **respondeo, respondere, respondi, responsum**	reply
resto, restare, restiti	make a stand against, stay behind
restringo, restringere, restrinxi, restrictum	bind tight
resumo, resumere, resumpsi, resumptum	take up again, take back
* **retineo, retinere, retinui, retentum**	keep, hold on to
retro	backwards
reus -i *m.*	defendant, man accused
* **rex, regis** *m.*	king
ritus -us *m.*	rule
robur, roboris *n.*	strength
Romanus -a -um	Roman
rumor, rumoris *m.*	(general/private) opinion
sacer, sacra, sacrum	sacred

A Level

* sacerdos, sacerdotis *m./f.*	priest, priestess
saepio, saepire, saepsi, saeptum	enclose
saevitia -ae *f.*	savagery
* saevus -a -um	savage
sanctitas, sanctitatis *f.*	chastity, purity
* sanguis, sanguinis *m.*	blood
* sapientia -ae *f.*	wisdom
Sardinia -ae *f.*	Sardinia
* satis	enough
scando, scandere, scandi, scansum	climb
* scelus, sceleris *n.*	crime
scientia -ae *f.*	knowledge, skill
* scribo, scribere, scripsi, scriptum	write
* se, sui	himself, herself, itself, themselves (reflexive pronoun)
secessus -us *m.*	retreat, retirement
secretus -a -um	secret
* secundus -a -um	second, favourable
securitas, securitatis *f.*	security
* sed	but
* sedes -is *f.*	base
seditio, seditionis *f.*	riot, civil disturbance
segnis -e	lazy
* semper	always
* senatus -us *m.*	senate
Seneca -ae *m.*	Seneca, Nero's tutor and the famous philosopher
senecta -ae *f.*	old age
* senex, senis *m.*	old man
septuaginta	seventy
* sequor, sequi, secutus sum	follow
sermo, sermonis *m.*	conversation
servilis -e	of a slave

A Level

servio, servire, servivi, servitum	be a slave
servitium -i *n.*	slavery (*pl.* slaves)
* **servo, servare, servavi, servatus**	save
* **servus** -i *m.*	slave
severitas, severitatis *f.*	severity, strictness
sexus -us *m.*	sex, gender
* **si**	if
* **sic**	thus, in this way
* **signum** -i *n.*	signal, military standard
sileo, silere, silui	be silent
Silurae -arum *m. pl.*	the Silures, a tribe who inhabited modern-day South Wales and Herefordshire
* **silva** -ae *f.*	wood
similitudo, similitudinis *f.*	similarity
* **simul**	at the same time
simulacrum -i *n.*	statue
* **sine** (+ *ablative*)	without
* **sino, sinere, sivi, situm**	allow
socio -are	make one's ally
* **socius** -i *m.*	ally
solitus -a -um	accustomed, usual
* **solum**	only
* **solus** -a -um	alone
sonor, sonoris *m.*	sound
* **soror, sororis** *f.*	sister
spargo, spargere, sparsi, sparsum	scatter, sprinkle
species -ei *f.*	appearance, image
* **sperno, spernere, sprevi, spretum**	scorn
* **spes** -ei *f.*	hope
spolio -are	strip, plunder
* **statim**	immediately

* statuo, statuere, statui, statutum	decide, set up
sterilis -e	unable to bear children
sterilitas, sterilitatis *f.*	sterility
sterno, sternere, stravi, stratum	strike to the ground
stimulo -are	goad, urge on
* sto, stare, steti, statum	stand
strages, stragis *f.*	butchery
strepitus -us *m.*	noise
* studium -i *n.*	devotion, enthusiasm
stuprum -i *n.*	rape, sexual violation
subicio, subicere, subieci, subiectum	set under, bring under someone's (*dative*) control
suboles, subolis *f.*	offspring
subsidium -i *n.*	help, aid
subvenio, subvenire, subveni, subventum	come to one's aid
subverto, subvertere, subverti, subversum	overthrow
successor, successoris *m.*	successor
suggredior, suggredi, suggressus sum	approach
Sulla -ae *m.*	Sulla, son-in-law to the emperor Claudius
* sum, esse, fui	be
* sumo, sumere, sumpsi, sumptum	take up
super (+ *accusative*)	beyond
superstitio, superstitionis *f.*	superstition
supplicatio, supplicationis *f.*	(a formal act of) thanksgiving
supplicium -i *n.*	punishment
supremus -a -um	last
suspicio, suspicionis *f.*	suspicion
* suus -a -um	his (own), her (own), its (own), their (own)

* **talis -e**	such, of this sort
* **tamen**	however, nevertheless
tamquam	as if
* **tandem**	at last
* **tantum**	only
* **tantus -a -um**	so great, such great
tardus -a -um	slow
* **telum -i** *n.*	weapon, missile
temeritas, temeritatis *f.*	rashness
Tamesa -ae *m.*	the river Thames
tempero -are (+ *dative*)	act with restraint towards, hold back from
* **templum -i** *n.*	temple
* **tempus, temporis** *n.*	time
* **tergum -i** *n.*	back, rear
* **terror, terroris** *m.*	terror
testamentum -i *n.*	will
testis -is *m./f.*	witness
testor -ari	bear witness to, demonstrate
theatrum -i *n.*	theatre
Tiberius -i *m.*	Tiberius, the second emperor of Rome
tibiae -arum *f. pl.*	tibia (a pipe-like wind instrument)
tibicen, tibicinis *m.*	flute-player
Tigellinus -i *m.*	Tigellinus, commander of the Praetorian Guard and advisor to Nero
* **timor, timoris** *m.*	fear
tolero -are	sustain
* **tollo, tollere, sustuli, sublatum**	lift up
tormentum -i *n.*	torture
* **tot**	so many
totiens	so often, just as often

A Level

* trado, tradere, tradidi, traditum	hand over, hand down
* traho, trahere, traxi, tractum	pull, drag, interpret
tramitto, tramittere, tramisi, tramissum	send across
transeo, transire, transii, transitum	cross
transigo, transigere, transegi, transactum	drive through, stab
trepidus -a -um	anxious
Trinovantes, Trinovantum *m. pl.*	the Trinovantes, a tribe based in the east of England
tueor, tueri, tuitus sum	protect, defend
* tum	then, next, at that time
* tumultus -us *m.*	uproar, disturbance
tunc	at that time
turbidus -a -um	wild, disturbed
turbo -are	throw into confusion
turma -ae *f.*	cavalry squadron
tutela -ae *f.*	protection
uberrimus -a -um	most fruitful
* ubi	where, when
ulciscor, ulcisci, ultus sum	take vengeance on
ultio, ultionis *f.*	revenge
ultra	further
ululatus -us *m.*	howl, shriek
umbo, umbonis *m.*	shield boss
umerus -i *m.*	shoulder
* unda -ae *f.*	wave
* unde	from where
universus -a -um	whole, all together, all
unus -a -um	one
* urbs, urbis *f.*	city, Rome
* usus -us *m.*	use, practice
* ut (+ *indicative*)	as, in a way in which, when

* **ut** (+ *subjunctive*)	that, with the result that
* **uterque, utraque, utrumque**	each (of two), both
* **uxor, uxoris** *f.*	wife
vadum -i *n.*	shallow water
vaecordia -ae *f.*	malice
* **valeo, valere, valui**	be strong
* **validus** -a -um	strong, powerful
vallum -i *n.*	defensive palisade, barrier
vapor, vaporis *m.*	steam
varius -a -um	various
vasto -are	lay waste, ravage
* **-ve**	or
vehiculum -i *n.*	vehicle, cart
* **veho, vehere, vexi, vectum**	bear, convey
* **vel**	or
* **velut**	as if
vena -ae *f.*	vein
venenum -i *n.*	drug, poison
veneror, venerari	worship
venundo -are	sell
Veranius, Veranii *m.*	Veranius, consul in AD 48 and governor of Britain in AD 58
verbera, verberum *n. pl.*	blows, beatings
* **verbum** -i *n.*	word
* **verto, vertere, verti, versum**	turn
Verulamium -i *n.*	Verulamium (modern-day St Albans)
verum	but
* **verus** -a -um	true
* **vestis** -is *f.*	clothes, clothing
veteranus -i *m.*	military veteran
* **vetus, veteris**	old, experienced
vexillariius -a -um	veteran reservists, soldiers in a detachment (rather than a legion)

A Level

vicesimani -orum *m. pl.*	soldiers of the twentieth legion
vicesimus -a -um	twentieth
* **victor, victoris** *m.*	victor, winner
* **victoria -ae** *f.*	victory
* **video, videre, vidi, visum**	see
* **videor, videri, visus sum**	seem
viduus -a -um	without a husband
vinclum -i *n.*	cord, chain
* **vinco, vincere, vici, victum**	defeat, win
vindicta -ae *f.*	vengeance, punishment
violo -are	violate, abuse
* **vir, viri** *m.*	man
virginitas, virginitatis *f.*	virginity
* **virtus, virtutis** *f.*	courage, military skill
* **vis, vi** (*ablative sg.*) *f.*	force, violence
viso, visere, visi, visum	visit, view
* **vita -ae** *f.*	life
* **vivo, vivere, vixi**	live, be alive
* **vix**	with difficulty
vulgus -i *n.*	the crowd, the masses
* **vulnero -are**	wound, injure
* **vulnus, vulneris** *n.*	wound

A Level

Apuleius

Metamorphoses VI.7–21

A Level

Introduction

Apuleius: The author and his context

His life and works

The eighteenth-century historian Edward Gibbon famously designated the Roman empire of the second century AD as 'the period in the history of the world, during which the condition of the human race was most happy and prosperous'. Without uncritically accepting Gibbon's judgement, it was certainly into a peaceful, comfortable North Africa under Roman rule that Apuleius was born sometime in the 120s. In that cosmopolitan empire, he carved out a career for himself as a celebrated writer, orator, Platonic philosopher and professional intellectual.

What information we have of his life comes from his own works and from comments by St Augustine of Hippo, a fellow North African writer clearly familiar with the writings of Apuleius several centuries later. He was born into a wealthy provincial family in a city (*colonia*) called Madauros in the province of Africa Proconsularis (now M'daurouch in modern-day Algeria), several hundred kilometres inland of Carthage (modern Tunis); his father achieved the highest political office in the *colonia* and left Apuleius and his brother a sizeable fortune at his death.

Although there had been Roman influence in this part of North Africa since the days of Massinissa, ally of the great Roman general Scipio in the Second Punic War (late third century BC), Punic culture and language (that is, the language and culture of Carthage) remained strong. It is not unlikely that the first language Apuleius spoke was Punic, rather than Latin, as was the case with Apuleius' own stepson Pudens (*Apology* 98) and, a generation later, the North African-born emperor, Septimius Severus.

It is Apuleius' facility with and mastery of the language of Rome for which he is famous, and around which he made his career, however. The empire had made its language the standard for the literary and legal worlds, and Apuleius' Latin education would have begun in Madauros. For more serious studies he was sent to Carthage, learning grammar and rhetoric, and probably also developing a grounding in Platonic philosophy. From there his enquiring intellect took him further afield, to Athens, where his Greek (started in Carthage) was perfected, and then later to Rome. There is some likelihood that he also travelled to other centres of imperial intellectual life such as Smyrna, Pergamum and Ephesus; he undoubtedly had contact with the major intellectuals and writers of his time at these hubs of culture and learning. This kind of wide educational travelling among the literary elite was not uncommon in the empire – his Roman contemporary Aulus Gellius studied and lived in Athens, and similar educational journeys are recorded by the Greek sophist Lucian and the second-century Alexandrian Christian author Clement.

On his way back to North Africa, at Oea (modern Tripoli), Apuleius met and married a wealthy and much older widow, Prudentilla, mother of Pontianus, a fellow student he had met on his travels. The match was not as pleasing to other members of her family as it was to his friend Pontianus, and he was taken to court in 158/9, with the accusation that Prudentilla had been induced to marry him by witchcraft. His defence, which still survives, is a rhetorical *tour de force*, a speech called *Pro se de magia* ('In self-defence on a charge of magic'; more commonly called his *Apology*). It laid the grounds for a triumphant return to Carthage, where he seems to have enjoyed a prosperous career as a speaker and writer, was elected to a priesthood, and voted a public statue. A collection of extracts from his speeches survives under the title of the *Florida*; and a number of other works of disputed authenticity (*De deo Socratis*, *De Platone* and *De Mundo*) suggest his development as a philosophical expositor of Greek ideas to a Roman audience.

Where in this career does his most famous work, the *Metamorphoses*, fit? Nothing in the text itself gives conclusive evidence, although some scholars have seen in the exuberant fiction the creation of a young and frivolous Apuleius writing for a more cosmopolitan Roman audience.

On the other hand, the themes in the *Metamorphoses* of magic and sorcery do not seem to have been brought up in accusation against him at his trial in 158/9. Further, various episodes in the work seem to play with his successful defence: there are episodes of trumped-up charges, defended by brilliant rhetoric, after which the speaker is awarded an honorific statue (III.11). Within this selection of the text, Venus makes particularly apposite remarks about the suspicions aroused by a country wedding, which had formed part of the concern around Apuleius' marriage to Prudentilla (VI.9). These seem too similar to biographical fact to be coincidental, and so sometime after his return to Carthage in the 160s or later seems the most plausible date.

The intellectual context

Although Apuleius' education and (extant) literary output was in Latin, his educational and cultural outlook is fundamentally shaped by the major intellectual currents of his day. Greek was regarded as the premier language and, more particularly, rhetorical performance in Greek by orators, harking in content, style and literary allusion back to the glory days of fifth-century Greece, shaped the intellectual atmosphere of the Roman empire at this period. This efflorescence of Greek rhetoric and writing is referred to as the Second Sophistic, a term coined by Philostratus (*c*. 170–250) and named after the self-conscious revival of the culture of the first so-called Sophists, intellectuals who made their home in the cultural melting-pot of Classical Athens, teachers of rhetoric and philosophy. Apuleius is a contemporary of these (second) Sophists – Lucian, Aelius Aristides, Dio of Prusa and those in their circles.

In broad terms, the key themes and features of this kind of literature were a concern for linguistic purity, usually in the form of almost hyper-Atticized Greek, and a focus on rhetorical performance, particularly extempore epideictic rhetoric (off-the-cuff show speeches). Culturally, this literature pivots around the negotiation between Greek and Roman identity and power, with the concept of *paideia*, culture or education, as the hinge. This immensely important property was wielded like a weapon or spent like currency by the elite Sophists, and traded in, on a smaller scale, by the penumbra of the *pepaideumenoi* (cultured elite) surrounding them. Apuleius has been referred to as a 'Latin Sophist', working through the same themes but in the language of the empire, and we see the key concerns of the Second Sophistic through the extracts of the *Metamorphoses* here: deep concern for literary and linguistic tradition, with complex and subtle allusions and intertextual play, a showy, performance-like use of language with a taste for archaisms, and rhetorical flourishes like ecphrases.

The *Metamorphoses*

Overview

The *Metamorphoses*, also known as *The Golden Ass*, is the most well-known of Apuleius' works. It tells the story of a wealthy, educated young man (in many respects remarkably similar to the author) called Lucius, who is introduced after an anonymous prologue promising a series of entertaining Greek tales. The novel is divided into eleven books – an unusual number for ancient literature – but the main narrative of Lucius' transformation and adventures often plays second fiddle to a series of embedded tales: some comic, some bawdy, some violent, but all entertaining.

Book I: Lucius (the narrator) tells of his journey to Thessaly; along the way he is told a tale of a man called Socrates who was murdered by magic after an affair with a witch. Lucius arrives at Hypata, his destination, and meets his host Milo.

Book II: The next day, Lucius meets and visits the house of Byrrhaena, a family friend; an ecphrasis (a literary description of an artwork; see IV.3 for discussion of this feature) of a statue of Diana and Actaeon foreshadows his own bestial metamorphosis. He is warned about the magical practices of Pamphile, Milo's wife, which only arouses Lucius' curiosity (his characteristic vice). Back at Milo's house, Lucius begins to embark upon a love affair with Photis, Milo's slave-girl. At a dinner party he hears another tale of witchcraft, this time about a man called Thelyphron, who has been humiliated and maimed by the action of witches. On his way back home, the drunken Lucius is set upon by thieves, but he kills them all at Milo's door.

Book III: The following morning Lucius is arrested and charged with the murder of the three thieves; despite a passionate rhetorical defence, he is convicted and made to uncover his victims' corpses: to his astonishment, they turn out to be merely wineskins. In his embarrassment, it is explained that the practical joke is part of the town's celebrations of the festival of laughter, and a statue is erected in honour. (This section is usually read as based on Apuleius' own experience of the sham charge regarding his wife and his successful defence, although modulated to a comic key.) Photis confesses that she aided Pamphile in magically animating the wineskins and, several nights later, she allows Lucius to see Pamphile turn herself into a bird; Lucius attempts to undergo the same magical transformation, but Photis, using the wrong ointment, accidentally turns him into an ass instead. She promises to cure him at dawn, but during the night, Lucius the ass is stolen by robbers.

Book IV: Lucius is taken to the robbers' cave, and we are treated to three tales of their exploits, all ending in comic failure, which they tell over dinner. The robbers go out the same night and return with a prisoner, a beautiful young girl. The robbers' housekeeper tells the tale of Cupid of Psyche to try to calm the distraught girl. This tale, from which our selection is taken, is the longest embedded tale in the *Metamorphoses* and continues through to the middle of the sixth book. The following section of this introduction will cover it in more detail.

Book VI: At the conclusion of the tale, Lucius attempts to escape, carrying the girl with him on his back, but they are caught and the robbers plan a grim fate for the escapees.

Book VII: A stranger arrives at the robbers' cave, claiming to be the infamous bandit Haemus. He tells several tales of derring-do and offers to become their leader; they accept and take his advice to sell the girl rather than kill her. Lucius realizes (eventually) that Haemus is, in fact, the girl's fiancé in disguise. 'Haemus' drugs the robbers and effects an escape, with Lucius' assistance, and the couple (Tleptolemus and Charite) are married. As a reward, Lucius is sent to their country estate – but there he is mistreated by a woman and a cruel boy. The boy is eaten by a bear and Lucius, blamed for the misfortune, is attacked by the boy's mother, but he successfully wards her off with a stream of liquid dung.

Book VIII: A messenger brings the news that Tleptolemus has been murdered and Charite has killed herself. The slaves, panicked at the news, run off, taking Lucius with them. Their journey is beset with disasters: they risk an attack by wolves, are chased by dogs and have to escape a devouring serpent disguised as an old man. They sell Lucius on to a group of travelling charlatans, disreputable priests of the Syrian goddess, who make their money duping credulous and superstitious peasants. At the close of the book, it looks as though the priests might slaughter Lucius to make up for a stolen joint of venison.

Book IX: Lucius escapes his fate by pretending to be rabid and, as he travels on, hears an extremely lewd tale of a cheating wife. The priests are arrested for theft from a temple, and Lucius is again sold and put to work in a mill. Lucius hears another two bawdy tales of adultery, and then assists in revealing the adultery of the miller's wife. The miller punishes her lover in a surprising way; but the miller's wife, thrown out of the house, takes her revenge, killing the miller by witchcraft. Lucius is sold to a gardener, and then commandeered by a soldier.

Book X: Lucius is left temporarily by the soldier at a house, where he hears another tale, this one of murder and medicine. Lucius is sold by the soldier to a pair of cooks, who discover him eating their food; his strange eating habits are turned into a public spectacle, and he is taught more tricks and taken to Corinth. An aristocratic lady takes her pleasure with Lucius, which encourages his owner to contemplate using him for display in the arena: to have sexual intercourse with a woman condemned for poisoning. Lucius, not enthused at this plan for a career on the stage, escapes and falls asleep on a beach at Cenchreae, just outside Corinth.

Book XI: Lucius, awaking at night on the beach, prays to the moon, who appears in the form of the goddess Isis and gives him instructions for his cure by participating in her festival. The cure is successful; Lucius finally regains human form and becomes an initiate and devotee of the goddess. After a trip home, he goes to Rome to be further initiated into the mysteries of Osiris, where he ends the tale as a minor priest of the cult, financing his devotion to the Egyptian deities by his career as a lawyer.

Genre and sources

The *Metamorphoses* is the only 'novel' to survive by Apuleius, and one of the very few exemplars of this genre in Latin to survive from antiquity. I use inverted commas because the connotations that the term conveys in the present day are quite different to what we see in the ancient form which goes under the name. One of the reasons for the interpretative disagreements which mark scholarship on the *Metamorphoses* is that there are so few works which might help us as comparisons or contrasts.

Whilst there are a small number of Greek prose works written under the Roman empire, known as the Greek novels, their swashbuckling romantic tales of lovers separated by pirates, adventures and other various trials, before inevitably they find each other and live happily ever after, read quite differently to the (very few) Roman novels. Indeed, along with the *Satyrica* of Petronius, the *Metamorphoses* is the only Latin prose fiction (before the advent of fanciful but still purportedly 'historical' Christian texts) which is not a direct translation from Greek; in both, the setting is a realist backdrop of the Roman empire, with a mostly first-person narration but including extensive inserted tales. The content of these tales is often bawdy and gritty, comic tales of everyday, common life. Despite this realism, the novels are also highly literary, with extensive allusion to other literary genres, and notable parody of the romantic themes of the Greek novels.

The form and content of the *Metamorphoses* was undoubtedly influenced by a genre of stories called 'Milesian tales'; the first sentence of the work begins: *at ego tibi sermone isto Milesio varias fabulas conseram* ('but I will stitch together for you various tales in that Milesian style'). Here again we have the problem that almost none of this genre actually survives from the ancient world, although the references to it suggest that the content was earthy and comic. Ovid (*Tristia* II.413, 443–4) makes reference to the famous Greek writer of Milesian tales, Aristides of Miletus, and his Latin translator, Sisenna, in these terms. The idea of a framing narrative, into which self-contained ribald stories were stitched, and possibly the use of a first-person narrator, are elements which Apuleius may have borrowed from the Milesian tales.

The framing narrative of the man turned into an ass also has a more direct literary antecedent: at the close of the prologue, we are promised a *fabulam Graecanicam* ('a Grecian tale') and it seems that Apuleius has borrowed the key points of the narrative wholesale from a Greek original, known as the *Onos* (the Greek for ass). Whilst the Greek original doesn't survive, an epitome of the tale has come down to us, falsely attributed to the Sophistic author Lucian, and there is a comparison drawn up by the Byzantine patriarch Photius comparing this version to a longer version of the ass tale-type, called (like Apuleius') the *Metamorphoses*, attributed to Lucius of Patrae. The character of Lucius, the framing story of the transformation into an ass and many of the inserted tales are likely to have come from this Greek original, although scholars generally agree that the Cupid and Psyche episode (among other features) is an original Apuleian addition.

Apuleius' eleventh book, however, strikes quite a different note to the Greek *Onos*: the Greek version finishes with a ribald episode absent from our text, in which the human lover of Lucius-ass expresses her disappointment with his transformation back into human form, because of his now human-sized body parts. Apuleius' account of the Isiac initiation, references to mystery cults and closure on a note of seeming joy and lasting fidelity are elements unique to his version.

Interpretations

Appropriately for a work titled for fluidity of form, the *Metamorphoses* has always confused and divided critics. It has been misread as autobiography (by no less an autobiographer than St Augustine, at *De civitate dei* XVIII.18), lauded as an edifying spiritual work by its first English translator, derided as derivative patchwork of earlier sources and praised as a rich example of deeply ironic comedy. For the first half of the twentieth century, the literary quality of the work went underappreciated, judged as possessing no unity and little artistic value. More recent scholarship has been more positive in its assessment, emphasizing the cleverness and complexity of its literary techniques and, in particular, its sophisticated narrative strategies. Secondly, the work's engagement with religious and philosophical content and symbolism has been reassessed. Many of the issues in its interpretation hinge on the relationship between Book XI and the rest of the work, but also key to many of the overall interpretations has been the Cupid and Psyche episode, with its possibilities of its religious and/or philosophical interpretation.

In terms of the narrative structure, the application of seemingly complex narratological theory, at first rather overwhelming in its complexity, makes sense when the text's own concern for narrative complexity, reliability and the role of the narrator is noted. The hugely influential work of Jack Winkler (1985) and the exhaustive commentaries of the Groningen group (see Further Reading below) both use narratological theory extensively in their interpretations: this kind of theory is, in simple terms, the recognition that the framing and method of telling of stories influences how readers approach them – how the narrator (Lucius, or any of the other embedded narrators, like the old woman in the Cupid and Psyche episode) is involved in the action, whether the narrator is trustworthy, or influenced by the narrator's later experiences in the re-telling of the story and so on. The question becomes more complex when we consider the process of reading and the reader's partial knowledge: does our perspective on the narrative change retrospectively as we discover more about the narrator. Does our realization that Lucius the narrator is now an Isiac devotee (after we have finished reading Book XI) change how we reread his retelling of his earlier adventures? Does our interpretation of the Cupid and Psyche story change when we see its themes mirrored in Lucius' own fall and redemption?

In particular, the distance between the perspective of the narrator, Lucius, and the author, Apuleius, has been often debated. Two passages have been at the heart of this debate: the prologue at the very beginning of the work; and the infamous 'man from Madauros' passage in Book XI. Both passages pivot around the relationship between Lucius, the narrator, and the author: thus, the unnamed speaker in the prologue has been variously identified as Lucius, Apuleius, a combination of the two, an anonymous prologue-voice or the voice of the book itself. At XI.27, the priest Arsinius Marcellus relates to Lucius that he was expected, as a dream had warned him that 'the man from Madauros' (the home town of Apuleius, but not of Lucius) would come to him for initiation. Various solutions for the puzzling slippage have been to emend the words out of the text; to treat them as a clever *sphragis* ('seal') or in-built acknowledgment of authorship; or as a mark of the autobiographical seriousness of the Isiac initiation; or as a deliberately playful complication of the convention of the fictive first-person narrator, balancing the ambiguity of the prologue.

This is linked to the vexing question of the relationship between the eleventh book and the first ten. From the very outset, an eleventh book is unexpected: an ancient audience was used to the division of longer works into books, but generally in balanced and symmetrical ways. Epic tended to favour multiples of three (the *Iliad* and the *Odyssey* with twenty-four, and the *Aeneid* with twelve) and the Augustan poets, schemes in multiples of five (Ovid's *Metamorphoses* has fifteen, for instance); even those Greek novels favouring a different schema at least are divided into an even number of books. Thus, from the outset, Apuleius seems to have meant his eleventh book to be a surprise.

What kind of surprise is it, though? Scholars have noted the similarity between Lucius' waking on the beach at Cenchreae and praying to the rising moon and other accounts of serious personal conversion. The first fifteen chapters of Book XI present the longest stretch of consistently elevated prose in the work, but this could be argued either to rule out or, conversely, to highlight irony.

The history of interpretation of the *Metamorphoses* as a serious allegorical moral tale is a surprisingly long one: starting with Fulgentius in the fifth or sixth century and continuing into the Renaissance and even to modern readers, the whole novel has been interpreted as a cautionary moral tale. In this reading, Lucius' initiation into Isis provides the serious key for deeper meanings of the seeming bawdiness of the preceding eleven books. Although this might seem far-fetched, the allegorical interpretation of apparently profane subject matter was a common tool of the Middle Platonists from whom Apuleius developed his philosophical outlook; the suggestion of hidden, secret meaning is embedded in the narrative by Lucius' own initiation into the hidden mysteries of the cult of Isis.

Several issues make this kind of reading problematic, however: whilst the embedded stories in the first three books, and the tale of Cupid and Psyche, can be read as part of an overall moralizing drive, it is more difficult to fit in the more loosely connected and generally more ribald tales of the last third of the novel into such a schema.

Rather than seeing his initiation into the mysteries as delivery from the disasters into which his curiosity has pitched him, it is possible to read his enthusiasm for his new cults as yet another trap which his credulity has led him into – we might question his uncritical acceptance of the new rites, his surprise when he has to undergo (and pay for) further initiations, the figure he cuts as a shaven-headed advocate in the forum (as a buffoon, in Winkler's reading). Photius, writing about the original Greek *Onos*, Apuleius' source-text, describes it as a satire on superstition and credulity: is this Apuleius' new take on the original theme? Lucius' stylistically elevated and rhetorically impassioned account of his Isiac conversion might instead be read as epideictic: a showing off of obscure religious knowledge in a Sophistic manner, designed to entertain rather than to convert.

A
Level

Lastly, increasing attention has been paid to the philosophical underpinnings of the novel; Apuleius presented himself (in his *Apology*), and was known to both contemporaries and posterity, as a Platonic philosopher (as attested by a statue of him erected in Madauros and the witness of St Augustine). The Cupid and Psyche tale shows clear dependence on Plato's account of the soul in the *Phaedrus* (*Metamorphoses* V.24 and *Phaedrus* 248c), and the centrality of *curiositas* connects with Platonic themes, particularly as developed by the Platonist Plutarch (with whom Lucius claims kinship at I.2) in his work, *De curiositate*. Platonic texture and allusions, however, do not mean that the work is necessarily philosophical. Again, the focus might be on the entertainment of literary games, with playful readings showing off erudition, rather than serious philosophy hidden in narrative form.

The last words on the interpretation of the *Metamorphoses*, however, can be given over to Jack Winkler, universally acknowledged as the most significant and influential interpreter of the text to date: in his words (1985: 187), the *Metamorphoses*: 'was originally written not to be a hermetically sealed monument, to be admired only from a respectful distance, but as an open text, one that encourages participation – real embarrassment, puzzlement, disgust, laughter, tentative closures of meaning and surprising entrapments, mental rewriting ("Oh, he must mean . . ."), and physical rewriting'.

The tale of Cupid and Psyche

Summary

The tale of Cupid and Psyche is the longest of the embedded narratives in the *Metamorphoses* and is almost certainly an Apuleian addition. It is the only tale which takes place outside the recognizable everyday world of the Roman empire, and we are taken instead to a mythical, idealized Greek world. The tale is embedded in the overarching narrative as a tale told by the robbers' housekeeper, attempting to calm the grief of the kidnapped Charite, stolen away at the very point of her marriage. The whole tale can be summarized as follows:

Psyche (Greek for 'soul') is a princess so beautiful she is worshipped by the people as an earthly Venus (IV.28); jealous, the goddess herself orders her son Cupid ('Desire') to punish Psyche (IV.30–1). Despite her beauty, therefore, she is admired but never loved and her parents, in despair, consult an oracle. They are given the answer that she must be exposed on a mountain top, where she will be taken in marriage by a monster (IV.33–4). She is duly left on the mountain but, rather than the expected awful fate, she is conveyed by Zephyr (the personified god of the west wind) to a magnificent palace where she is waited on by invisible attendants (IV.35–V.3). An equally invisible bridegroom comes to her at night (V.3–4). Against the advice of her unseen lover, she invites her sisters to visit her and her good fortune excites their jealousy (V.5–11). They attempt to convince her that her husband is actually a serpent, who intends to devour her, and urge her to kill him to protect herself (V.12–20).

Psyche, gullible (but also culpably curious), is convinced and, dagger and lamp in hand, discovers her husband is not a serpent, but the incomparably handsome Cupid (V.21–2). A drop of oil from the lamp awakens (and wounds) him and he flees, despite the fact that Psyche is now pregnant with his child. Psyche unsuccessfully tries to kill herself (V.24–5); she takes her vengeance on her sisters, who die by throwing themselves from a cliff, convinced that Cupid is going to take them on as his lover (V.26–7).

This is the point at which the text with which A-Level candidates ought to be familiar in translation begins. In V.28–31, Venus is informed of what has happened to Cupid by a seagull, who also informs her that both she and Cupid are being accused of abandoning their duties, causing havoc on earth. Embarrassed at the affront to her reputation, and particularly enraged that it is her enemy Cupid who has caused her son's fall from grace, she vows revenge. Both Juno and Ceres attempt to calm her down, but to no avail. Book VI.1–6 starts with a shift of focus back to Psyche. Now aware of the divine nature of her lover, she reasons that she can at least worship him as a god, if not comfort him as a wife, and she approaches two temples in turn, dedicated to Ceres and Juno. She wins the sympathy of both, but they both claim to be unable to help her because of their close familial and personal relationship with Venus.

We return to Venus (at the start of the text to be read in Latin). Taking the role of a scorned mother-in-law, she now persecutes Psyche (VI.7–10) by setting her impossible tasks, which Psyche manages to complete with the help of other creatures (VI.10–15). The final task, a descent to the underworld, Psyche accomplishes with supernatural help (VI.16–20). At the final moment, however, carrying back a casket from Proserpina to Venus, she again succumbs to her vice of curiosity and opens its lid (VI.21), which sends her into a death-like sleep (this is the end of the specification's Latin text). By this time, Cupid has recovered from his wound and escaped the watch of his mother; he finds Psyche, restores the casket to Proserpina and pleads for his love at the throne of Jupiter (VI.22); Venus is reconciled with Psyche, and the tale ends with a happy wedding feast amongst the gods, capped by the birth of a daughter to Cupid and Psyche, Voluptas ('Pleasure', VI.23–4, where the text to be read in English also finishes).

Structure

Several attempts have been made to identify the internal structure of the tale; the fact that no one system has gained general acceptance suggests that there is no clear and obvious way of understanding its structure. Given that the book divisions are Apuleius' own, the tripartite structure based around them suggested by Zimmerman et al. (2004) is perhaps the most plausible:

> A. (IV.28–35) Introduction of the main characters, and the problems which lead to the drama of the tale.
> B. (V) Rise and fall of Psyche: her awakening as Cupid's lover, and her fall due to over-curiosity.
> C. (VI.1–24) Trials of Psyche, leading to her reunion with Cupid.

Within this broader understanding, there are clear structural features within the tale; a key feature is the inclusion of ecphrases (artistic descriptive scenes; see IV.3 below) at four pivotal points in the tale. The first, at IV.31, describes Venus' departure to the sea: the splendour of her retinue contrasting with the loneliness of Psyche. The second occurs at the opening of Book V, where Cupid's palace is explored by Psyche. The ecphrasis dramatizes the fact that Psyche has entered an entirely new world, and the gloomy end of Book IV is reversed by the discovery of this wonderland. The third ecphrasis is Psyche's discovery of the beauty of Cupid at V.22, the pivotal point of Psyche's fall. Lastly, a fourth ecphrasis (VI.6) returns us to Venus, describing her ascent to Olympus. The overall structure is chiastic: Venus' two different retinues, one of the sea and one of the sky, bookend two descriptions of wonder, seen through Psyche's eyes. There are two more, minor ecphrases in the trials of Psyche which parallel each other: at VI.13, Venus gives an ecphrasis of the location of Psyche's third task and then, at VI.14, we see it focalized through Psyche's eyes. These descriptive scenes serve to give colour and charm to the tale, as well as provide it with structural balance and coherence.

The story-within-a-story

Although the tale stands up perfectly well when removed from its surrounds and has often been edited or translated as a stand-alone story, it has been carefully embedded within the larger narrative. In many interpretations it provides the key, or at least a significant piece of the puzzle, for an overarching interpretation of the novel as a whole. Walsh, in a much-quoted observation, notes that Apuleius 'has here adopted the Alexandrian technique exploited by Callimachus in his *Hecale* and taken over by Catullus in his sixty-fourth poem; *Cupid and Psyche* is a story within a story, and designed to illuminate the larger whole' (1970: 190).

Embedding the tale across three books (a technique characteristic of Ovid in his *Metamorphoses*) secures and embeds it integrally within the work as a whole; moreover, the introduction of the tale by the old woman, *sed ego te narrationibus lepidis anilibusque fabulis protinus avocabo* ('But come, now let me take your mind off your troubles: here's a pretty fairy tale, an old woman's story'), clearly echoes the prologue of the *Metamorphoses*: *at ego tibi sermone isto Milesio varias fabulas conseram auresque tuas benivolas lepido susurro permulceam* ('Now what I propose in this Milesian discourse is to string together for you a series of different stories and to charm your ears, kind reader, with amusing gossip'; Kenney's translation). The analogy suggested between the two stories is complex: Lucius, as a hearer of the Cupid and Psyche tale, does not realize its relevance and parallel to his own situation until his salvation by Isis; equally, the reader of the *Metamorphoses* will not realize that there might be instruction beneath the 'amusing gossip' until that same point in Lucius' retelling, his narration of his Isiac conversion.

The fable recapitulates the core elements of the story of Lucius: his transformation into an ass is the result, like Psyche's troubles, of inordinate curiosity, and his transformation back into human form takes place after a series of misfortunes which echo Psyche's trials. Resolution comes as a result of divine intervention, and Psyche's journey to the underworld and opening a secret casket echo elements of the Eleusinian mysteries and thus prefigure Lucius' mystic initiations into the Isis and Osiris cults in Book XI. Further support for this position is offered by the central positioning of the tale within the *Metamorphoses*: the tale itself sits in the middle of the first ten books, but Psyche's *katabasis*, her descent to the underworld, is the centre of the whole work. This is partly a reference to the centrality of similar *katabases* in Homer's *Odyssey* and Virgil's *Aeneid*; it also points forward to Lucius' own *katabasis* in Book XI, after which he is united to Isis, as Psyche is joined to Cupid.

On another level, the tale fits into a carefully interwoven complex of narratives and themes which binds together the disparate elements and characters of IV.23–VIII.14. The so-called 'Charite-complex', identified by Carl Schlam (see Further Reading), integrates three strands of the narrative in a delicate counterpoint: Charite and Tlepolemus, Cupid and Psyche, and the story of Lucius himself. The Cupid and Psyche tale echoes Charite's own interrupted wedding and prefigures her eventual liberation and successful marriage (though without the subsequent reversal of fortune that befalls both Lucius and Charite). Narratologically, the balance between Charite's back-story (told by Charite herself to the old woman) and the tale of Cupid and Psyche (told by the old woman to Charite) rests on a series of opposites: narrator and audience swap places, from opposite perspectives – young/old, rich/poor, real-life tragedy/mythic happily-ever-after fairytale. As a binding recurrent theme, a series of clever deceits tie the stories together: Psyche is deceived by her sisters but, in turn, causes their deaths by a clever deceit of her own; Tlepolemus deceives the robbers by an Odyssean trick (getting them drunk) but is himself later undone, deceived by a rival, who himself, tricked by drugged wine, is exposed by Charite before her death.

The sources of the tale

Whilst the tale is an Apuleian insertion into the Greek *Onos*, it is clearly not just an imaginative *tour de force* of the author's creative powers; elements of the story clearly have predecessors, models and sources in earlier variants. Accounts of the tale (especially in the first half of the twentieth century) have attempted to find an exclusive source in folktale, myth or literature. Certainly, the overall narrative seems to have connections with folklore: at the very beginning of modern research into folk traditions, the Brothers Grimm noted the folkloric elements of Apuleius' tale and, with the technical development of what is called the Finnish historical-geographical method, hundreds of parallel folk stories could be found for Cupid and Psyche. Core motifs are the search for a lost husband, who initially appears as an animal or monster, and whose loss follows the violation of a taboo (elements of this can be seen in the tales of Beauty and the Beast and even Cinderella), and the fulfilment of impossible tasks set by a witch.

What is lacking from this account, however, is the importance of the figures of Cupid and Psyche themselves: the folklore parallels give us tales of anonymous or, at least, generic husbands and wives, rather than the Soul and Love personified and, whilst many motifs and elements are shared, the narrative as a whole is largely unparalleled. More serious criticisms have been levelled at the attempted scientific nature of folklore research in general, critiquing the attempts to look for origins for particular tale-types in some pure, non-elite, non-literary, historically unbroken oral tradition. In the most strident objection, folklore is itself a literary genre created in the sixteenth to eighteenth centuries, developed by writers drawing on written material of the middle ages and antiquity: in this view, traces of Cupid and Psyche in fairytales are just as likely to be dependent on the Apuleian tale as they are evidence for a pre-existing oral source.

Looking towards myth rather than folklore, suggestions that Apuleius was drawing on an earlier source are supported by the iconographic tradition of Cupid and Psyche as a pair, a representation which was popular from the sixth century BC onwards. When the oracle warns Psyche's parents of her monstrous lover as 'a creature of no mortal stock, but a cruel, wild, and fiery evil, who, flying above the sky, wearies all things, and cripples each with flame and iron, before whom Jupiter himself trembles' (*Metamorphoses* IV.33; trans. in Schlam 1992), the mystery of her lover is only conventional: this imagery of Eros/Cupid is familiar both from literature and from art, and even expected after the introduction of our heroine as Psyche (at IV.30).

The iconography with which the audience would have been familiar depicted both Cupid and Psyche as winged creatures, part of a tradition which saw the soul figured as a butterfly, particularly in contexts suggestive of the life of the soul after death. Often the relationship between the two characters represents Eros as a *daemon* who draws the soul towards the divine, and the embracing pair became 'an enduring expression of the goal of reunion with the divine within man with God' (Schlam 1992: 91). These representations were particularly common as funereal motifs on sarcophagi at the time of the *Metamorphoses*' composition, as an emblem of the survival or salvation of the soul after death, and this theme clearly links into Isiac interpretations of the tale as discussed below. But, while this iconography is certainly part of what Apuleius is playing with, these images do not seem to have been attached to a particular narrative, certainly not one as complex as the tale we have here.

Over the top of whatever elements Apuleius has taken from myth or folklore are much more literary elements: foremost, the Platonic tradition of philosophical myth-making but, more playfully, borrowing elements from genres as diverse as epic, satire and, in particular, Alexandrian poetry. The literary texture is just as much part of Apuleius' tale as any of the putative sources for it: thus, Venus' opening speech (IV.30) is reminiscent of Lucretian style, but is deliberately playing on Virgil's Juno, particularly her first speech at *Aeneid* I.34–49, already parodied by Ovid in his *Metamorphoses* (III.262–72). The sisters' description of the snake at V.26 is another Virgilian pastiche, and the most extended play with the *Aeneid* is in Psyche's *katabasis* in the selection here, 'virtually a mosaic of Virgilian phrases' (Walsh 1970: 57). This kind of intellectual game-playing is part of the competitive literary culture which formed Apuleius' cultural backdrop, and, whilst an audience does not need to recognize an intertextual allusion to understand the story, often it adds an extra level of characterization, emotion or wit to the narrative.

The meaning(s) of the tale

There have been readings of the tale which see in it quite specific Isiac resonances and incorporate the tale into an overall interpretation of the work as serious Isiac propaganda: a 1953 article by a German scholar, Reinhold Merkelbach, stands at the head of this tradition ('Eros und Psyche', *Philologus* 102 [1953]: 103–16). Although his reading is not the mainstream one, it still has adherents in more recent scholarship. Merkelbach notes that Isis has both transcendent and narrative mythic forms: the former as the personified hand of fortune and the latter as the itinerant goddess, searching for the dismembered parts of Osiris; thus, the heavenly Venus represents the first aspect, and the wandering Psyche the second.

More influential and convincing a reading, however, is based on the known philosophical leanings of Apuleius. It is the tale of Cupid and Psyche more than any other part of the *Metamorphoses* which has given rise to Platonic readings of the work. Kenney (1990) has noted the influence of the discussion of love in Plato's *Symposium*. In this work, Venus and Eros (i.e. Cupid) are discussed as each having a heavenly and an earthly form (Venus Urania and Venus Pandemos, with Erotes to match): one for the love of souls, the other for love of bodies (180d–181b). Apuleius himself paraphrased the work in his *Apology* (12) and the argument runs that the fable dramatizes the conflict between earthly Venus and heavenly Eros, and thus is an allegory of the competition between, and the victory of, spiritual love (the love of virtue) over physical lust. Mark Edwards ('The Tale of Cupid and Psyche', *Zeitschrift für Papyrologie und Epigraphik* 94 [1992]: 77–94) gives a detailed account of parallels to Apuleius' story in Neo-Platonist, Gnostic and eastern mythic traditions, and shows how such complex allegorical story-telling was part and parcel of the spiritual and intellectual milieu of the second century. Even if we do not read the tale as straightforward, serious, philosophical mythic allegory, therefore, it seems more than likely that Apuleius deliberately plays with features of this kind of writing. As so often in the *Metamorphoses*, whether Apuleius is sermonizing or jesting is difficult to tell.

Apuleius' style

General stylistic features

It can never be far from the reader's mind that Apuleius was trained and practised as an orator and professional rhetorician. His writing is constructed with an ear for its effect when read aloud, for the delight in the sounds and the images created by them: it strikes the reader as exuberant, over the top, showy and intricate. It used to be common to refer to Latin of the first century BC as 'golden' and that of the first century AD as 'silver' (being inferior) and, following this pattern, it was a common literary judgement to see both Latin and Greek literature of the later empire as degenerate, derivative and second-rate. More recently, however, critical scholarship has been more positive in its assessment, underscoring the creativity, playfulness and complexity of imperial literature; Apuleius has benefitted from a serious reconsideration of his literary value over the generations.

The key features of Apuleius' language are 'exuberance and richness' (Kenney 1990: 29): you will notice that reading and translating Apuleius is quite a different experience to reading and translating Caesar, Cicero, Tacitus or the other prose authors you may have studied up to this point. With Apuleius, it is worthwhile, once you have got over the initial hurdle of unpicking the syntax and vocabulary, to go back over the sentence, paragraph or passage (whether it be a speech, narrative description or other set-piece) and read it out aloud. The characteristic features of Apuleius you might be able to spot occur on a number of levels within the text:

- **Vocabulary**: hugely varied, with frequent poetic usages, archaisms, neologisms (often formed from poetic or archaic forms) or words used in unfamiliar or unusual senses and diminutives.
- **Sentence structure**: tends to be paratactic rather than hypotactic, that is, independent clauses (often balanced in contrast or parallelism) rather than strings of subordinate clauses. Apuleius is also much given to different kinds of repetition: pleonasm, variation and amplification. In both of these habits, Apuleius should be more reader- and translator-friendly than many Classical authors (like Cicero, Livy or Tacitus, all of whom tend to more complex periodic construction). For a clever example of amplification, or *amplificatio*, the enhancements or exaggeration of an argument to maximize its impact, see VI.10: *discerne seminum*

istorum passivam congeriem, singulisque granis rite dispositis atque seiugatis ante istam vesperam opus expeditum approbato mihi ('Sort out this random heap of seeds, and let me see the work completed by this evening, with each kind of grain properly arranged and separated.' [trans. Kenney]). The piled-up heap (*passivam congeriem*) of grain echoes the technical definition of the device (e.g. in Quintilian) as a *congeries verborum*, which we see here in the repetition of synonymous words and phrases: *discerne . . . singulis . . . rite dispositis . . . seiugatis.*

- **Attention to sound**: Apuleius frequently uses alliteration and assonance to adorn his sentences. Sometimes the effect of this is obvious and striking: e.g. at VI.8, Mercury's message is delivered with an obvious alliteration of *p* and assonance of *o, per omnium ora populorum* ('through the mouths of the whole population') which echoes the sound of running feet and the plosives give a sense of shock and surprise. In the same speech, Venus' reward, *septem savia suavia* ('seven sweet kisses'), is sensual in its sibilance. At other times, however, although alliteration might be obvious, its particular effect is harder to pin down and interpret. As a general rule for interpretation, attempting to claim a representative or symbolic function for particular kinds of sounds is often weak and unconvincing (although this is precisely what I have done with my first two examples!); much better is to note that alliteration or assonance draws attention to particular combinations of words and gives them particular weight or stress to echo, subvert or complement the face-value meaning of the words. In the commentary, I shall draw attention to such alliteration without necessarily imposing my own interpretation on the passage: part of the skill students ought to be developing is how to posit and defend their own interpretations.
- **Rhythm**: Apuleius one of most attentive authors to prose rhythm – the use of metrical formulae (like you may be familiar with in poetry), particularly to mark the conclusion of sentences (called

clausulae), on which see below. There are two strands which feed into Apuleian style here: first, his primary training (and professional life) is as an orator – the sound of delivery is key to a successful performance and, therefore, of primary concern. Just as important, however, is Apuleius' close literary relationship to poetry; his key intertexts (see below) are poetic authors – particularly Vergil and Ovid in our selection, and hence there is a bleeding of poetic features into his prose.

- *Topoi* (literary commonplaces): you will find a large number of set rhetorical pieces. Often these are straightforwardly in the form of formal speeches, but also, for example, in ornate descriptive passages (ecphrases); the best examples of these in our text are the twinned descriptions of the underworld in VI.13 and VI.14; the former opens with a clear, recognizable marker of ecphrasis, a verb of seeing, *vides*.

- **Allusion and intertextuality**: Apuleius is often consciously and deliberately playing with a rich literary tradition. An audience does not need to be highly educated and intimately familiar with the Latin literary tradition to appreciate the *Metamorphoses*, but without such knowledge hearers will miss a large number of jokes, ironies, wry comparisons and general literary play. In our selection, there are several narratives that Apuleius plays with, not just as general myths, but as specific literary versions which he alludes to at numerous points by specific verbal echo. The characterization of Venus early in our selection plays with Ovid's jealous Juno in the *Metamorphoses* and Psyche's descent to the underworld; he evokes Aeneas' catabasis in Vergil's *Aeneid* VI, the tale of Orpheus and Eurydice, again from Vergil, *Georgics* IV (see the Commentary for more detailed references). His intertextuality includes Greek as well as Latin texts, so Odysseus' descent to the underworld is at times subtly referenced as well, and the *Argonautica* of Apollonius of Rhodes gets a look-in during the episode of the sheep with the golden fleece (VI.11).

Prose rhythm

From at least the Classical period, Roman authors were clearly conscious of the aural effect created by patterns of heavy and light syllables in formal spoken prose. Cicero records that a particularly apt rhythm could bring about spontaneous applause (*Or.* 214) and his use of different rhythmical patterns set the standard for later authors. Part of this tradition is based on Greek models and theories of prose rhythm, but Latin developed its distinctive tradition and style. In particular, the ends of sentences, called *clausulae*, were the particular focus for judicious use of sonorous patterns; partly for purely aesthetic reasons, but undoubtedly also for practical purposes: in a tradition where literature was still fundamentally meant to be read aloud, but in which scribal convention did not often show sense divisions in sentences, or even divisions between words, rhythmical markers for the ends of periods or *cola* (natural sense breaks within sentences) were useful, particularly in complex periodic sentences.

It is important to note that the patterns are quantitive, rather than (as is common in English poetry or prose) stress-based – i.e. they are based on length of syllables (heavy or light, marked ¯ and ˘, respectively, or ^{x} where a syllable can be long or short), rather than emphasized syllables within words; so neither word-accent nor word-division make a difference to the use of these rhythms. As in verse, elision is taken into account: a vowel ending a word, if followed by one starting with a vowel, is not pronounced – so *totisque illis* in the first section from the set text would have been pronounced *totisqu~illis* with four syllables.

The basic *clausula* patterns preferred by Cicero are the ditrochee (¯ ˘ ¯ ^{x}), especially with a preceding cretic (¯ ˘ ¯ | ¯ ˘ ¯ ^{x}), the double cretic (¯ ˘ ¯ | ¯ ˘ ^{x}) and the cretic followed by either a trochee or a spondee (¯ ˘ ¯ | ¯ ^{x}). These patterns can also be varied by resolution – the replacement of a long syllable by two short syllables. The pattern of *ēssĕ vĭdĕātūr* (a resolved version of the third form above) even became such a trademark of Cicero's that later writers avoided it unless deliberately trying to evoke Cicero.

Apuleius, as a rhetorician, and as an author distinctly conscious of his literary heritage, is remarkably consistent in his usage of these *clausulae*: depending on the method of counting used, up to 92.5 per cent of Apuleius' sentences end in a recognized rhythm; another analysis suggests that Apuleius follows Ciceronian principles just under seventy per cent of the time (Kenney 1990: 31). A sense of prose rhythm is clearly also present in the careful manipulation of the lengths of clauses (in terms of number of syllables); clauses can build to a climax with ascending numbers of syllables or be balanced in equal lengths. For example, at VI.14 the 'savage dragons', *saevi dracones,* are described by two parallel phrases: *inconivae vigiliae luminibus addictis et in perpetuam lucem pupulis excubantibus* ('with their eyes devoted to unsleeping watch and with their pupils awake into an everlasting vision'); each clause is fifteen syllables in length, using allusive rather than straightforward vocabulary for eyes, and the word order in both ablatives absolute; it finishes with a recognizable *clausula* made of a cretic followed by an iamb. Whilst prose rhythm analysis doesn't often tend to make for the same examination-ready commentary notes as other rhetorical features, it is important, nonetheless, to keep in mind that throughout the composition of the *Metamorphoses* the aural effect of the prose was consistently one of Apuleius' fundamental considerations.

Glossary of stylistic terms

Alliteration: repetition of consonant sounds.
Anaphora: repetition of a word, especially at the beginning of successive clauses.
Apostrophe: breaking out from narration to make a direct address.
Asyndeton: lack of connective particles between clauses.
Assonance: repetition of vowel sounds.
Bathos: an effect of anticlimax, by dropping from elevated speech to colloquial or ridiculous.
Chiasmus: inverted parallelism – i.e. any arrangement of words in a pattern of A–B–B–A (e.g. by part of speech, by case, by sound).
Diminutive: a form of a noun denoting that it is a small or immature version; like the English 'booklet' or 'piglet' for small forms of book and pig.

Enallage (also **hypallage**): transferring an element from what it agrees with in sense to another part of the sentence; also referred to as a transferred epithet. E.g. the final verse of *Adeste fideles* reads: 'Yea, Lord, we greet thee, born this happy morning' – in sense, we are happy, rather than the morning.
Homoioteleuton: similar endings, giving the effect of rhyme.
Hyperbaton: an inversion of the normal order of words, usually for emphasis.
Hypotaxis: construction of periodic sentences using subordinate clauses.
Isocolon: a succession of sentences or phrases of equal length.
Juxtaposition: the placing of contrasting words or ideas next to each other.
Makarismos: a *topos*, common in ancient religious contexts, of declaring someone or something blessed: the most well-known example being the 'Beatitudes' from the Sermon on the Mount, with its list of 'Blessed are . . .'.
Neologism: a newly invented word.
Onomatopoeia: words which make the sound they describe, like 'whirr' or 'buzz'.
Oxymoron: a seeming contradiction in terms; literally 'sharp-dull' in Greek. E.g. *festina lente*, 'hasten slowly'.
Parataxis: constructing sentences by parallel clauses, rather than by subordination.
Paronomasia: play on words, punning.
Pleonasm: the use of more words than are necessary, usually for emphasis.
Polyptoton: repetition of a word in multiple grammatical forms.
Tetracolon: a series of four parallel clauses.
Topos: a traditional or formulaic theme or element in literature.
Tricolon: a combination of three parallel clauses, often building up to a significant, emphasized third element.
Zeugma: also known as *syllepsis*; where a single word or phrase is used with two other parts of a sentence, but must be understood differently in relation to each. The Flanders and Swan music-hall song 'Have Some Madeira, M'Dear' is an education in zeugma; for example, 'by raising her glass, her courage, her eyes, and his hopes'.

The text

The text of the *Metamorphoses* depends on a single source, an eleventh-century manuscript held at Florence, catalogued as Laurentianus 68.2, known as 'F'; all other extant copies derive from this single survival, although some copies were clearly made when F when was in a better condition than it is now and, where wear and tear have defaced the reading, we can often supply the deficiency from these copies. Emendations to the text have therefore been made by editors on the basis of difficulties with the Latin rather than conflicting witnesses. I have not provided an *apparatus criticus* with this text, as being unnecessary for the purposes of a school text; the edition I have mainly followed is the Oxford Classical Text (2012), edited by Maaike Zimmerman.

Further reading

I shall attempt here to give a (necessarily rather subjective) selection of the texts which would be most useful for a teacher preparing the text to consult, and which a particularly interested and capable student might be directed towards for extension. Full bibliographical references are given at the end. The most important further reading is to read the rest of the tale of Cupid and Psyche in translation, and ideally the whole of the *Metamorphoses*. There are several readily available good translations. The Penguin Classics version, Kenney (2004), is lively and readable, with an excellent brief introduction. The Loeb edition, with facing English and Latin, Hanson (1989), in two volumes, and the Oxford World's Classics edition, Walsh (1994), are both also eminently accessible without sacrificing accuracy.

There are two excellent modern commentaries on Cupid and Psyche, both with translations: the Cambridge 'green and yellow' commentary (although oddly not actually green and yellow, in this case), Kenney (1990), has an extensive introduction (a fuller version than that in his Penguin translation) and brief but very useful notes. The magisterial volume on the tale of Cupid and Psyche in the Groningen Commentaries on Apuleius, by Zimmerman et al. (2004) is exhaustive in its treatment, including an English translation. Its cost, however, is prohibitive, unless you have access to a university library, and its depth is well beyond that needed even at undergraduate level. Given their significance and usefulness, I refer to both numerous times in the text of the commentary (using the simple terms Kenney and GCA). Surprisingly useful still is Purser's 1910 commentary, available in reprint (and helpfully also online), which gives more help than Kenney at the appropriate level for sixth-form students.

For more general reading on Apuleius, Harrison (2000) provides an excellent overview and sets the *Metamorphoses* within the context of Apuleius' wider oeuvre and his intellectual context. A broader outlook on Antonine literature, including a chapter by Kenney on Cupid and Psyche, is given by Russell (1990). The best single-volume studies on the *Metamorphoses* are Tatum (1979), Schlam (1992), both highly readable and accessible texts, and most influentially (though a more challenging read) Winkler (1985). For those interested in the literary allusiveness of Apuleius, Finkelpearl (1998) is outstanding. Walsh (1970) is useful for placing the *Metamorphoses*, and its genre as a novel, in the context of Roman literature more broadly.

Lastly, one area left untouched by this introduction has been the rich afterlife of the *Metamorphoses*, and the Cupid and Psyche episode in particular, in later literature and art. The field of Classical reception is one growing in importance and visibility in the world of academic Classics but, quite apart from that, the story of later receptions of Apuleius is a fascinating one, with some particular interesting by-ways to tread, especially for those interested in renaissance literature or art. There are two books from the last decade or so which provide excellent coverage of the field, Carver (2007) and Gaisser (2008); the overview of Cupid and Psyche in renaissance art in De Jong (1998) is also well worth perusing, as is the more recent volume on the reception of the tale since 1600 by May and Harrison (2020).

References

Apulei (2012), *Metamorphoseon Libri XI*, ed. Maaike Zimmerman, Oxford Classical Texts, Oxford: Oxford University Press

Apuleius (2018), *Metamorphoses V: A Selection*, Introduction, notes and vocabulary by Stuart R. Thomson, London: Bloomsbury.

Carver, Robert H. F. (2007), *The Protean Ass: The Metamorphoses of Apuleius from Antiquity to the Renaissance*, Oxford Classical Monographs, Oxford: Oxford University Press.

De Jong, J. L. (1998), '"Il Pittore a le Volte è pure Poeta": Cupid and Psyche in Italian Renaissance Painting', in M. Zimmerman et al. (eds), *Aspects of Apuleius' Golden Ass II: Cupid and Psyche*, 189–216, Groningen: Egbert Forsten.

Finkelpearl, Ellen D. (1998), *Metamorphosis of Language in Apuleius: A Study of Allusion in the Novel*, Ann Arbor: University of Michigan Press.

Gaisser, Julia H. (2008), *The Fortunes of Apuleius and the Golden Ass: A Study in Transmission and Reception*, Martin Classical Lectures, Princeton: Princeton University Press.

Hanson, J. A., ed. and trans. (1989), Apuleius, *Metamorphoses (The Golden Ass)*, Loeb Classical Library, 2 vols, Cambridge, MA: Harvard University Press.

Harrison, S. J. 2000. *Apuleius: A Latin Sophist.* Oxford: OUP.

Kenney, E. J., ed. (1990), Apuleius, *Cupid and Psyche*, Cambridge: Cambridge University Press.

Kenney, E. J., trans. and intro. ([1998] 2004), Apuleius, *The Golden Ass*, rev. edn, London: Penguin.

May, Regine, and Stephen J. Harrison, eds (2020), *Cupid and Psyche: The Reception of Apuleius' Love Story since 1600: Trends in Classics – Pathways of Reception 1*, Berlin; Boston: De Gruyter.

Purser, Louis C., ed. (1910), *The Story of Cupid and Psyche: As Related by Apuleius*, with Introduction and notes, London: George Bell & Sons.

Purser, Louis C. (1913), *Apulei Psyche et Cupido*, Scriptorum Classicorum Bibliotheca Riccardiana, London: Lee Warner.

Russell, D. A., ed. (1990), *Antonine Literature*, Oxford: Oxford University Press.

Schlam, Carl C. (1992), *The Metamorphoses of Apuleius: On Making an Ass of Oneself*, London: Duckworth.

Tatum, James (1979), *Apuleius and* The Golden Ass, Ithaca and London: Cornell University Press.

Walsh, P. G. (1970), *The Roman Novel*, Cambridge: Cambridge University Press.

Walsh, P. G., ed. and trans. (1994), Apuleius, *The Golden Ass*, with an Introduction, Oxford World's Classics, Oxford: Clarendon Press.

Winkler, J. J. (1985), *Auctor and Actor: A Narratological Reading of Apuleius's Golden Ass*, Berkeley, Los Angeles; London: University of California Press.

Zimmerman, M., S. Panayotakis et al. (2004), *Apuleius Madaurensis: Metamorphoses: Book IV 28–35, V and VI 1–24: The Tale of Cupid and Psyche*, Text, Introduction and Commentary, Groningen Commentaries on Apuleius, Groningen: Egbert Forsten.

Text

Book VI, Chapters 1 to 6: Psyche, hunted by Venus, seeks refuge in the temples of Ceres and Juno but is refused sanctuary. Meanwhile Venus, having searched for Psyche on earth, ascends to the heavens to look for her there.

[7] tunc se protinus ad Iovis regias arces dirigit, et petitu superbo Mercuri, dei vocalis, operae necessariam usuram postulat. nec rennuit Iovis caerulum supercilium. tunc ovans ilico, comitante etiam Mercurio, Venus caelo demeat eique sollicite serit verba:

'Frater Arcadi, scis nempe sororem tuam Venerem sine Mercuri praesentia nil umquam fecisse, nec te praeterit utique quanto iam tempore delitescentem ancillam nequiverim repperire. nil ergo superest quam tuo praeconio praemium investigationis publicitus edicere. fac ergo mandatum matures meum et indicia qui possit agnosci manifeste designes, ne, si quis occultationis illicitae crimen subierit, ignorantiae se possit excusatione defendere.' et simul dicens libellum ei porrigit, ubi Psyches nomen continebatur et cetera. quo facto protinus domum secessit.

[8] nec Mercurius omisit obsequium. nam per omnium ora populorum passim discurrens, sic mandatae praedicationis munus exequebatur: 'si quis a fuga retrahere vel occultam demonstrare poterit fugitivam regis filiam, Veneris ancillam, nomine Psychen, conveniat retro metas Murtias Mercurium praedicatorem, accepturus indicivae nomine ab ipsa Venere septem savia suavia et unum blandientis adpulsu linguae longe mellitum.'

ad hunc modum pronuntiante Mercurio tanti praemii cupido certatim omnium mortalium studium adrexerat. quae res nunc vel maxime sustulit Psyches omnem cunctationem. iamque fores eius dominae proximanti occurrit una de famulitione Veneris nomine Consuetudo, statimque quantum maxime potuit exclamat: 'tandem, ancilla nequissima, dominam habere te scire coepisti? an pro cetera morum tuorum temeritate istud quoque nescire te fingis, quantos labores circa tuas inquisitiones sustinuerimus? sed bene quod meas potissimum manus incidisti et inter Orci cancros iam ipsos haesisti datura scilicet actutum tantae contumaciae poenas.'

[**9**] et audaciter in capillos eius immissa manu trahebat eam nequaquam renitentem. quam ubi primum inductam oblatamque sibi conspexit Venus, latissimum cachinnum extollit et qualem solent furenter irati, caputque quatiens et ascalpens aurem dexteram, 'tandem' inquit 'dignata es socrum tuam salutare? an potius maritum, qui tuo vulnere periclitatur, intervisere venisti? sed esto secura; iam enim excipiam te, ut bonam nurum condecet.' et: 'ubi sunt' inquit 'Sollicitudo atque Tristities, ancillae meae?'

quibus intro vocatis torquendam tradidit eam. at illae sequentes erile praeceptum Psychen misellam flagellis afflictam et ceteris tormentis excruciatam iterum dominae conspectui reddunt. tunc rursus sublato risu Venus 'et ecce' inquit 'nobis turgidi ventris sui lenocinio commovet miserationem, unde me praeclara subole aviam beatam scilicet faciat. felix vero ego, quae in ipso aetatis meae flore vocabor avia, et vilis ancillae filius nepos Veneris audiet. quamquam inepta ego frustra filium dicam. impares enim nuptiae et praeterea in villa sine testibus et patre non consentiente factae legitimae non possunt videri, ac per hoc spurius iste nascetur, si tamen partum omnino perferre te patiemur.'

[**10**] his editis involat eam vestemque plurifariam diloricat, capilloque discisso et capite conquassato graviter affligit. et accepto frumento et hordeo et milio et papavere et cicere et lente et faba commixtisque acervatim confusis in unum grumulum, sic ad illam: 'videris enim mihi tam deformis ancilla nullo alio sed tantum sedulo ministerio amatores tuos promereri. iam ergo et ipsa frugem tuam periclitabor. discerne

seminum istorum passivam congeriem, singulisque granis rite dispositis atque seiugatis ante istam vesperam opus expeditum approbato mihi.'

sic assignato tantorum seminum cumulo ipsa cenae nuptiali concessit. nec Psyche manus admolitur inconditae illi et inextricabili moli, sed immanitate praecepti consternata silens obstupescit. tunc formicula illa parvula atque ruricola, certa difficultatis tantae laborisque, miserta contubernalis magni dei socrusque saevitiam execrata, discurrens naviter convocat corrogatque cunctam formicarum accolarum classem. 'miseremini, terrae omniparentis agiles alumnae, miseremini, et Amoris uxori, puellae lepidae, periclitanti prompta velocitate succurrite.' ruunt aliae superque aliae sepedum populorum undae, summoque studio singulae granatim totum digerunt acervum, separatimque distributis dissitisque generibus, e conspectu perniciter abeunt.

[11] sed initio noctis e convivio nuptiali, vino madens et fraglans balsama, Venus remeat totumque revincta corpus rosis micantibus, visaque diligentia miri laboris, 'non tuum,' inquit 'nequissima, nec tuarum manuum istud opus, sed illius cui tuo, immo et ipsius, malo placuisti.' et frusto cibarii panis ei proiecto cubitum facessit.

interim Cupido solus interioris domus unici cubiculi custodia clausus coercebatur acriter, partim ne petulanti luxurie vulnus gravaret, partim ne cum sua cupita conveniret. sic ergo distentis et sub uno tecto separatis amatoribus taetra nox exanclata.

sed Aurora commodum inequitante, vocatae Psychae Venus infit talia: 'videsne illud nemus, quod fluvio praeterluenti ripisque longis attenditur? cuius ubi frutices vicinum fontem despiciunt, oves ibi nitentes aurique colore florentes incustodito pastu vagantur. inde de coma pretiosi velleris floccum mihi confestim quoquo modo quaesitum afferas censeo.'

[12] perrexit Psyche volenter non obsequium quidem illa functura, sed requiem malorum praecipitio fluvialis rupis habitura. sed inde de fluvio

musicae suavis nutricula, leni crepitu dulcis aurae divinitus inspirata, sic vaticinatur harundo viridis: 'Psyche, tantis aerumnis exercita, neque tua miserrima morte meas sanctas aquas polluas, nec vero istud horae contra formidabiles oves feras aditum, quoad de solis flagrantia mutuatae calorem truci rabie solent efferari cornuque acuto et fronte saxea et nonnumquam venenatis morsibus in exitium saevire mortalium. sed dum meridies solis sedaverit vaporem et pecua spiritus fluvialis serenitate conquieverint, poteris sub illa procerissima platano, quae mecum simul unum fluentum bibit, latenter abscondere. et cum primum mitigata furia laxaverint oves animum, percussis frondibus attigui nemoris lanosum aurum repperies, quod passim stirpibus convexis obhaerescit.'

[13] sic harundo simplex et humana Psychen aegerrimam salutem suam docebat. nec auscultatu paenitendo, diligenter instructa, illa cessavit, sed observatis omnibus furatrina facili flaventis auri mollitie congestum gremium Veneri reportat. nec tamen apud dominam saltem secundi laboris periculum secundum testimonium meruit, sed contortis superciliis subridens amarum sic inquit: 'nec me praeterit huius quoque facti auctor adulterinus. sed iam nunc ego sedulo periclitabor an oppido forti animo singularique prudentia sis praedita. videsne insistentem celsissimae illi rupi montis ardui verticem, de quo fontis atri fuscae defluunt undae proxumaeque conceptaculo vallis inclusae Stygias inrigant paludes et rauca Cocyti fluenta nutriunt? indidem mihi de summi fontis penita scaturrigine rorem rigentem hauritum ista confestim defers urnula.' sic aiens crustallo dedolatum vasculum, insuper ei graviora comminata, tradidit.

[14] at illa studiose gradum celerans montis extremum petit tumulum, certe vel illic inventura vitae pessimae finem. sed cum primum praedicti iugi conterminos locos appulit, videt rei vastae letalem difficultatem. Namque saxum immani magnitudine procerum et inaccessa salebritate lubricum mediis e faucibus lapidis fontes horridos evomebat, qui statim proni foraminis lacunis editi perque proclive delapsi et angusti canalis exarato contecti tramite proxumam convallem latenter incidebant.

dextra laevaque cautibus cavatis proserpunt ecce longa colla porrecti saevi dracones, inconivae vigiliae luminibus addictis et in perpetuam lucem pupulis excubantibus. iamque et ipsae semet muniebant vocales aquae. nam et 'discede!' et 'quid facis? vide!' et 'quid agis? cave!' et 'fuge!' et 'peribis!' subinde clamant. sic impossibilitate ipsa mutata in lapidem Psyche, quamvis praesenti corpore, sensibus tamen aberat et inextricabilis periculi mole prorsus obruta lacrimarum etiam extremo solacio carebat.

[15] nec Providentiae bonae graves oculos innocentis animae latuit aerumna. nam supremi Iovis regalis ales illa repente propansis utrimque pinnis affuit, rapax aquila, memorque veteris obsequii, quo ductu Cupidinis Iovi pocillatorem Phrygium substulerat, opportunam ferens opem deique numen in uxoris laboribus percolens, alti culminis diales vias deserit et ob os puellae praevolans incipit:

'at tu, simplex alioquin et expers rerum talium, sperasne te sanctissimi nec minus truculenti fontis vel unam stillam posse furari vel omnino contingere? diis etiam ipsique Iovi formidabiles aquas istas Stygias vel fando comperisti, quodque vos deieratis per numina deorum, deos per Stygis maiestatem solere? sed cedo istam urnulam.'

et protinus adrepta complexaque festinat, libratisque pinnarum nutantium molibus inter genas saevientium dentium et trisulca vibramina draconum remigium dextra laevaque porrigens, nolentes aquas et ut abiret innoxius praeminantes excipit, commentus ob iussum Veneris petere eique se praeministrare, quare paulo facilior adeundi fuit copia.

[16] sic acceptam cum gaudio plenam urnulam Psyche Veneri citata rettulit. nec tamen nutum deae saevientis vel tunc expiare potuit. nam sic eam maiora atque peiora flagitia comminans appellat renidens exitiabile: 'iam tu quidem magna videris quaedam mihi et alta prorsus malefica, quae talibus praeceptis meis obtemperasti naviter. sed adhuc istud, mea pupula, ministrare debebis. sume istam pyxidem', et dedit;

'protinus usque ad inferos et ipsius Orci ferales penates te derige. tunc conferens pyxidem Proserpinae: "petit de te Venus" dicito "modicum de tua mittas ei formonsitate vel ad unam saltem dieculam sufficiens. nam quod habuit, dum filium curat aegrotum consumpsit atque contrivit omne." sed haud immaturius redito, quia me necesse est indidem delitam theatrum deorum frequentare.'

[**17**] tunc Psyche vel maxime sensit ultimas fortunas suas, et velamento reiecto ad promptum exitium sese compelli manifeste comperit – quidni? – quae suis pedibus ultro ad Tartarum manesque commeare cogeretur. nec cunctata diutius pergit ad quampiam turrim praealtam, indidem sese datura praecipitem. sic enim rebatur ad inferos recte atque pulcherrime se posse descendere. sed turris prorumpit in vocem subitam, et 'quid te' inquit 'praecipitio, misella, quaeris extinguere? quidque iam novissimo periculo laborique isto temere succumbis? nam si spiritus corpore tuo semel fuerit seiugatus, ibis quidem profecto ad imum Tartarum, sed inde nullo pacto redire poteris. mihi ausculta.

[**18**] Lacedaemo, Achaiae nobilis civitas, non longe sita est. huius conterminam deviis abditam locis quaere Taenarum. inibi spiraculum Ditis, et per portas hiantes monstratur iter invium, cui te limine transmeato simul commiseris, iam canale directo perges ad ipsam Orci regiam. sed non hactenus vacua debebis per illas tenebras incedere, sed offas polentae mulso concretas ambabus gestare manibus, at in ipso ore duas ferre stipes. iamque confecta bona parte mortiferae viae, continaberis claudum asinum lignorum gerulum cum agasone simili, qui te rogabit decidentis sarcinae fusticulos aliquos porrigas ei; sed tu nulla voce deprompta tacita praeterito. nec mora cum ad flumen mortuum venies, cui praefectus Charon protinus expetens portorium, sic ad ripam ulteriorem sutili cumba deducit commeantes. ergo et inter mortuos avaritia vivit, nec Charon ille Ditis sectator, tantus deus, quicquam gratuito facit, et moriens pauper viaticum debet quaerere, et aes si forte prae manu non fuerit, nemo eum expirare patietur. huic squalido seni dabis nauli nomine de stipibus quas feres alteram, sic tamen ut ipse sua manu de tuo sumat ore. nec setius tibi pigrum

fluentum transmeanti quidam supernatans senex mortuus putris adtollens manus orabit ut eum intra navigium trahas; nec tu tamen inlicita adflectare pietate.

[19] transito fluvio modicum te progressam textrices orabunt anus telam struentes, manus paulisper accommodes; nec id tamen tibi contingere fas est. nam haec omnia tibi et multa alia de Veneris insidiis orientur, ut vel unam de manibus omittas offulam. nec putes futile istud polentarium damnum leve: altera enim perdita, lux haec tibi prorsus denegabitur. canis namque praegrandis, teriugo et satis amplo capite praeditus, immanis et formidabilis, tonantibus oblatrans faucibus mortuos, quibus iam nil mali potest facere, frustra territando, ante ipsum limen et atra atria Proserpinae semper excubans servat vacuam Ditis domum. hunc offrenatum unius offulae praeda facile praeteribis ad ipsamque protinus Proserpinam introibis, quae te comiter excipiet ac benigne, ut et molliter assidere et prandium opipare suadeat sumere. sed tu et humi reside et panem sordidum petitum esto; deinde nuntiato quid adveneris, susceptoque quod offeretur rursus remeans canis saevitiam offula reliqua redime; ac deinde, avaro navitae data quam reservaveras stipe transitoque eius fluvio, recalcans priora vestigia ad istum caelestium siderum redies chorum. sed inter omnia hoc observandum praecipue tibi censeo, ne velis aperire vel inspicere illam quam feres pyxidem, vel omnino divinae formonsitatis abditum curare thensaurum.'

[20] sic turris illa prospicua vaticinationis munus explicuit. nec morata Psyche pergit Taenarum, sumptisque rite stipibus illis et offulis, infernum decurrit meatum. transitoque per silentium asinario debili et amnica stipe vectori data, neglecto supernatantis mortui desiderio et spretis textricum subdolis precibus et offulae cibo sopita canis horrenda rabie, domum Proserpinae penetrat. nec offerentis hospitae sedile delicatum vel cibum beatum amplexa, sed ante pedes eius residens humilis cibario pane contenta, Veneriam pertulit legationem. statimque secreto repletam conclusamque pyxidem suscipit, et offulae sequentis fraude caninis latratibus obseratis residuaque navitae reddita stipe,

longe vegetior ab inferis recurrit. et repetita atque adorata candida ista luce, quamquam festinans obsequium terminare, mentem capitur temeraria curiositate. et 'ecce' inquit 'inepta ego divinae formonsitatis gerula, quae nec tantillum quidem indidem mihi delibo, vel sic illi amatori meo formonso placitura.'

[**21**] et cum dicto reserat pyxidem; nec quicquam ibi rerum nec formonsitas ulla, sed infernus somnus ac vere Stygius, qui statim coperculo revelatus invadit eam crassaque soporis nebula cunctis eius membris perfunditur, et in ipso vestigio ipsaque semita conlapsam possidet. et iacebat immobilis et nihil aliud quam dormiens cadaver.

Chapters 22 to 32: For a summary of the rest of the speech, see Introduction pp. 194–7.

Commentary Notes

Note: This commentary is heavily indebted to both the Cupid and Psyche volume in the Groningen Commentaries on Apuleius series, by Zimmerman et al. (2004), and Kenney (1990); their influence should be assumed throughout but, where I have thought it worthwhile to draw out their particular insights, I have abbreviated them as GCA and Kenney, respectively. Students ought to be familiar with *Metamorphoses* V.28–VI.24 in translation and a brief summary of those chapters is included below; see the Introduction for a more general overview of the narrative.

Book V, Chapters 28 to 31: Venus is informed of Cupid's injury; moreover, she is told that rumours have been circulated that both she and Cupid had been neglecting their duties. Venus, angry, demands to know who is responsible for her son's waywardness, is even more enraged to find it is Psyche. She swears to have her revenge on her son – whom she threatens to disinherit, and comically talks of replacing by having another child, or adopting one of her slave-boys – as well as Psyche. Juno and Ceres try to assuage her anger, but to no avail.

Book VI, Chapters 1 to 6: The narrative switches to Psyche. Now she is aware of his divinity, she hopes at least to appease him as a worshipper if not comfort him as his wife and, hence, seeing a hill-top temple, she approaches it in the hope it might be his. When she enters, it is full of jumbled-up agricultural implements. Reasoning that, even if she cannot please Cupid, she can at least please another of the gods, she sets about tidying the temple up. Ceres, whose temple it is, finds her and lets her know that Venus is seeking her to exact revenge; Ceres is moved by her plight, but says she cannot help because of her close relationship to Venus.

Psyche then finds another temple, this one belonging to Juno, to whom she likewise prays for protection: the excuse of close family relationship between the gods is used to deny her a goddess' protection. Psyche, desperate, considers handing herself over to Venus as the only option.

We return to Venus in her search for Psyche; having failed to find her on earth, she starts to search the heavens and in charming ecphrasis we see her depart for the skies in a golden chariot drawn by doves. She is received with joy at Jupiter's citadel.

Chapter 7

dirigit: we start (and continue) in the historic present, giving a sense of vivid immediacy; translating as a present or perfect are both acceptable choices (as long as you are consistent).

petitu: fourth declension noun, agreeing with *superbo*; it is only in post-Classical Latin that it means, as here, 'request', i.e. 'with an arrogant request'.

Mercuri ... operae necessariam usuram: 'the essential loan of the services of Mercury'; *necessarius* can also mean 'connected by familial ties'; both are appropriate here. Mercury is often connected with Venus, see e.g. Horace, *Odes* I.30, or (in a very different way) Vergil, *Aeneid* IV, where Mercury is sent to convey the message that Aeneas must leave Carthage. There were even joint cults of the two in antiquity at Argos, Megalopolis, Cnidos and Lesbos.

dei vocalis: appropriate as Mercury is the messenger of the gods, here to be used as a kind of town crier.

nec rennuit: litotes, where the double negative strongly affirms.

caerulum supercilium: the tone is epic, echoing Homer, *Iliad* 1.528, in an almost literal translation into Latin: 'the son of Cronus spoken, and nodded his dark brows in assent'. There, Zeus is acceding to the request of Thetis to punish the Greeks for their disrespect of her son, Achilles.

comitante ... Mercurio: ablative absolute (evident from the ending of the participle in -*e*, rather than -*i*).

caelo: ablative denoting motion away from the following *demeat*, which is a particularly Apuleian word. There is possibly a hint also that she is descending from 'Heaven', i.e. Uranus, flagging her change from Venus Caelestis to Venus Vulgaris (see further in the Introduction).

sollicite serit: notice the alliteration (for the purposes of alliteration in Apuleius more generally, see the Introduction, section 'Apuleius' style').

Frater Arcadi: Mercury was born on Mount Cyllene in Arcadia, hence 'Arcadian brother'. This presupposes a genealogy of Venus which sees her as the daughter of Jupiter and Dione – e.g. in Homer, *Iliad* 5.370–1, or Cicero, *De natura deorum* III.59.

sororem ... fecisse: accusative + infinitive following *scis*. The sentiment relies on the close association between Venus and Mercury; as well as a messenger, he was a notorious thief and liar in Latin literature – see e.g. Horace, *Odes* I.10.

praesentia: not a participle, but the noun meaning 'presence' (in the ablative depending on *sine*).

utique: adverb, 'certainly'.

nequiverim: perfect subjunctive (following sequence of tenses) in an indirect question, introduced by *quanto ... tempore*, 'for how long', an ablative of time within which.

publicitus: adverb.

fac ... matures: a common way of expressing what would otherwise just be the simple imperative, most commonly in colloquial contexts; the construction continues with *designes*. It could be translated as 'see to it that ...' or (more colloquially) 'go and ...'.

qui: 'whereby', an archaic ablative of the relative, which can be used for all genders and both singular and plural.

A Level

si quis: after *si*, *quis* is used to mean 'anyone'.

possit: present subjunctive in a relative clause of characteristic (see *Kennedy's Revised Latin Primer* §452).

subierit: future perfect in a future open conditional; although best translated in English as a present tense, the future perfect must be used in Latin as the condition must precede the apodosis in future time (see *Kennedy's* §§437–43; Taylor, *Essential GCSE Latin*, p. 80).

ignorantiae: although this was not generally a defence in Roman law, there were exceptions, so we get the first hint of Venus' legalism (see below on **impares . . . nuptiae** in Chapter 9).

possit: present subjunctive following *ne*, negative purpose clause, functioning as the apodosis of the conditional.

libellum: a small placard, notice or handbill.

Psyches: a Greek genitive.

et cetera: 'and her other details', nominative like *nomen*.

quo facto: ablative absolute with a connecting relative (see Taylor, p. 8).

Chapter 8

nec . . . omisit: another example of litotes.

per omnium ora populorum: Mercury and the message he carries are treated as one; *ora* here means 'eyes' or 'faces'. Notice the alliteration and assonance, with *passim . . . praedicationis*, echoing the sounds of running feet.

passim discurrens: there is a possible play on an etymology of Hermes (evidenced in Varro) from *medius currens*.

si quis: 'if anyone', modelled on other examples of public proclamations. The proclamation is modelled is Moschus 1.1–5 (a Greek pastoral poet), in which Aphrodite is searching for Eros.

occultam: agreeing with *filiam ... Psychen* (a Greek accusative); could here be a little loosely translated as 'the hiding place of Psyche, the daughter ...'.

poterit: simple future of *possum*.

conveniat: iussive subjunctive, 'let him meet' (referring back to *quis*, which continues as the subject).

retro metas Murtias: the Murtian turning-posts were fixtures in the Circus Maximus in Rome, named after the shrine of the goddess Murcia, sometimes given as a cult name for Venus. This was an infamous haunt of prostitutes.

accepturus: the future participle here (as often in Greek) represents purpose, 'to receive'.

indicivae nomine: 'by way of reward'; the former is a rare word, and the latter used in an unusual sense.

septem savia suavia: the alliteration is obvious! There might be a foreshadowing of Lucius' seven ritual immersions before his invocation of Isis (who is Venus Caelestis) in Book XI; on the other hand, read in a baser fashion, it makes Venus little better than the slave-girl Photis who causes the troubles for Lucius in the first place – cf. II.10.

longe to be taken with **mellitum**: 'deeply honeyed'; Apuleius often uses *longe* as a synonym for *valde*.

ad hunc modum: 'after this fashion', 'in this way', taken with the following phrase.

pronuntiante Mercurio: ablative absolute.

tanti praemii: genitive, following *cupido*, 'desire for ...'.

mortalium: genitive plural (agreeing with *omnium*), depending on *studium* (nominative).

quae res: connective relative, literally 'Which thing ...' but, more smoothly, 'This situation ...'.

vel maxime: *vel* can be used as an intensifier, and, with a superlative, 'as much as possible', 'to the greatest possible degree'.

sustulit: perfect of *tollo*, here, 'removed'.

Psyches: Greek genitive.

fores eius dominae: 'the doors of her mistress'. The geography of the story is fantastical – the house of Venus must clearly be an earthly abode not far from Taenarum.

proximanti: *occurrit* takes the dative, referring to Psyche: 'came up to her as she was nearing ...'.

famulitione: a rare form, used elsewhere (II.2) by Apuleius; *una de* simply translates as 'one of ...'.

Consuetudo: an abstract noun 'Habit', personified as one of Venus' servants. The word can mean 'intercourse' or 'marriage', but here seems to function to accustom Psyche to the pains of love.

quantum maxime potuit: 'as greatly as she could', a very overdetermined superlative and, here, clearly means 'as loudly as possible'.

dominam habere te: accusative infinitive, dependent on *scire*; *te* is the subject-accusative and *dominam* the object of *habere*.

coepisti: take as a pure perfect, 'have you begun ... ?'.

pro: here, 'as one might expect from'.

istud: object of *nescire* and expanded on by the indirect question introduced by *quantos*.

nescire te: accusative infinitive, dependent on *fingis*.

circa tuas inquisitiones: 'concerning searchings for you' or, more naturally, 'in looking for you'. The possessive pronoun here is functioning in an objective sense (i.e. the object of the *inquisitiones*).

sustinuerimus: perfect subjunctive in an indirect question (introduced by *quantos*).

sed bene quod: sc. *est*; 'It [is] well that …', *quod* here introducing an explanatory noun clause.

potissimum: adverbial, 'before all'; effectively, here, 'rather than anyone else's'.

Orci cancros: 'the claws of Orcus'; Orcus was a god of the underworld, a punisher of broken oaths, envisaged as a kind of monster with crab-like claws. Though the word *cancer* is not attested in quite this sense elsewhere, it seems likely this is the force here – it parallels *meas … manus* and the generally monstrous description of Orcus, rather than, what some other interpreters have opted for, 'the barriers of Orcus'.

haesisti: translate as a pure perfect, 'have become stuck'.

datura … poenas: the future either conveys a sense of purpose ('to pay the penalty') or stands for a relative ('you, who will pay the penalty').

tantae contumaciae: technically a genitive, but best translated 'for such great stubbornness'.

Chapter 9

audaciter: adverb from *audax*; the usual Classical form is *audacter*.

eam nequaquam renitentem: the violence of the scene is underscored by Psyche's passivity, emphasized by the alliteration and assonance here.

quam: connecting relative, referring to Psyche; can be translated as 'her' (object of *conspexit*).

ubi primum: 'as soon as'.

cachinnum: Venus' laughter (in this tale) is almost always malevolent – see below **rursus sublato risu** and again in Chapter 13 (**subridens amarum**).

qualem: 'of the sort which', relative clause further describing Venus' laughter.

solent furenter irati: sc. *extollere*: 'angry people are accustomed [to give/emit] furiously'. *furenter* is an extremely rare word.

caput ... quatiens: typical of Apuleius' Venus: she first appears *capite quassante* in IV.29, and tosses her again while torturing Psyche in VI.10.

ascalpens aurem dexteram: a sign of barely controlled anger; Venus is marked by these histrionic gestures which ancient authorities on rhetoric warned their students against (like her head-tossing above). There was an ancient association with touching of the ear with admonition, and Pliny the Elder (*Historia naturalis* XI.251) associates the spot behind the right ear with the goddess of retribution, Nemesis. This is the only attested use of *ascalpere*.

periclitatur: although this verb is deponent, here it is used passively, 'is put in peril'.

intervisere: infinitive being used for purpose with *venire*; this is common in old and colloquial Latin, found in poetry, but increasingly common in later Latin.

esto: future imperative of the verb *esse*.

bonam nurum: note that *nurus* is second declension feminine; the tone of *bonam* is obviously sarcastic.

Sollicitudo atque Tristities: more personified attributes as attendants of Venus; like Consuetudo earlier, there are no parallels to these particular personifications, so they are likely Apuleian innovations. This language is, however, traditional of the tortures of love.

quibus ... vocatis: Connecting relative (referring back to the *ancillae*) in the dative, governed by *tradidit*.

torquendam: gerundive of obligation, here with the verb *tradidit*, 'handed her over to be tortured'.

misellam flagellis afflictam: notice the alliteration of 'l' and 'm'; the diminutive *misella* is often used of Psyche and adds extra pathos.

There is a possibility that there is a connection here to mystery cults, initiation into which sometimes involved ritual flagellation (e.g. in the wall painting in the Villa of the Mysteries in Pompeii). The tortures suffered by Psyche are a common theme of visual representations of the tale.

rursus sublato risu: see note above on **cacchinnum**.

turgidi ventris sui: Psyche's pregnancy, like her beauty, is threatening to Venus, who in this Apuleian tale is possessed by angst at her own inability to become pregnant (see earlier in the tale at V.29). It is a strikingly odd phrase used to describe pregnancy and is probably meant to sound insulting, given that *turgidus* is often used of disease. Ovid, *Metamorphoses* II.471ff. and III.268ff., provides a striking parallel in Juno's anger at the pregnancy of Callisto and Semele.

commovet: the subject must be understood as 'she', i.e. Psyche; the force of the present tense here is conative – 'she is trying to move'.

unde ... faciat: effectively a relative clause, referring back to Psyche's *venter*; the subjunctive is for a relative clause of characteristic; translate as 'she might make'.

praeclara ... beatam: both bitingly ironic, as underlined by *scilicet*. Note that *praeclara* is ablative, with *subole*.

felix vero ego: again ironic; supply *sum* or *ero*, and take as an exclamation: '[How] lucky I am!'. The language used is playing with a traditional form of prayer to a divinity called a *makarismos* (from the Greek for 'blessed' or 'happy'): the best-known surviving examples are the Beatitudes from the Gospels: 'Blessed are the poor ...' (see Matthew 5.3-12). The same sarcastic use of the form is made by Psyche's sisters earlier in the story (at V.17).

ipso aetatis meae flore: 'in the very prime of my life'; English sometimes uses 'flower' in the same metaphorical sense, e.g. 'flower of youth'.

audiet: used here to mean 'will be called', as variation for *vocabor*.

quamquam: used at the beginning of a sentence to correct a preceding statement.

inepta ego ... filium dicam: the adjective is used predicatively here; render 'I will be foolish to call him a son'; *dicam* is future tense (following in sense *audiet* from the sentence before).

impares ... nuptiae et ... in villa: Venus, in casting doubts on the legitimacy of the marriage and the offspring, is playing with a number of things. There is a hint of 'contemporary legalism' (Kenney), as marriage across social divides could be illegal, but the underlying concepts of illegitimacy (like the reference to the marriage being in secret, without witnesses) seem to be Greek, rather than Roman (see below on **spurius**). Apuleius is playing more with literary than legal language. There might be a slight autobiographical joke on Apuleius' part, too – part of his prosecution (see his *Apology* 67, 87–8) was on the basis that his wedding took place in the country, out of public view.

et patre non consentiente: the father's consent was necessary in Roman law; it adds to the 'legalese' of Venus' attack, but also allows a sly authorial joke at Venus' expense: mythologically, the parentage of Cupid was notoriously unclear.

factae legitimae: agreeing with *nuptiae*, used predicatively with *possunt videri*, 'not able to be viewed as made legitimately'.

spurius: although the technical Latin term for a bastard, with the same insulting connotations, in Roman understanding and law this is not correct – the child of a free man and a slave (as Venus suggests) is not a bastard, but simply a slave, which requires the father not just to not be wedded to the mother, but unknown.

si ... patiemur: future indicative in an open future conditional. Note the alliteration of 'p', with *partum ... perferre*, 'to carry the child to term'; the terminology is medical. Abortion (not a crime in the Graeco-Roman world) did happen but generally only when the health of the mother was threatened (though the fact that medical writing advises against abortion for social reasons like extra-marital pregnancy suggests it did happen) and often resulted in the death of the mother, hence the threat is double-edged.

Chapter 10

his editis: ablative absolute; the force of *edo* here is 'to utter solemnly' and echoes the formal legal language that Venus has been using.

involat: literally, 'flies in' (vivid present); a similar metaphor can be used in English, 'she flies at'. The presentation of Venus here echoes both Ovid's account of Juno's treatment of Callisto in *Metamorphoses* II.476–7 and traditional literary representations of a difficult mistress – e.g. in Ovid, *Ars Amatoria* III.239–42, Juvenal (VI.487–93) and Martial (II.66).

capilloque discisso et capite conquassato: both ablatives absolute; note the pointedly violent alliteration.

accepto … commixtisque … confusis: a (rather lengthy) ablative absolute, best taken as all the participles in sense agreeing with all the grains mentioned, though grammatically *accepto* agrees with *frumento*, and *commixtis* and *confusis* are plural, coming after the mention of a large number of collective singular nouns. Note the polysyndeton emphasizing the volume of grain.

sic ad illam: sc. *inquit*; Apuleius very rarely leaves out the verb of speaking; here, it may emphasize the speed and emotion of Venus.

enim: not explanatory but a 'consensus particle' (GCA), used by a speaker to gain (or imply) agreement from the audience and, hence, often used with verbs like *videor, opinor* etc. Translate as 'now'.

deformis ancilla: in apposition to the second person subject, 'as a hideous slave-girl'. Of course, we as the audience of this tale are well aware of Psyche's extraordinary beauty, so Venus here is betraying her own jealousy.

A Level

nullo alio: ablative of means, dependent on *promereri*, 'by no others means'.

sedulo ministerio: has double connotations; in Venus' terms, it refers to Psyche's servile state (and may also play insultingly with the idea of prostitution – see below on **promereri**); but the terminology is also religious; since Cupid left, Psyche has been trying to win him back with devoted prayer, a possible interpretation of this phrase, and *sedulis ... ministeriis ... numen promerueris* is used of Lucius devoting himself to Isis in Book XI.6.

promereri: this word is often used in romantic or sexual contexts as 'winning the favour of' lovers; it is etymologically connected with *meretrix*, 'prostitute', which Venus might be hinting at here; on another level, see the note above for its use in religious contexts (appropriate as Cupid is a divinity), first found in Apuleius but later used extensively, especially by Christians.

discerne ... approbato mihi: this sentence is a rhetorical *tour de force*; see the Introduction (section Apuleius' style) for a closer look at this sentence.

congeriem: in VI.2, a similar heap of grain was a potential hiding place for Psyche; there, at the temple of Ceres, Psyche diligently sorted out the confused mass in the temple of Ceres, demonstrating in advance the piety and virtue towards the gods Venus now tests.

singulisque granis rite dispositis atque seiugatis: ablative absolute with a temporal force, 'after the individual grains have been correctly arranged ...'.

istam: is odd, where we would expect *hanc* or *ipsam*; it might suggest Venus' forcefulness and relentlessness.

opus ... approbato mihi: future third person imperative with a dative of agent, 'let the work be examined by me'.

tantorum seminum: not 'such great seeds', as Classical usage would suggest, but 'so many', with *tantorum = tot*.

cenae nuptiali: a dative of purpose, 'for a marriage feast', or possibly of direction, 'to a wedding feast'; note the irony!

admolitur: takes a dative (*inconditae . . . moli*); note the assonance and alliteration.

immanitate: ablative of means, 'by the immensity'; this is the only Apuleian usage of the word, and it can refer to both the size of the heap and the immensity of the task.

consternata silens obstupescit: note the sibilance; the final two words are a Vergilian formula – see *Aeneid* II.120.

formicula . . . parvula: diminutives are common in Apuleius, but here emphasize the smallness of the ant; note also the homoioteleuton here. On the tradition of both the task at hand and animal helpers in folklore, see the Introduction.

certa: here means 'knowing' or 'understanding'; here it takes the genitives *difficultatis tantae laborisque*. Ancient authors credited ants with exceptional perception and even foresight – e.g. Horace, *Satires* I.1.33; Augustine, *Epist.* 137.3.

miserta: this is a rare contracted form of the participle (for *miserita*), used probably for the similarity to *certa*. This participle ('having taken pity upon'; active, since it comes from a deponent verb) takes a genitive here, *contubernalis*.

contubernalis: significantly, she is not referred to as *uxor*, but rather as 'bedfellow' or 'partner'; the term *contubernium* could describe slaves living in a union sanctioned by their master, fitting the servile presentation of Psyche by Venus.

magni dei: this is the first indication that Cupid is behind the help given to Psyche.

convocat corrogatque: these two alliterating synonyms are both drawn from the vocabulary of the military, and are followed by further martial-sounding alliteration of 'c'.

classem: not 'fleet' here, but 'a body of citizens summoned for military service'.

miseremini: imperative (of a deponent verb; hence, passive in form).

terrae omniparentis ... alumnae: Apueilus is echoing Vergil, *Aeneid* VI.595, which refers to the giant Tityos; the contrast in size, now referring to ants, is undoubtedly subtle literary comedy.

Amoris uxori: the choice of *Amoris* rather than *Cupidinis* is probably motivated by the sound-play with *uxori*; this is in the dative, depending on *succurrite*, 'run to the aid of ...'.

prompta velocitate: ablative of manner, 'with ready speed'.

aliae superque aliae ... undae: literally, 'other and in addition other waves'; trans. 'wave upon wave'. The metaphor of waves as indicative of vast numbers (usually of people) goes all the way back through Homer and is most often found in military contexts, building up the mock epic feel here.

digerunt ... distributis dissitisque: note the repeated compounds with prefix *di-* to underscore the ants' diligence; this section parallels the earlier description of the heap in this passage with the same rhetorical features of *amplificatio*.

Chapter 11

initio noctis: ablative of time, i.e. 'at nightfall'; the phrase is used three times in the *Metamorphoses* and both other instances are connected with witchcraft.

vino depends on **madens**: 'dripping with wine'; in chiastic arrangement with the following phrase. The same words are used twice elsewhere in the *Metamorphoses* (II.16 and X.11), both in the context of sexual desire.

fraglans balsama: accusative of respect depending on the participle, 'fragrant with balsam'; this aromatic was associated both with Venus and with weddings. *flaglo* is an alternative spelling for *flagro*.

totum ... revincta corpus: accusative of respect depending on the participle, 'wreathed in respect of her whole body', i.e. 'her whole body wreathed'.

rosis micantibus: roses in the ancient world, like the modern, were associated with romance. They play a role in the wider narrative of the *Metamorphoses*: the slave-girl Fotis (the cause of Lucius' troubles!) comes wreathed in roses at II.16, and Lucius' cure at the end of his trials (turning him from an ass back into a human) requires him to eat roses. Roses are often described as 'shining' by Apuleius.

visa: ablative, agreeing with *diligentia* in an ablative absolute.

diligentia miri laboris: although grammatically *miri* agrees with *laboris*, in sense it should be taken with *diligentia* (an example of enallage, or a transferred epithet).

non tuum: predicative use of the adjective, agreeing with *opus* – 'the work is not yours'.

nequissima: vocative, addressing Psyche.

illius: i.e. Cupid, genitive to parallel *tuarum manuum*, describing whose *opus* it was.

cui ... placuisti: *placeo* takes a dative – 'whose fancy you have taken' (GCA); it can often have the connotation of sexual attraction.

tuo, immo et ipsius, malo: 'to your harm – and, indeed, to his as well'.

frusto ... proiecto: ablative absolute.

cibarii panis: a coarse type of bread given to slaves; Psyche again is being treated as a slave.

facessit: *facessire* is an archaism, used for *abire*.

interim: a clear shift of scene, from Psyche to Cupid, also underscored by the change from the historic present to the imperfect *coercebatur*.

A Level

Cupido solus: the adjective emphasizes Cupid's own isolation; note the fierce alliteration of 'c' in this sentence and the abundant over-emphasis on the strictness of his imprisonment.

interioris domus: both genitives, to be taken with *unici cubiculi*, 'of a single room in [literally, 'of'] the inside of the house'; the whole is an expanded description of **custodia** (below).

custodia: ablative of place where, 'in the prison'.

petulanti luxurie: in agreement (remembering that third declension adjectives end in *-i*, not *-e*), 'with wanton extravagance'.

vulnus: accusative; the subject (implied) continues to be Cupid.

sua cupita: technically a perfect passive participle being used as a noun (as we do in English), 'his beloved'; the choice of term is obviously based on the play with his own name.

sub uno tecto separatis: the theme of lovers apart but under the same roof is a commonplace in Greek novels, and emphasized here by the repetition of the theme of separation in two synonymous participles (*distentis ... separatis*). The participles (with *amatoribus*) could either be ablatives, in ablative absolute, or datives, of (dis)advantage.

exanclata: sc. *est*. An archaism favoured by Apuleius.

Aurora ... inequitante: ablative absolute; Apuleius is playing with Homeric formulae here (e.g. the beginning of *Odyssey* 2, 7 and 17), continuing to lend an epic feel to Psyche's labours.

vocatae Psychae: dative, dependent on *infit*; the verb is poetic.

vides ...: used to introduce a brief ecphrasis. It is paralleled by another description of a landscape in VI.13. This landscape has features of a traditional *locus amoenus*, the literary trope of a 'pleasant place' – the river and nearby spring, a grove of trees; here, though, rather than an idyll, the scene is a nightmarish vision.

fluvio praeterluenti ripisque longis: hendiadys (i.e. 'the river flowing past and the long banks' = 'the long banks of the river flowing past'); the dative is dependent on *attenditur* ('is stretched toward').

ubi frutices: the text here is corrupt; as printed, this is taken as a subordinate clause (start with *ubi*, picked up by *ibi* in the main clause), with a connecting relative referring to the grove, but this is a conjectural emendation.

nitentes ... florentes: cleverly ambiguous; *niteo* can mean 'shine', referencing their golden fleece; but it can also mean (of animals) 'to be sleek, in good condition'; likewise, *floreo* can mean 'to be bright with colour' but also, more generally, 'to flourish, be in one's prime'.

aurique colore: Apuleius is playing here with the tale of the Golden Fleece, and particularly with Apollonius of Rhodes' *Argonautica*. It also echoes *Odyssey* 6.363ff., where Menelaus captures Proteus, following Idothea's advice, and Vergil's repurposing of the episode in the Aristaeus tale in *Georgics* IV.387ff. In all these, the protagonist, at his wits' end, succeeds by the tactic of lying in ambush while a flock takes its rest from the midday heat.

incustodito pastu: ablative of circumstance or location; 'in unguarded pasture'.

inde de coma: slightly pleonastic, an adverb reinforcing a preposition of place. Literally, 'from there, from the hair'; the first word can effectively be left out in a smooth English translation.

pretiosi velleris: a genitive phrase, which applies equally well to both *coma* and *floccum*.

quoquo modo: 'in any way you can'.

quaesitum: perfect passive participle, agreeing with *floccum*.

afferas: present subjunctive in an indirect command (introduced by *censeo*); supply *ut*, which Apuleius frequently omits in indirect commands.

Chapter 12

perrexit: from *pergo*.

illa: grammatically unnecessary; called the pleonastic or resumptive use of the pronoun, it is a poetic feature.

functura ... habitura: future participles used, as in Greek, to express purpose.

praecipitio fluvialis rupis: 'by a jump from a river-rock' (GCA); the grammar of the genitive is murky – either a genitive of separation (following Greek) or possessive. The image reminds the audience of IV.35, where Psyche was abandoned on a rock by her father; this is the third attempted suicide of Psyche, after V.22 and 25. Jumping from a rock is a stereotypical literary way for a desperate person to attempt suicide, 'not without a touch of grandeur' (GCA). In total, Psyche attempts suicide five times.

inde de fluvio: see note on **inde de coma** in Chapter 11 above; GCA translates 'from the river below'.

musicae suavis nutricula: *suavis* is genitive, agreeing with *musicae*; the reed is introduced by two riddle-like descriptions before its identity is revealed. This first description refers to the role of the reed in the creation of panpipes. The use of the diminutive (*nutricula*) is characteristic of Apuleius and later Latin in general.

leni crepitu: in agreement; ablative of means following *inspirata*, 'inspired/blown by the light rustling'. The participle is carefully ambiguous; it refers literally to the blowing of the breeze, but plays with the idea of inspiration, as well as the notion of the playing of reed pipes. Prophecy was often connected to singing, and particularly the verb *vaticinari*, etymologically connected to *canere*.

dulcis aurae: we are reminded of the assistance of Zephyr, who earlier transported Psyche and her sisters to and from Cupid's palace.

divinitus: adverb.

tantis aerumnis exercita: an elevated opening tone (as befitting musical prophecy); *aerumnis* is archaic, and the line recalls *Aeneid* III.182.

neque ... polluas ... nec ... feras: present subjunctives, used for negative commands.

tua miserrima morte: ablative.

istud horae: 'at this moment'.

formidabiles oves: this is the first indication that the sheep are somehow dangerous.

feras aditum: literally, 'bring an attack/approach'; a smooth translation might render it 'attempt to approach'.

quoad: 'as long as' + indicative (solent); the subject remains *oves*.

de solis flagrantia: the genitive *solis* is positioned in between the preposition and the noun it governs.

calorem: object of the deponent participle *mutuatae*. The heat of the midday sun was seen as particularly dangerous in the ancient world, when Pan might strike; the reed is suggesting that the heat of the sun is 'borrowed' by the sheep and translated into their madness.

truci rabie: taken with *efferari*, 'to be made fierce with a savage madness'.

solent: governs both the infinitives *efferari* and *saevire*.

cornuque acuto et fronte saxea et nonnumquam venenatis morsibus: tricolon of ablatives of means. The double negative (another example of litotes) usually, as here, intensifies.

in exitium: expressing purpose, 'for the ruin'.

dum ... sedaverit ... conquieverint: *dum* + future perfect = until.

meridies: cannot here mean 'midday' but, rather, 'afternoon'.

solis: depends on *vaporem* (rather than *meridies*), 'the heat of the sun'.

A Level

spiritus fluvialis: in agreement, 'of the river breeze'.

serenitate: ablative of means, 'by the peacefulness'.

platano: note that trees are commonly second declension feminine nouns (hence, in agreement with *illa procerissima*). Resting beneath a pleasant plane tree in the heat of the day is stereotypical of the literary trope of the *locus amoenus*, and reminds us of pastoral and lyric poetry; more significantly, it is reminiscent of Plato's *Phaedrus*, a key dialogue in which the nature of the soul (Psyche) is discussed.

unum fluentum: 'the same stream'.

abscondere: the verb is used here intransitively (as if a Greek middle); infinitive dependent on the earlier *poteris*.

cum primum . . . laxaverint: future perfect in a temporal clause; Latin is strictly logical with the tense, where English tends to use a perfect: 'as soon as [they] have relaxed'.

mitigata furia: ablative absolute.

percussis frondibus: another ablative absolute.

stirpibus convexis: dative, dependent on *obhaerescit*.

Chapter 13

salutem suam: *suus* ought normally to refer back to the subject of the sentence, but here the referent must clearly be Psyche, 'her own safety'.

auscultatu paenitendo: gerundive of obligation; 'with an obedience she would have had to regret' (GCA).

cessavit: the verb must have the force of 'be inactive'.

furatrina facili: 'with an easy theft'.

flaventis auri mollitie: literally, 'with the softness of yellow gold'; hendiadys for 'with the soft yellow gold', to be taken with *congestum*, i.e. 'loaded with'.

saltem: scholars differ on what to take this with; either *apud dominam*, 'in her mistress' eyes at least' (Kenney), or *secundi laboris periculum*, 'even the danger of her second task' (GCA).

secundi ... secundum: plays with the two meanings of the word; in the first instance, 'second', and in the latter, 'favourable'.

contortis superciliis: a sign of annoyance.

subridens: see note on the danger of Venus' laughter above (Chapter 9, **cachinnum**).

amarum: adverbial (technically an internal accusative, echoing Greek usage).

praeterit: usually impersonal, but here is used with *auctor* as its subject; it is, however, best translated as: 'it does not escape my notice that ...'.

auctor adulterinus: deliberately ambiguous and difficult to render into English; the adjective could either (like the connotations of 'adulterous' in English) be an insulting reference to Cupid's licentiousness, or simply suggest Cupid's unseen ('false, counterfeit') action in the salvation of Psyche.

an ... sis: indirect question following *periclitabor*, 'I shall test whether ...'; we might expect *num*, but here there is an unexpressed but implied 'or not'.

praedita: nominative, agreeing with the second person subject, Psyche; 'endowed with' + ablatives (*oppido forti animo singularique prudentia*).

videsne: the following is another mini-ecphrasis, this time dark and sombre from the beginning, again (like in VI.11) introduced by the verb of seeing.

celsissimae illi rupi: dative, depending on *insistentem*; 'standing upon ...'.

proxumaeque conceptaculo vallis inclusae: the word order, and unpicking agreement, can be confusing; 'and shut in by the enclosure of the nearby valley'. The subject continues to be *undae*.

rauca ... fluenta: accusative plural, object of *nutriunt* (the subject still being *undae*).

mihi: indirect object, with *defers*.

rorem rigentem: note the alliteration (with *scaturrigine*); *rigeo* can be used of water to mean 'be icy cold'.

hauritum: an alternative to the more common *haustum*, participle of *haurio*.

defers: a rare form of the singular imperative of *defero*, in place of the usual *defer*.

ista ... urnula: 'in this little jar'. Hesiod's *Theogony* 782–7 identifies the ice-cold water of the stream as a divine lie-detector used by Zeus, who sends Iris to fetch it in a golden pitcher. Although Apuleius plays with that passage in a number of details, there seems to be no significance in its mythic function for the tale – simply that it is extremely difficult for Psyche to get.

aiens: a rare participle from the verb *aio*, 'say'.

crustallo dedolatum: 'hewn from crystal'.

ei graviora comminata: *comminor* takes a dative of the person threatened, and an accusative of the threat; 'having threatened her with more serious punishments'.

Chapter 14

gradum: here, 'pace', rather than 'a pace/step'.

extremum ... tumulum: 'highest mound'; the word is commonly associated with graves, hence is pointedly appropriate here.

certe vel illic: 'sure [to find] there at least'.

inventura: future participle used to express purpose.

cum primum ... appulit: temporal clause with a perfect indicative, 'as soon as she has landed ...'.

conterminos: takes the genitive *praedicti iugi*.

immani magnitudine procerum: 'lofty with immense size', an appropriately over-the-top emphasis on magnitude.

inaccessa salebritate lubricum: the construction is parallel to the preceding one, i.e. 'slippery with ...', and mirrors it in length, with twelve syllables balanced against eleven. Whereas the first phrase is notable for its pleonasm, this one is marked by *recherché* vocabulary and compactness of expression.

mediis: agrees with *faucibus*.

qui ... editi ... delapsi ... contecti: a tricolon of nominative plural participles; the antecedent is *fontes*.

proni foraminis: in agreement; 'of the sloping fissure'.

lacunis: ablative of separation, 'from the hollows'.

per ... proclive: nominal phrase, 'along the downward slope'.

exarato contecti tramite: 'hidden by the ploughed-up track'.

incidebant: from *in-cado* ('fall/flow into/upon'), rather than *in-caedo* (which both produce *incido*).

dextra laevaque: ablatives of place, 'on the right and on the left'.

cautibus cavatis: ablatives of place from which, 'from the hollowed crags'.

A Level

longa colla porrecti: perfect passive participle with an accusative of respect (a Greek usage, characteristic of Apuleius); the participle is also echoing a Greek middle, rather than acting as a true passive. Best translated, 'their long necks stretched out', as if it were an ablative absolute; avoiding the construction enables *variatio* for the tricolon which Apuleius goes on to compose.

luminibus addictis: ablative absolute; *lumina* here refer to eyes; *addico* takes the dative ('dedicate to') *inconivae vigiliae*.

in perpetuam lucem: 'into an everlasting vision', a strange expression, almost unparalleled, gives a strange and unnerving quality to the beasts.

pupulis excubantibus: the second phrase focusing on the eyes of the dragons also avoids using the prosaic *oculus*; the two descriptions carefully balance one another, both fifteen syllables in length, with parallel grammatical structures.

semet: strengthened form of *se*.

vocales aquae: like the reed earlier, the waters are given human qualities.

et 'discede!' et . . .: The waters speak short sentences in quick succession, emphasized by the polysyndeton.

ipsa mutata in lapidem: 'having been into stone herself'. Note the theme of metamorphosis, obviously significant to the work as a whole.

praesenti corpore: ablative of accompanying circumstance, 'with her body being present', to form a contrast with the following phrase.

sensibus: ablative of specification, 'absent from/in her senses'.

carebat: takes an ablative of the thing lacked; here, *lacrimarum . . . extremo solacio*.

Chapter 15

Providentiae bonae: an important concept in the *Metamorphoses*; often, as here, coupled with a positive adjective, it marks out good fortune, whereas *Fortuna* tends to be used for cases of bad luck or ill fortune. In the broader tale, nine out of twenty-one occurences of *Providentia* are in Book XI, referring to the divine action of Isis, possibly hinting at a parallelism between Lucius and Psyche.

graves oculos: object of *latuit*, 'lay hidden from', which takes a simple accusative.

innocentis animae: depends on *aerumna*, which is the subject of the sentence. There is a pun here on Psyche's name (*anima* in Greek being *Psyche*).

nam supremi Iovis regalis ales: the description of the eagle is an Apuleian *tour de force*; the tricolon of main verbs (*affuit ... deserit ... incipit*) alternates with participial, adjectival and one relative constructions, with some marked alliteration of 'r' and 'p'. Even before the clear identification of the bird as *aquila* the reference would have been clear; note the play on sound in *regalis ales*. Note that, although both *ales* and *aquila* are grammatically feminine nouns (hence agreement with *illa*) the eagle is implicitly thought of as masculine – hence *innoxius* near the end of this chapter.

quo: 'when/at which time'.

ductu: ablative of means, 'by the leading [of Cupid]', i.e. 'led by Cupid'.

Iovi pocillatorem Phrygium: a reference to the myth of Ganymede, the mortal youth carried off to be Jupiter's cup-bearer because of his surpassing beauty.

dei ... numen: 'the power/divinity of the god', referring to Cupid.

in uxoris laboribus: 'in his wife's labours', i.e. Psyche's trials.

alti culminis diales vias: *dialis* is an archaic adjective, with the connotation of brightness, day, sky and Jupiter, most often used with the title *flamen dialis*. The etymological link is here most significant; hence, 'Jove's ways' is a poetic way to refer to the heavens, reminding us of the link to Jupiter; 'of the high summit' could feasibly refer to the mountain peak above Psyche but, more likely, *culmen* here means the highest point of the sky.

ob os puellae: 'before the girls' eyes'.

simplex: Psyche throughout the tale has been defined by her simplicity and naivety.

sperasne: introduces an indirect statement, with accusative *te* and infinitives *posse furari . . . contingere*.

sanctissimi nec minus truculenti fontis: 'most holy and no less dangerous spring'.

vel . . . vel: used in the sense of *saltem*, 'or even'.

diis etiam ipsique Iovi: datives dependent on *formidabiles*, 'terrifying to . . .'.

aquas istas Stygias: direct object of *comperisti*, 'have you heard about . . .'; the construction then shifts to an accusative infinitive in the second half of the question, '[have you heard] that . . .'.

vel: as above, used in the sense of *saltem*, 'at least/even just'.

fando: 'from speaking', i.e. by hearsay.

quodque vos deieratis: 'and just as you [i.e. humans] swear', a use of the neuter singular of *qui* to equate to *quantum*.

deos . . . solere: sc. *deierare*; accusative infinitive following *comperisti*.

cedo: not a first person present tense, but an imperative, 'give, hand over'.

A Level

et protinus . . .: this period is another elaborate construction, this time built around two main verbs (*festinat . . . excipit*); two participial phrases, the ablative absolute *libratis . . . molibus*, and *inter genas . . . porrigens* describing the eagle, paralleled by two participial phrases describing the water (*nolentes* and *praeminantes*); the eagle's lie is introduced by another participial phrase (*commentus . . .*) and the whole concluded by a relative clause (*quare . . .*). The sentence is full of balanced pairs (e.g. *genas . . . vibramina*; *dextra laevaque* etc.), technically referred to as syndetic dicola.

adrepta complexaque: sc. *urnula*, forming a double ablative absolute.

libratisque pinnarum nutantium molibus: note the chiasmus in this ablative absolute, giving a sense of balance and making a word-picture for *libro*.

inter genas . . . et . . . vibramina: 'between the jaws and fangs'; *gena* usually means 'cheek' but, in the context of wild beasts, often has a more dangerous connotation. The two halves of this phrase, divided by *et*, are almost equal in length (twelve and eleven syllables, respectively).

saevientium dentium: descriptive genitive, 'the jaws with their ferocious teeth' (Kenney); the sound effect of the homoioteleuton is notable.

remigium: the imagery of rowing for flying is commonplace, going all the way back to at least Aeschylus' *Agamemnon* 52.

nolentes: concessive use of the participle, 'although unwilling'.

ut abiret: indirect command depending on the following *praeminantes*.

innoxius: translate as 'while still unharmed', predicative use of the adjective in the indirect command (Kenney supplies 'while the going was good'); note that it is masculine, referring to the eagle (see above on **ales**).

commentus: perfect active participle as *comminiscor* is deponent; it takes an accusative infinitive construction, *se* being the accusative

A Level

subject with infinitives *petere* and *praeministrare*, 'pretending to seek ... and that he was in her service'. English needs to supply an object for *petere* (sc. 'the water').

eique: refers to Venus, dative following *praeministrare*, 'to be in one's service'.

quare: 'whereby'.

paulo facilior: ablative of degree of difference with comparative adjective, 'a little easier'.

adeundi ... copia: subject of the clause; *adeundi* is a gerund; 'the means of approaching' (NB the meaning of *copia* in the singular here, different to the normal usage in the plural).

Chapter 16

citata: nominative, but used adverbially.

nutum: the basic meaning is 'nod', but Apuleius frequently uses it to mean 'will, power' (especially in connection with deities). Note the reference back to **rennuit** at Chapter 7 above.

vel tunc: 'even then'.

expiare: a formal word of religious significance, for propitiation of angry divinities.

eam maiora atque peiora flagitia comminans: echoing Venus' threats in Chapter 13 (**ei graviora comminata**); here, the grammar has been constructed rather differently, with a double accusative, 'threatening her with greater and worse outrages'.

renidens exitiabile: Venus' laughter or smile is invariably threatening; see above in Chapter 9 (**cachinnum** and **rursus sublato risu**) and Chapter 13 (**subridens amarum**).

magna . . . quaedam . . . et alta . . . malefica: 'some great and profound witch'; predicative nominatives to be taken after *videris*, 'you seem [to be] . . .'.

obtemperasti: = *obtemperavisti*; the verb, 'to comply with, obey', takes the dative *talibus praeceptis meis*.

mea pupula: an alternative spelling to *pupilla*, this can mean both the 'pupil' of an eye and (rarely, as here) 'little girl'; the diminutive is in ironic contrast to the earlier *magna et alta*.

debebis: future tense; take with *adhuc*, 'you will still have to' (+ infinitive).

ipsius Orci: see note on Orcus above at Chapter 8.

ad inferos . . . te derige: Psyche's final task is a combination of familiar mythic and literary themes; the *catabasis* (also spelt *katabasis*), descent to the underworld, is prominent in the *Odyssey*, echoed in the *Aeneid*, and a key element in the Hercules narrative, among others, but its mythic spread is geographically and temporally much wider and broader. This is not just literary play, but engagement with one of the most common motifs of Mediterranean folklore.

petit de te Venus: in Classical Latin, this would be *ex* or *ab*; this is indicative of Late Latin. Apuleius inverts the usual trope whereby Venus lends charms or objects to enhance beauty to others: most famously in the episode of the 'Deception of Zeus' (Διὸς ἀπάτη) in *Iliad* 6, enabled by Aphrodite's loan of her girdle to Hera; but also in the enhancement of Penelope's beauty at *Odyssey* 18.190–4 granted by Athena, which likewise comes from Aphrodite. In this passage, Aphrodite's beauty is figured as a salve with which the goddess anoints herself for dancing, which probably influenced this passage with its conceptualization of *formonsitas* as a kind of ointment.

dicito: a form of imperative, effectively = *dic*; forms in -*to* are regularly found in Venus' speech; cf. Chapter 9 (**esto**) and below in this section,

redito. They are an archaism; possibly they remind the audience of Old Comedy but, more likely, give a feeling of legal command and formality.

mittas: present subjunctive, iussive in parataxis with the verb of asking (*petit*); this is a construction by which both a verb of request is given but, instead of being followed by the expected subordinate clause, the request is also phrased directly. Alternatively (which amounts to the same thing in translation) with the *ut* understood as an indirect command.

modicum de tua ... formonsitate: the only occurence of this abstract noun as if it is a beauty cream; see note above on **petit de te Venus**.

ad unam ... dieculam sufficiens: 'enough for at least one little day'. The diminutive is very rare; it has the function of minimizing what Venus asks for, but, more importantly, in its almost babyish language denotes feminine familiarity between the goddesses and provides a striking contrast to the terrifying danger it represents for Psyche.

quod habuit ... omne: 'all that she had'.

consumpsit atque contrivit: it is not clear whether the *formonsitas* was used up as some kind of salve for Cupid, or as a beauty cream for Venus, worn out by caring for her son; the alliteration is marked.

haud immaturius: an unparalleled expression; most obviously, it must mean 'in good time', but a literal rendering is 'not too soon'. The ambiguity might represent Venus' desire for Psyche to spend more time in the underworld.

redito: imperative; see above on **dicito**.

me ... frequentare: accusative + infinitive, following *necesse est*.

theatrum deorum frequentare: the phrase is ambiguous as to Venus' role at the the *theatrum*; some commentators suggest she is presented as a Roman matron, keen not to present herself as a spectacle at the games; but the use of this verb might equally suggest that she will be present as a performer: this is the context of the allusion to the *Odyssey* passage noted above (18.190–4), where the beauty which Aphrodite lends Penelope is that with which she anoints herself when she dances with the Graces; later, at VI.24, she performs as a dancer at the wedding of Cupid and Psyche. *theatrum* can also mean 'assembly', taken by some translators.

Chapter 17

vel maxime: as in Chapter 8 above, *vel* is used as an intensifier with the superlative, 'to the greatest possible degree', or, more loosely, 'more than ever' (GCA).

ultimas fortunas suas: accusative and implied infinitive *esse* after *sensit*; the adjective is predicative, 'she felt her fortunes were the worst'; as noted earlier (on **Providentiae bonae**, Chapter 15), *fortuna* is generally negative in connotation.

velamento reiecto: ablative absolute, and clearly metaphorical language of literary heritage, first used by Tacitus, *Annales* XIII.47; *velamentum* is used by Apuleius of a blindfold at IX.15, so the connection to realizing clearly after a period of ignorance is clear.

promptum: the core meaning is 'at hand', so it can have temporal connotations, 'immediate', or the sense of 'manifest, evident'; it can also carry the connotation of 'prepared, planned'; all are appropriate here.

sese compelli: emphatic form of *se* in an accusative + (passive) infinitive construction, following *comperit*.

quidni?: The short interjecting sentence is borrowed either from comedy or rhetorical practice; it focalizes the passage from Psyche's point of view; even though it is in the third person, it functions effectively as direct speech.

quae ... cogeretur: subjunctive in a relative clause of characteristic, 'she, who would be forced'.

suis pedibus: 'on her own feet'.

A Level

ultro: here, 'actually, even'.

turrim praealtam: the scene of seeking a high tower to jump from is borrowed from Attic comedy (e.g. Aristophanes, *Frogs* 130); there is also a suggestion that it might be a parody of Zoroastrian funeral rites with which Apuleius would have been familiar.

sese datura: future participle again acting as a purpose clause; 'give herself' is the equivalent of 'throw herself' here.

praecipitem: death by *praecipitium* is Psyche's favourite solution to difficult situations, as at VI.12, and further back, V.25. Four of Psyche's five suicide attempts involve *praecipitium*.

ad inferos recte … se posse descendere: accusative + infinitive after *rebatur*; the reasoning is obviously comical, further marked by the clearly ironic *pulcherrime*; a direct allusion to or borrowing from Aristophanes' *Frogs* 127ff., where this method is raised as a possible means of entering the underworld. Note the marked assonance of 'e' here.

prorumpit in vocem subitam: the unexpected animation of the tower is marked by the verb, first used in this context here, but afterwards common in Late Latin, as well as the adjective 'sudden'. Talking objects have a strong literary pedigree: e.g. the wall, addressed in Ovid *Metamorphoses* IV.73, and a talking door in Catullus 67. However, this is simply a continuation of increasingly far-fetched characters given speech: an ant, an eagle, a reed and now a tower.

quid: here, 'why'.

te … praecipitio … quaeris extinguere: *te* is the object of *extinguere*. Almost exactly the same phrasing is used of Lucius at VII.24, implying a parallelism of Psyche and Lucius.

misella: vocative; a frequent epithet of Psyche.

novissimo periculo laborique isto: *isto* is a deviant form of *isti*, either as archaism or colloquialism; the dative is used after *succumbis*, 'succumb to', 'collapsing in view of …'. Note the chiasmus of the phrase.

si . . . fuerit seiugatus: future perfect indicative; required in the protasis as it refers to future time, and by necessity precedes the future verb of the apodosis, *ibis*.

spiritus: nominative.

corpore tuo: ablative of separation following *seiugatus*, 'separated from your body'.

quidem profecto: the combination of two emphatic particles is probably colloquial, but certainly dramatic.

ad imum Tartarum: poetic; *Tartarus* is usually plural in prose.

nullo pacto: ablative of means; 'in no manner' or 'under no condition'. *nullo pacto = nullo modo* is frequent in comedy, but there may be a hint of the usual meaning of *pactum* 'agreement', by which Apuleius is playing with mythical agreements for returning from Hades, like that of Orpheus.

Chapter 18

Lacedaemo: nominative; although masculine, it is in apposition to civitas, hence the verbal form *sita est* is feminine.

huius: genitive because of *conterminam*, 'adjacent to this'; normally the adjective takes a dative, and the genitive seems to echo Greek usage, giving a literary feel to the tower's speech.

deviis . . . locis: ablative of location with *abditam*, 'hidden in remote places'; notice the clever word picture.

Taenarum: though second declension, feminine, hence agreeing with *conterminam . . . abditam*. Taenarus is one of the southern promontories of the Peloponnese and of significant literary fame as an entrance to the underworld, connected to the myths of both Orpheus (especially in Vergil's *Georgics* 4) and Hercules.

inibi: an archaic term well used by Apuleius, continuing the literary feel of the speech.

spiraculum Ditis: an allusion to Vergil, *Aeneid* VII.568, describing the dwelling-place of Allecto.

portas hiantes: the phrase is unusual and personifies the gates of Hades; these gates of the underworld are prominent from Homer on (e.g. *Iliad* 5.646) and borrowed into Latin as a commonplace (e.g. Lucretius, *De rerum natura* III.67), including in Vergil's famous *catabasis* at *Aeneid* VI.552, though in the singular there.

monstratur: continues to echo verbally the same passage from the *Aeneid* referenced above, VII.569, there, the subject is *lugentes campi*.

iter invium: a striking oxymoron, suggestive of both the impossibility of access for the living and return for the dead.

cui: dative after *commiseris*, 'as soon as you have committed yourself to it'. te

limine transmeato: ablative absolute.

canale directo: ablative of means, 'by a straight path'; *canalis* here must simply be a synonym for *via*.

regiam: Hades is often figured as a 'palace'; e.g. Ovid, *Metamorphoses* IV.438, 716.

vacua: 'empty-handed, unprovided', modified by the adverb *hactenus*, either meaning 'in this way' or 'utterly'.

offas polentae mulso concretas: 'cakes of barley, kneaded together with honeyed wine'; these are food for Cerberus, in Vergil's terms, *Aeneid* VI.420f.

ambabus: feminine ablative form of *ambo*, agreeing with *manibus*, 'in both hands'.

in ipso ore: i.e. 'right in your mouth'.

duas ... stipes: i.e. the fee to cross twice, there and back; the regular literary fee for passage is one (e.g. Lucian, *De luctu* 10 etc.), though archaeological finds record larger amounts, too.

confecta bona parte: ablative absolute; *bona* here (as is possible in English) = *magna*, 'a good [i.e. large] part'.

claudum asinum ... cum agasone simili: these mysterious characters resist easy identification; proposed answers include Ocnus and his donkey, known from literary and iconographic sources. Ocnus was punished in the underworld by ever plaiting a rope which his donkey is ever eating up and, hence, became proverbial for pointless labour. Other options are as an alter ego for Lucius the ass, or a personified representation of malignity. In general, the three traps designed by Venus for Psyche are not based in myth of folklore and sound more like ritual ordeals.

decidentis ... fusticulos: in agreement (*-is* is an alterantive to *-es* in the accusative plural, though systematically rooted out from GCSE set texts!). The diminutive is a rare form and lessens the significance of the task.

sarcinae: 'from his load', genitive with *decido*.

porrigas: present subjunctive in an indirect command, with the *ut* elided; see above on **afferas** at Chapter 11.

nulla voce deprompta tacita: pleonastic; the ablative absolute phrase is synonymous with *tacita*. Compulsory silence was a common element in mystery religions and religious (especially initiation) ceremonies.

praeterito: imperative form with the ending *-to*.

nec mora cum: an idiom common in Apuleius meaning 'soon after this', 'directly afterwards'. Usually it is with a present indicative but, here, the future indicative.

mortuum: the adjective is used metonymically for *mortuorum*.

A Level

cui: dative of possession, 'whose'.

praefectus Charon protinus expetens portorium: the beginnings of the comic characterization of Charon as a greedy old man, underlined by the alliteration and the choice of the unexpectedly officious *praefectus*.

sic: i.e. 'on these terms'.

sutili cumba: ablative, 'in his patchwork boat'.

commeantes: nominal use of the participle, object of *deducit*, 'leads down those travelling'.

inter mortuos avaritia vivit: the oxymoron is obvious and highlighted by alliteration of 'v'. Aemilianus, the main target of Apuleius in his *Apology* (see the Introduction) in which *avaritia* is a significant theme, is nicknamed Charon partly because of his enrichment from inheriting from sudden death (*Apology* 23.7).

Ditis sectator: 'attendant of the underworld'.

tantus deus: in apposition to Charon; clearly ironic.

aes si: take *si* first; with *non*, 'unless'.

prae manu: an idiom, 'at hand'.

fuerit: future perfect, by necessity in a future conditional where the protasis logical precedes the apodosis.

squalido seni: the same appelation is used by Seneca, *Hercules furens* 764, but the phrase is closely modelled again on Vergil's description of the underworld and its inhabitants, *Aeneid* VI.299.

nauli nomine: ablative of specification, plus genitive, 'for the payment of the fare'. *naulum* is a borrowing of the Greek ναῦλον, like many seafaring words.

alteram: i.e. 'one of the two'.

ipse sua manu: an emphatic pleonasm; possibly a reference to religious ritual.

nec setius: 'no less', hence, 'likewise'.

supernatans senex mortuus: possibly modelled on Aeneas' pilot, Palinurus, who appears (dead) at *Aeneid* VI.370; other commentators suggest it is instead a reference to Plato's presentation of Hades in *Phaedo* 114b, where numerous dead souls desperately attempt to cross the divide.

putris ... manus: in agreement (accusative plural, object of *adtollens*).

adflectare: passive imperative.

inlicita ... pietate: 'by forbidden pity'.

Chapter 19

modicum te progressam: 'you, having advanced a little'.

textrices ... anus: in apposition; 'weavers, old women'. Again, the identity of these figures is opaque. They are not the Fates, who are not generally imagined to live in the underworld and are not weavers, but spinners. There is a traditional connection between deception and weaving.

telam struentes: technical weaving terms, but used in an unclear way; 'constructing a warp'.

manus ... accommodes: an idiom, 'to lend a hand'; another present subjunctive in an indirect command (following *orabunt*) with an unexpressed *ut*.

de Veneris insidiis: 'from Venus' ambushes', i.e. 'because of the traps set by Venus' (GCA).

vel unam ... offulam: *offula* is a diminutive of *offa*, the word used for the two cakes at VI.18; the Vergilian reference is replaced by a more colloquial term: 'just one piece of cake' (GCA).

A Level

nec putes: iussive subjunctive, instead of *noli putare*, placed emphatically.

polentarium damnum: the adjective is used as if it were a genitive noun, i.e. = *polentae damnum*.

leve: predicative; 'do not consider the loss light'.

altera ... perdita: ablative absolute, 'with either lost', functioning conditionally.

praeditus: takes the ablative *teriugo et satis amplo capite*, 'endowed with ...'. *satis* (adverbial) with the adjective here doesn't mean 'tolerably, moderately' but 'very'. *teriugus* is very rare (appearing only once elsewhere in Latin literature). This whole description of Cerberus is clearly playing with Vergil's description of Cerberus at *Aeneid* VI.400ff.

oblatrans: 'barking at' with the direct object *mortuos*.

nil mali: partitive genitive, 'nothing bad'.

territando: gerund in the ablative (of means), with *servat*, 'he guards by terrifying'.

vacuam Ditis domum: echoing *Aeneid* VI.269; in Vergilian terms, the underworld is *vacuus* because its inhabitants are immaterial, lacking substance.

unius offulae praeda: 'with the reward of one cake'.

ad ipsamque: take the *-que* before the preposition.

prandium ... sumere: those who eat the food of the dead are bound to stay in the underworld, according to common mythic logic (e.g. the myth of Persephone herself, in a deliberately ironic twist).

humi reside: imperative; this is the position of a beggar, 'on the ground' (locative).

esto: imperative not of *sum* but of *edo, esse*, 'eat'.

nuntiato: ablative absolute, with the indirect question standing for the noun in the clause; likewise with *susceptoque quod offeretur*.

quid adveneris: perfect subjunctive in an indirect question, 'why you have arrived'.

quod offeretur: imperfect subjunctive in an indirect question, 'what is being offered'.

rursus remeans: the return journey is described in a single sentence, unlike the two full chapters in which the descent is described; it is replete with compounds of *re-*, some (like here) doubly strengthened. Even where the prefix doesn't have the sense of 'back, again' (like in **reside** above, the combination overall gives a rhythmic repetition of the idea of return.

canis: genitive (with *saevitiam*).

avaro navitae: i.e. Charon; *navita* is a first declension masculine noun, a variant of *nauta*, chosen doubtless for alliteration as well as assonance.

quam reservaveras stipe: *stipe* is the antecedent to the relative clause, part of an ablative absolute with *data* and is best translated before; e.g. 'having the coin which you had preserved'.

redies: = *redibis*, future of *redeo*.

hoc observandum: gerundive of obligation, 'this is to be observed'. The use of *observo* in a command to not look is undoubtedly deliberate irony.

ne velis aperire vel inspicere: forceful prohibition, 'do not open' (rather than 'do not desire to open'; *ne velis* here is fulfilling the same function as *noli* in a normal prohibition). The command to refrain from looking is a common *topos* in underworld stories (as in Orpheus and Eurydice).

illam quam feres pyxidem: take *pyxidem* before the relative clause, of which it is the antecedent; note *feres* is future.

A Level

Chapter 20

turris illa prospicua: all in agreement.

munus: here in the sense, 'duty', 'office', with the genitive *vaticinationis*.

nec morata: perfect active participle, agreeing with Psyche; i.e. 'without delay . . .'.

Taenarum: accusative without a preposition for motion towards a city or town.

sumptis . . . stipibus: the first of a series of six ablatives absolute in this section, containing in total nine clauses, building up to the climax of *penetrat* at the end of the following sentence, which is intimately linked – many editors print it as a single sentence, which structures a single period around a tricolon of three main verbs (*pergit . . . decurrit . . . penetrat*). Like the description of the return journey by the tower, it is far more compressed and brisk than the advice for descending to the underworld in the preceding chapters. The repetition of a previous speech in action is Homeric, though the lack of exact verbal repetition is less so. In particular, Apuleius is playing with *Odyssey* 11.1–50, Odysseus' own *catabasis*, which sees the hero undertake the tasks set out in Circe's advice in the preceding book.

infernum: a poetic alternative for *ad inferos*.

decurrit meatum: an internal accusative, 'she ran down her course', or (GCA) 'made her crossing'.

per silentium: i.e. 'in silence'.

debili: ablative, agreeing with *asinario*.

amnica stipe: 'the river fare', ablative in an ablative absolute with *data*.

neglecto . . . desiderio: another of the ablatives absolute; *negligo* is stronger than the English 'neglect' and implies active avoidance.

offulae cibo: ablative of means (and dependent genitive) following the participle *sopita*, itself part of another ablative absolute with *horrenda rabie*.

offerentis hospitae: genitive of possession, following both *sedile* and *cibum*; 'the chair and food of her hostess, who was offering them'. This is the expected behaviour of a normal host in the Roman world. The irony is surely deliberate – Persephone, who herself was trapped in the underworld by taking the offer of food, is now playing the same trick herself.

sedile: both Theseus and Pirithous were trapped in the underworld after sitting down on thrones, according to some traditions, which Apuleius may allude to here; cf. Vergil, *Aeneid* VI.617.

vel: Classical Latin would expect *nec* here (to correlate with the first *nec*), but this usage is normal for Apuleius.

amplexa: perfect active participle in the nominative, agreeing with the (implied) subject, Psyche.

sed ante pedes eius residens humilis: the traditional posture of a suppliant; *humilis* is both literal, 'on the ground', and figurative, 'humble'.

legationem: drawn from the vocabulary of formal diplomacy, perhaps chosen for ironic contrast with the image of her eating common bread, seated on the ground.

secreto repletam conclusamque: the pleonastic emphasis on the sealing of the box foreshadows the significance of Psyche's opening of it.

offulae sequentis fraude: ablative of means with dependent genitive, 'by the trick of the second piece of cake'.

caninis: adjective (agreeing with *latratibus*, in an ablative absolute with *obseratis*), standing for the genitive *canis*.

longe vegetior: 'far more lively', agreeing with Psyche – ironic, in view of the following disaster.

repetita atque adorata candida ista luce: ablative absolute; (loosely) 'having found again and worshipped that light'. There are verbal parallels with Lucius' Isiac inititation in Book XI.23, one of a number of connections in this passage between the two.

obsequium: either abstract, referring to her servitude to Venus, 'duty of obedience', or more concretely referring to the task set.

mentem: accusative of respect (sometime 'Greek' accusative); 'she is seized in respect of her mind'.

temeraria curiositate: the word order holds this noun to the end for emphasis, drawing attention to the fault Psyche has been subject to since the beginning of the tale, her rash curiosity. This again links to Lucius, whose chief fault is also curiosity, and who specifically seeks to avoid *temeraria curiositas* at his initiation.

inepta ego: an exclamatory nominative, with *gerula* in apposition; the noun has archaic colour to it. There is maybe a subtle play on words here, as Psyche, pregnant with Cupid's child, is truly a 'bearer of divine beauty'.

quae: a causal relative; can be translated simply as 'who', but has the force here of 'if I . . .'.

nec . . . quidem: 'not even'.

indidem: 'from that same source'.

mihi: 'for myself'.

vel sic: should be taken closely with *placitura*, 'to be pleasing [to Cupid], at least by that means'. The force of the future participle is purposive.

illi amatori meo: all in agreement, dative after *placeo*.

Chapter 21

cum dicto: 'with her speech', 'as she spoke'.

reserat pyxidem: the actual error is briefly stated, with the noun emphatically placed, in contrast to the rhetorically rich periodicity of her speech. This is a reversal of the pattern so far, where Psyche succeeds in seemingly impossible tasks despite the odds; the opening of the box after explicit orders not to echoes the Orpheus and Eurydice myth, especially as related by Vergil, *Georgics* IV.485–93, as well as the story of Pandora's box (actually a jar) in Hesiod, *Works and Days* 94ff.

quicquam ... rerum: partitive genitive, literally 'anything of things'; i.e. 'anything at all', an emphatic way to show the emptiness of the box.

formonsitas: the third use of this word (or variant thereof) in as many lines, flagging the gap between expectation and reality.

infernus somnus: the 'sleep of death' and death-like sleep are recurring motifs in the *Metamorphoses* – in the tale of Thelyphron at II.25, among others – and an apparent death is a recurrent plot device in the Greek novels (Xenophon, *Ephesiaca* III.6–7, Chariton I.6–10), folklore in general (e.g. Sleeping Beauty and Snow White) and can also be seen in Shakespeare's *Romeo and Juliet*. Kenney notes that the overtones here are philosophical and that this sleep represents 'the spiritual death of the soul that is wholly given over to the wrong kind of love, and from this plight only Love in its higher guise can rescue it', citing Plutarch's *Amatorius* 764–5, a Platonizing dialogue on love of the early second century.

qui ... invadit ... perfunditur ... possidet: the effect of the sleep is given in this lengthy relative clause, structured around a tricolon with ascending numbers of syllables (fifteen, nineteen and twenty); variation is maintained by lack of parallelism; the first colon ends in *eam* rather than the verb, and the connecting participles vary, with *-que* followed by *et*.

coperculo: ablative of separation after *revelatus*, 'laid bare from its cover'.

crassa ... soporis nebula: could feasibly be either nominative, in apposition to *somnus*, 'as a thick mist of sleep', or ablative, 'with a thick mist'; both GCA and Kenney translate as the latter.

A Level

cunctis eius membris: 'over all her limbs'.

perfunditur: used as a Greek middle voice, 'pours itself out', part of a generally poetic feel to this line.

ipsaque semita: ablative with *in*, 'on the path itself', paralleling *in ipso vestigio*, 'on the very spot'.

et iacebat: this sentence, dramatically short after the complex colon preceding, starts with the verb emphatically placed, and *cadaver* equally emphatically at its conclusion.

dormiens cadaver: again, playing with the ambiguity of sleep and death.

Chapters 21 to 24: The scene is shifted to Cupid's bedroom; with his scar healed, he escapes out the window, and wipes the sleep from Psyche, returning it to the jar. Waking her with a touch of his arrow, he gently chides her for again falling prey to curiosity, bids her to finish the task, and flies off to Jupiter's throne. The scene between him and Jupiter depicts the relationship as between a spoilt favourite child and a doting father; despite all Cupid's lawbreaking, and the trouble he causes by Jupiter's own romances, the king of the gods acquiesces to his request (with the proviso that a similarly beautiful girl be provided for Jupiter's own pleasure!).

Chapters 23 and 24 are therefore the triumphant marriage rites of Cupid and Psyche; Jupiter invites all the gods and, to allay Venus' concerns about an unequal match, grants Psyche immortality. In due course, a daughter is born to the couple, called Pleasure (Voluptas).

For a summary of the rest of the book, see Introduction pp. 194–7.

A Level

Vocabulary

While there is no Defined Vocabulary List for A-level, words in the OCR Defined Vocabulary List for AS-level are marked with * so that students can quickly see the vocabulary with which they should be particularly familiar.

***a**, **ab**, **abs**	from, by (+ *abl.*)
abdo, (3), **abdidi**, **abditus**	to hide
abeo, **-ire**, **-ivi**, **-itus**	to depart, disappear
abscondeo, (2)	to hide
***absum**, **abesse**, **afui**, **afuturus**	to be absent
ac	and in addition, and also, and, (+ *comparative*) than
***accipio**, (3), **accepi**, **acceptus**	to accept, hear, receive, take, hear
accola, **-ae** *f.*	a neighbour
accommodo, (1)	to apply
acervatim (*adv.*)	without order
acervus, **-i** *m.*	a heap
Achaia, **-ae** *f.*	Achaia, region in the northwest Peloponnese in Greece
acriter (*adv.*)	steadfastly
actutum (*adv.*)	without delay
acutus, **-a**, **-um**	sharp
***ad**	to, up to, towards (+ *acc.*)
addico, (3), **addixi**, **addictus**	to devote, dedicate (+ *dat.*)
adeo, **-ire**, **-ivi**, **-itus**	to approach
adflecto, (1)	to influence
***adhuc**	still
aditus, **-us** *m.*	an attack, approach
admolior, (4), **admolitus sum**	to exert oneself (to)
adoro, (1)	to adore
adpulsus, **-us** *m.*	an impact

A Level

adrigo, (3), **adrexi, adrectus**	to excite
adripio, (3), **adripui, adreptus**	to snatch
*****adsum, adesse, affui**	to arrive, be present, be at hand
adtollo, (3)	to raise
adulterinus, -a, -um	false
*****advenio**, (4)	to arrive
adventus, -us *m.*	an approach
aeger, -gra, -grum	sorrowful
aegrotus, -a, -um	love-sick
aerumna, -ae *f.*	task, toil, distress
aes, aeris *n.*	money
aetas, -atis *f.*	age
Aether, -eris, *n.*	Aether, upper air
affero, affere, attuli, allatus	to convey
affligo, (3), **afflixi, afflictus**	to throw down, afflict
agaso, -onis *m.*	a driver
agilis, -e	nimble
agnosco, (3), **agnovi, agnotum**	to recognize
*****ago, agere, egi, actum**	to drive, do, act
ales, -itis *f.*	a bird
alioquin (*adv.*)	in general
*****alius, -a, -ud**	other, another
*****alter, -era, -erum**	one (of two), either
altus, -a, -um	high, noble, profound
alumna, -ae *f.*	a nursling
amarum (*adv.*)	bitterly
amator, -oris *m.*	a lover
ambo, -ae, -o	both
amnicus, -a, -um	of a river
*****amor, -oris** *m.*	love; (capitalized) Amor, Cupid
amplector, (3), **amplexus sum**	to embrace
amplexus, -us *m.*	embrace, coil (snake)
amplus, -a, -um	ample
*****an**	or; (in questions) can it be that …?
	utrum … an: whether … or

*ancilla, -ae *f.*	a handmaid, slave-girl
*angustus, -a, -um	steep, narrow
anima, -ae *f.*	soul
*animus, -i *m.*	a heart, spirit, mind
*ante	before, in front of (*adv.* and *prep.* + *acc.*)
anus, -us *f.*	old woman
*aperio, (4), aperui, apertum	to open
appello, (1)	to address
appello, (3), appuli, appulsum	to land, arrive
approbo, (1)	to approve
*apud	in the view of (+ *acc.*)
*aqua, -ae *f.*	water
*aquila, -ae *f.*	an eagle
arduus, -a, -um	steep
arx, arcis *f.*	a citadel
ascalpo, (3), ascalpsi, ascalptum	to scratch
asinarius, -i *m.*	an ass-driver
asinus, -i *m.*	an ass, donkey
assido, (3), -sedi	to sit down
assigno, (1)	to assign
*at	but, but yet
ater, -tra, -trum	black, gloomy
atque	and in addition, and also, and
atrium, -i *n.*	atrium
attendo, (3), attendi, attentum	to stretch toward, extend
attiguus, -a, -um	adjoining, neighbouring
auctor, -oris *m.*	an originator
audaciter (*adv.*)	boldly
*audio, -ire, -ivi/-ii, -itum	to hear, listen to, obey
aura, -ae *f.*	breeze
aureus, -a, -um	golden, gleaming
auris, -is *f.*	ear
Aurora, -ae *f.*	Dawn
aurum, -i *n.*	gold

A Level

auscultatus, -us *m.*	listening, obedience
ausculto, (1)	to listen to (+ *dat.*)
*****autem**	moreover, but, however
avaritia, -ae *f.*	greed
avarus, -a, -um	greedy
avia, -ae *f.*	a grandmother
avis, -is *f.*	a bird
balsamum, -i *n.*	balsam
beatus, -a, -um	blessed, happy, fortunate
*****bene** (*adv.*)	well
benigne (*adv.*)	kindly
bestia, -ae *f.*	a wild beast, creature
*****bibo**, (3), **bibi**	to drink
blandio, (4)	to please
bonum, -i *n.*	a good (thing); (*pl.*) wealth
*****bonus, -a, -um**	good, noble
cachinnus, -i *m.*	a derisive laugh, guffaw
cadaver, -eris *n.*	a corpse
caelestis, -e	heavenly
*****caelum, -i** *n.*	sky, heavens
caerulus, -a, -um	sky-dark
calor, -oris *m.*	heat
canalis, -is *n.*	a channel
cancer, -cri *m.*	a barrier
candidus, -a, -um	bright
caninus, -a, -um	of a dog
*****canis, -is** *m.*	a dog
canorus, -a, -um	harmonious
cantito, (1)	to sing
capillus, -i *m.*	hair
*****capio**, (3), **cepi, captum**	to seize
*****caput, capitis** *n.*	head
careo, (2), **carui, caritum**	to be without, lack (+ *abl.*)
casus, -us *m.*	a fall; chance, accident
cautes, -is *f.*	a crag

A Level

cavatus, -a, -um	hollow
***caveo**, (2), **cavi, cautum**	to beware
***cedo**, (3), **cessi, cessum**	to grant, make way
celero, (1)	to quicken
celsus, -a, -um	high
***cena**, -ae *f.*	dinner
censeo, censere, censui, censum	assess, rate; think, decide, decree, advise
certatim	in competition
certe	certainly, surely
***certus, -a, -um**	certain of, knowledgeable of (+ *gen.*)
cesso, (1)	to be inactive
***ceteri, -ae, -a**	the rest, others
Charon, -onis, *m.*	Charon, ferryman of the dead
chorus, -i *m.*	a chorus
cibarius, -a, -um	common, plain
***cibus, -i** *m.*	food, morsel
cicer, -eris *n.*	chickpea
citatus, -a, -um	quick
***civitas, -atis** *f.*	a city
***clamo**, (1)	to shout out
classis, -is *f.*	a class, fleet
claudo, (3), **clausi, clausus**	to confine
claudus, -a, -um	lame
Cocytus, -i *m.*	Cocytus, the river of wailing
***coepi**, (3), **coepisse, coeptum**	to begin
coerceo, (2)	to restrain
***cogo**, (3), **coegi, coactum**	to compel
collum, -i *n.*	neck
color, -is *m.*	colour
coma, -ae *f.*	wool
comiter	(*adv.*) courteously
***comito**, (1)	to accompany
***commeo**, (1)	to go to, travel

A Level

comminiscor, (1), commentus sum	to pretend
comminor, (1), comminatus sum	to threaten
commisceo, (2), commiscui, commixtus	to combine
*committo, (3), -misi, -missus	to commit
commodum	(*adv.*) even now
commoveo, (2)	to provoke
compello, (3), -pulsi, -pulsum	to force
comperio, (4), comperi, compertus	to hear, discover
compleo, (2), -evi, -etum	to fill up
concedo, (3), concessi	to depart
conceptaculum, -i *n.*	a receptacle
concludo, (3), conclusi, conclusus	to shut up
condecet, (2), -uit	it is fitting
*confero, -ferre, -tuli, collatus	to confer, direct (a conversation)
confestim	(*adv.*) immediately
*conficio, (3), confeci, confectus	to complete, wear out
confundo, (3), confudi, confusus	to jumble
congeries, -ei *f.*	a heap
congero, (3), congessi, congestus	to pile on, gather
conlabor, (3), conlapsus sum	to collapse
conquasso, (1)	to shake violently
conquiesco, (3), conquievi	to take repose
consentio, (4)	to consent
*consilium, -i *n.*	a plan
conspectus, -us *m.*	a sight, contemplation
*conspicio, (3), conspexi, conspectum	to catch sight of
consterno, (1)	to confound
constrepo, (3), -strepui	to resound
Consuetudo, -inis *f.*	Habit

*****consumo**, (3), **consumpsi**, **consumptum**	to consume
contego, (3), **contexi**, **contectum**	to conceal
contentus, -a, -um	content
conterminus, -a, -um	neighbouring, adjacent to (+ *gen.*)
contero, (3), **contrivi**, **contritum**	to use up
contineo, (2), **-tinui**, **-tentum**	to contain
contingo, (3), **-tigi**, **-tactum**	to touch
continor, (1), **continatus sum**	to encounter
contorqueo, (2), **contorsi**, **contortum**	to twist
*****contra**	against, opposite (*adv.* and *prep.* + *acc.*)
contubernalis, -is *m.*	bedmate
contumacia, -ae *f.*	stubbornness
convallis, -is *f.*	valley, ravine
convenio, (4), **-veni**, **-ventum**	to approach, come together
convexus, -a, um	vaulted, curved
convivium, -i *n.*	a banquet
convoco, (1)	to assemble
coperculum, -i *n.*	a cover
*****copia**, -ae *f.*	supply, means
cornu, -us *n.*	a horn
*****corpus**, **corporis** *n.*	body
corrogo, (1)	to summon to a gathering
crassus, -a, -um	thick
crepitus, -us *m.*	rustling
*****crimen**, -inis *n.*	a charge
crustallum, -i *n.*	crystal
cubiculum, -i *n.*	a bedroom
cubitus, -us *m.*	a bed
culmen, -inis *n.*	height
*****cum**	with (*prep.* + *abl.*); when, since, although (*conj.* + *subj.*)
cumba, -ae *f.*	a small boat

A Level

cumulus, **-i** *m.*	a heap
cunctatio, **-onis** *f.*	hesitation
cunctor, (1), **cunctatus sum**	to delay
*****cunctus**, **-a**, **-um**	all, entire
cupido, **-inis** *n.*	desire, greed; (capitalized) Cupid
cupita, **-ae** *f.*	beloved
curiositas, **-atis** *f.*	curiosity
*****curo**, (1)	to take care of
custodia, **-ae** *f.*	prison
damnum, **-i** *n.*	loss
*****de**	down from, about, concerning (+ *abl.*)
*****debeo**, (2), **debui**, **debitum**	ought to, must (+ *inf.*)
debilis, **-e**	crippled
decido, (3), **decidi**, **decisum**	to fall
decurro, (3), **decucurri**	to hurry down
dedolo, (1)	to hew smooth
deduco, (3), **deduxi**, **deductum**	to escort
defendo, (3)	to defend
defero, **-ferre**, **-tuli**, **-latum**	to bring
defluo, (3), **defluxi**, **-fluxum**	to fall
deformis, **-e**	ugly
deiero, (1)	to swear
*****deinde**	next
delabor, (3), **delapsus sum**	to flow down
delibo, (1)	to skim off
delicatus, **-a**, **-um**	luxurious
delino, (3), **delivi**, **delitum**	to anoint
delitesco, (3), **-tui**	to hide
demeo, (1)	to descend
demonstro, (1)	to point out
denego, (1)	to deny
*****denique**	finally
dens, **-entis** *m.*	a tooth
depromo, (3), **deprompsi**, **depromptum**	to utter

Vocabulary

derigo, (3), **-rexi**, **-rectum**	to direct
*****descendo**, (3), **descendi**, **descensum**	to descend
desero, (3), **-rui**, **desertum**	to depart
desiderium, **-i** *n.*	a desire, request
designo, (1)	to describe
*****despicio**, (3), **-spexi**, **-spectum**	to look down on
*****deus**, **-i** *m.*; **dea**, **-ae** *f.*	god; goddess
devius, **-a**, **-um**	remote
*****dexter**, **-tra**, **-trum**	on the right side
dialis, **-e**	of Jupiter
*****dico**, **dicere**, **dixi**, **dictum**	to say, speak
dictum, **-i** *n.*	an utterance
diecula, **-ae** *f.*	little day
difficultas, **-atis** *f.*	difficulty, hardship
digero, (3), **-gessi**, **-gestum**	to organize
dignor, (1), **dignatus sum**	to deign to (+ *inf.*)
diligenter	(*adv.*) carefully
diligentia, **-ae** *f.*	diligence
dilorico, (1)	to tear apart
directo	(*adv.*) in straight line
dirigo, (3)	to direct (= **derigo**)
Dis, **Ditis** *m.*	Dis, the underworld
*****discedo**, (3), **-cessi**, **-cessum**	to withdraw
discerno, (3), **-crevi**, **-cretum**	to distinguish, sort out
discindo, (3), **discidi**, **discissum**	to cut in two, tear
discurro, (3)	to dash about, wander
dispono, (3), **disposui**, **dispositum**	to distribute
dissero, (3), **dissevi**, **dissitum**	to plant at intervals, distribute
distineo, (2), **distinui**, **distentum**	to keep apart
distribuo, (3), **distribui**, **distributum**	to divide
diutius	longer
divinitus	(*adv.*) divinely

A Level

*do, dare, dedi, datum	to give, pay
*doceo, (2), docui, doctum	to teach, show
*dominus, -i m; * domina, -ae f.	master, lord; mistress
*domus, -i/-us f.	a house, home
*dormio, (4)	to sleep
draco, -onis m.	a dragon, snake
ductus, -us m.	a leading, conducting
*dum	while (+ *indic.*); until (+ *subj.*)
*e, ex	out of, from (+ *abl.*)
ecce	behold!
*edo, (3), edidi, editus	to declare, eject
edo, esse	to eat
effero, (1)	to make wild, savage, fierce
effero, efferre, extuli, elatus	to raise; (*pass.*) to be carried away
*ego, mei, mihi, me	I, me
*enim	for, indeed
*eo, ire, ivi, itus	to go, pass
*ergo	therefore
erilis, -e	of a master or mistress
*et	and
*etiam	also, even
evomo, (3)	to vomit out
exanclo, (1)	to suffer, go through
exaro, (1)	to plough
*excipio, (3), excepi, exceptum	to receive, collect
exclamo, (1)	to exclaim
excrucio, (1)	torment
excubo, (1)	to be attentive, stay awake, keep watch
excusatio, -onis f.	excuse
exercito, (1)	to harass
exitiabilis, -e	deadly
*exitium, -i n.	death, destruction
expedio, (4), expedivi, expeditum	to be complete, make ready
expers, -ertis (*gen.*)	lacking experience of + *gen.*

expeto, (3), **-petivi**, **-petitum**	to ask for
expio, (1)	to expiate, appease
explico, (1), **explicui**	unfold, set forth
exsecror, (1), **exsecratus sum**	to detest
exsequor, (3), **exsecutus sum**	to execute, accomplish
exspiro, (1)	to die
extinguo, (3), **-nxi**, **-nctum**	to kill
extollo, (3)	to raise
extremus, **-a**, **-um**	extreme, farthest
faba, **-ae** *f.*	bean
facesso, (3), **facessi**	to go away
*__facilis__, **-e**	easy
*__facio__, **facere**, **feci**, **factum**	to do, make
factum, **-i** *n.*	deed, achievement
familia, **-ae** *f.*	household of slaves
famulatio, **-onis** *f.*	the servants of a house
fas	allowable, permitted (+ *inf.*)
faux, **faucis** *f.*	maw, chasm
*__felix__, **-icis** (*gen.*)	happy
feralis, **-e**	funereal
*__fero__, **ferre**, **tuli**, **latus**	to bear, carry
festino, (1)	to hurry (+ *inf.*)
*__filia__, **-ae** *f.*	daughter
*__filius__, **-i** *m.*	son
fingo, (3), **finxi**, **fictum**	to pretend
*__finis__, **-is** *m.*	an end
flagellum, **-i** *n.*	a whip
flagitium, **-i** *n.*	outrage
flaveo, (2)	to be yellow coloured
floccus, **-i** *m.*	a tuft
floreo, (2)	to flourish, be bright
flos, **-oris** *m.*	youthful prime
fluentum, **-i** *n.*	a stream
*__flumen__, **-inis** *n.*	a river
fluvialis, **-e**	of a river

A Level

fluvius, -i *m.*	a river
fons, fontis *m.*	a spring, source
for, (1), **fatus sum**	to speak, talk, say
foramen, -inis *n.*	a fissure
foris, -is *f.*	a gate
formica, -ae *f.*	an ant
formicula, -ae *f.*	a little ant
formidabilis, -e	terrifying
*****formonsitas, -atis** *f.*	beauty
formonsus, -a, -um	handsome
fors, fortis *f.*	chance
*****fortis, -e**	strong
*****fortuna, -ae** *f.*	fate, fortune
fraglantia, -ae *f.*	burning (also **flagrantia**)
fragrans, -antis (*gen.*)	smelling, fragrant (also **fraglans**)
*****frater, fratris** *m.*	a brother
fraus, fraudis *f.*	trickery
frequento, (1)	to visit
frons, -ondis *f.*	foliage
frons, frontis *m.*	a brow
*****frumentum, -i** *n.*	grain
*****frustra**	(*adv.*) in vain
frustum, -i *n.*	a morsel, crumb
frutex, -icis *m.*	a shrub
frux, -ugis *f.*	produce, virtue
*****fuga, -ae** *f.*	flight
*****fugio,** (3), **fugi**	to flee
fugitivus, -a, -um	fugitive
fungor, (3), **functus sum**	to perform
furatrina, -ae *f.*	theft
furenter	(*adv.*) furiously
furia, -ae *f.*	frenzy
furor, (1), **furatus sum**	to steal
fuscus, -a, -um	dark
fusticulus, -i *m.*	a little stick

futilis, -e	worthless
***gaudium**, -i *n*.*	joy
gena, -ae *f*.	a cheek, jaw
***genus**, -eris *n*.*	a variety
gero**, (3), **gessi**, **gestum	to carry on
gerula, -ae *f*.	a bearer
gerulus, -i *m*.	a bearer
gesto, (1)	to carry
gradus, -us *m*.	a step
granatim	grain by grain
granum, -i *n*.	grain
gratuitus, -a, -um	without pay
gravis, -e	grave, earnest, heavy
graviter	(*adv*.) violently
gravo, (1)	to aggravate, weigh down
gremium, -i *n*.	a lap, bosom
grumulus, -i *m*.	a little heap
habeo**, (2), **habui	to have
hactenus	(*adv*.) in this way
haereo, (2), **haesi, haesus**	to stick
harundo, -inis *f*.	a reed
***haud**	by no means
haurio, (4), **hausi, hauritus, -a, -um**	to draw out
hic, haec, hoc	this, these
hio, (1)	to be wide open, gape
***homo, hominis** *m*.*	a man, human being
***hora**, -ae *f*.*	time, hour
hordeum, -i *n*.	barley
horrendus, -a, -um	horrible
horridus, -a, -um	wild
hospita, -ae *f*.	a hostess
humanus, -a, -um	kind
***humi** (*loc*.)*	on the ground
humilis, -e	humble

*iaceo, (2), iacui	to lie
*iam, iamque	now; already
*ibi	there
*idem, eadem, idem	the same
ignorantia, -ae *f.*	ignorance
ilico	(*adv.*) immediately
*ille, illa, illud	that
*illic	in that place
immanis, -e	immense, monstrous
immanitas, -atis *f.*	frightfulness, vast size
immaturius	(*adv.*) more untimely, later
immo	indeed, rather
immobilis, -e	unmoving
impaeniteo, (2)	to not repent
impar, -aris (*gen.*)	unequal (in rank)
impossibilitas, -atis *f.*	impossibility
imus, -a, -um	deepest, lowest
*in	in, on (+ *abl.*); into, onto (+ *acc.*)
inaccessus, -a, -um	inaccessible
incedo, (3)	to walk
incido, (3), incidi, incasum	to happen, fall upon
incipio, (3), incepi, inceptum	to begin
includo, (3), inclusi, inclusus	to enclose
inconditus, -a, -um	disordered
inconivus, -a, um	unsleeping
incustoditus, -a, -um	unsupervised
*inde	from there, from then
indicium, -i *n.*	information, proof
indiciva, -ae *f.*	an informer's reward
indidem	(*adv.*) from the same place
induco, (3), induxi, inductus	to lead in
ineptus, -a, -um	foolish
inequito, (1)	to ride over
inextricabilis, -e	impossible to disentangle
infernus, -a, -um	infernal

inferus, **-i** *m.*	region below, the dead
infit	s/he begins
inibi	(*adv.*) in that place
*****initium**, **-i** *n.*	a beginning
inlicitus, **-a**, **-um**	unlawful, forbidden
inmitto, (3), **inmisi**, **inmissus**	to throw in
innocens, **-entis** (*gen.*)	innocent
innoxius, **-a**, **-um**	unharmed
*****inquam**, **inquis**, **inquit**, **inquiunt**	to say (used with direct speech)
inquisitio, **-onis** *f.*	search
inrigo, (1)	to irrigate
*****insidia**, **-ae** *f.*	a trap
insisto, (3)	to stand upon
*****inspicio**, (3), **inspexi**, **inspectum**	to look into
inspiro, (1)	to inspire
*****instruo**, (3), **instruxi**, **instructus**	to instruct, draw up
insuper	(*adv.*) in addition
*****inter**	between, among; during (+ *acc.*)
*****interea**/**interim**	meanwhile
interior, **-ius**	interior
interviso, (3), **-visi**, **-visum**	to visit
intro	(*adv.*) in, inside
introeo, **-ire**, **-ivi**, **-itus**	to enter
invado, (3)	to attack
*****invenio**, (4), **inveni**, **inventus**	to contrive, discover
investigatio, **-onis** *f.*	a search
invius, **-a**, **-um**	impassable
involo, (1)	to fly at, attack
*****iratus**, **-a**, **-um**	made angry, raging
*****is**, **ea**, **id**	he, she, it
iste, **ista**, **istud**	that, that of yours
*****iter**, **itineris** *n.*	a path, pass
*****iterum**	(*adv.*) a second time
*****iubeo**, **iubere**, **iussi**, **iussum**	to order, bid
iugum, **-i** *n.*	a ridge, summit

A Level

iussus, **-us** *m.*	an order
Lacedaemo, **-onis** *m.*	Lacedaemon, the region of Sparta
lacrima, **-ae** *f.*	tear (also **lacruma**)
lacuna, **-ae** *f.*	a hollow, cleft
laetus, **-a**, **-um**	glad, happy, joyful
laevus, **-a**, **-um**	on the left side
lanosus, **-a**, **-um**	woolly
lapis, **-idis** *m.*	a stone, milestone, jewel
lascivio, (4)	to frisk, frolic
latenter	(*adv.*) without being perceived, secretly
lateo, (2), **latui**	to lie hidden from
latratus, **-us** *m.*	barking
latus, **-a**, **-um**	extensive
laxo, (1)	to relax
legatio, **-onis** *f.*	a mission
legitimus, **-a**, **-um**	lawful
lenis, **-e**	light
lenocinium, **-i** *n.*	enticement
lens, **lentis** *f.*	lentil
lepidus, **-a**, **-um**	charming
letalis, **-e**	lethal
***levis**, **-e**	trifling, light
libellus, **-i** *m.*	a little book, defamatory publication
libro, (1)	to balance
licet	even though
lignum, **-i** *n.*	firewood
limen, **-inis** *n.*	a threshold
lingua, **-ae** *f.*	a tongue
longe	(*adv.*) far, by far
lubricus, **-a**, **-um**	slippery
lucerna, **-ae** *f.*	oil lamp
lumen, **-inis** *n.*	an eye
lumen, **luminis** *n.*	light
***lux**, **lucis** *f.*	daylight, light, vision, life

luxuries, -ei *f.*	extravagance
madeo, (2)	to be dripping
magnitudo, -**inis** *f.*	size
*****magnus**, -**a**, -**um**	large, great
maiestas, -**atis** *f.*	majesty
*****maior**, -**us**	larger
malefica, -**ae** *f.*	a witch
*****malus**, -**a**, -**um**	bad, evil
mandatum, -**i** *n.*	a command
*****mando**, (1)	to entrust, command
manifeste	(*adv.*) undoubtedly
manifestus, -**a**, -**um**	clear, plainly guilty
manis, -**is** *m.*	shades of dead (*pl.*)
*****manus**, -**us** *f.*	hand, band of men
*****maritus**, -**i** *m.*	husband
maturo, (1)	to hasten
meatus, -**us** *m.*	a passageway
*****medius**, -**a**, -**um**	middle, in the middle, central
melleus, -**a**, -**um**	of honey
mellitus, -**a**, -**um**	honey-sweet
membrum, -**i** *n.*	a limb
memor, -**oris** (*gen.*)	mindful
*****mens**, **mentis** *f.*	mind
Mercurius, -**i** *m.*	Mercury
mereo, (2), **merui**, **meritum**	merit
meridies, -**ei** *m.*	midday
meta, -**ae** *f.*	a turning post
metuo, **metuere**, **metui**	to fear, be afraid
*****meus**, -**a**, -**um**	my, mine
mico, (1)	to gleam
milium, -**i** *n.*	millet
ministerium, -**i** *n.*	service
ministro, (1)	to attend (to)
mirus, -**a**, -**um**	extraordinary
misellus, -**a**, -**um**	poor, wretched

miseratio, -onis *f.*	compassion
misereor, (2), **misertus sum**	to pity
mitigo, (1)	to soothe
*****mitto**, (3), **misi, missum**	to send
modicum, -i, *n.*	short distance, small measure
*****modo**	just, just now; **modo ... modo**: now ... now, at one moment ... at another, sometimes ... sometimes
*****modus, -i** *m.*	manner, means, way
moles, -is *f.*	a mass, burden
molliter	(*adv.*) calmly
mollities, -ei *f.*	softness
*****mons, montis** *m.*	mountain
*****monstro**, (1)	to reveal
*****mora, -ae** *f.*	delay
*****morior**, (3), **mortuus sum**	to die
*****moror**, (1), **moratus sum**	to delay
*****mors, mortis** *f.*	death
morsus, -us *m.*	teeth
mortalis, -e	mortal
mortifer, -a, -um	deadly
mortuus, -i *m.*	a corpse, the dead
*****mos, moris** *m.*	custom, habit
mox	soon
mulsum, -i *n.*	honeyed wine
*****munio**, (4)	to protect
*****munus, -eris** *n.*	duty, service
musica, -ae *f.*	music
*****muto**, (1)	to change
*****mutuor**, (1), **mutuatus sum**	to borrow
*****nam, namque**	for, indeed, really
*****nascor**, (3), **natus sum**	to be born
naulum, -i *n.*	a fare, passage money
navigium, -i *n.*	a vessel

navita, -ae *m.*	a sailor
naviter	(*adv.*) diligently
***ne**	lest, that not (+ *subj.*)
nebula, -ae *f.*	mist, cloud
***nec**	and not, nor; **nec** ... **nec**: neither ... nor
necessarius, -a, -um	indispensable
***neglego**, (3), **neglexi, neglectus**	to ignore
***nemo, neminis**	no one
nempe	of course
nemus, -oris *n.*	wood
nepos, -otis *m.*	a grandson
nequaquam	by no means
nequeo, (4), **-ivi, -itus**	to be unable
nequissimus, -a, -um	most vile, worst
***nescio**, (4)	to not know
***nihil/nil**	nothing
***nisi, ni**	if not, unless
niteo, (2)	to shine
nobilis, -e	noble
***nolo, nolle, nolui**	to be unwilling
***nomen, -inis** *n.*	a name, payment
***non**	not
***nos, nostrum/nostri, nobis, nos**	we
***nox, noctis** *f.*	night
nubes, -is *f.*	a cloud
***nullus, -a, -um**	not any, no one
***nunc**	now
***nunquam**	never
***nuntio**, (1)	to announce
nuptialis, -e	of a wedding
nurus, -us *f.*	daughter-in-law
nuto, (1)	to nod, flutter
nutricula, -ae *f.*	nurse
nutrio, (4)	to feed

A Level

nutus, **-us** *m.*	will
*****ob**	against, on account of (+ *acc.*)
obhaeresco, (3), **-haesi**	to adhere to (+ *dat.*)
oblatro, (1)	to bark at
obruo, (3), **obrui**, **obrutus**	to overwhelm
obsequium, **-i** *n.*	compliance, deference, service
obsero, (1)	to bolt, bar
observo, (1)	to heed
obstupesco, (3)	to be stupefied
obtempero, (1)	to comply
obvius, **-a**, **-um**	hostile
occulo, (3), **occului**, **occultum**	to conceal
occultatio, **-onis** *f.*	concealment
occurro, (3), **occucurri**	to run to meet
*****oculus**, **-i** *m.*	an eye
offa, **-ae** *f.*	a lump of food, cake
*****offero**, **offerre**, **obtuli**, **oblatum**	to present, offer, expose
offrenatus, **-a**, **-um**	tamed
offula, **-ae** *f.*	a piece of food, cake
*****omitto**, (3), **omisi**, **omissum**	to disregard, let go
omnino	(*adv.*) altogether, at all, generally, entirely
omniparens, **-entis** (*gen.*)	parent or creator of all things
*****omnis**, **-e**	all, every, as a whole
oncretus, **-a**, **-um**	dense, kneaded together
*****opera**, **-ae** *f.*	service, work, effort
opipare	(*adv.*) sumptuously
oppido	(*adv.*) exceedingly
opportunus, **-a**, **-um**	advantageous
*****ops**, **opis** *f.*	power, assistance, resources, wealth, help
*****opus**, **-eris** *n.*	work
Orcus, **-i** *m.*	Dis, god of the underworld
*****orior**, (3), **ortus sum**	to emerge, rise
*****oro**, (1)	to ask, beg, pray

***os, oris** *n.*	a mouth, face
ovis, -is *f.*	a sheep
ovo, (1)	to rejoice
pactum, -i *n.*	manner
palus, -udis *f.*	a swamp
pando, (3)	to spread out
panis, -is *m.*	bread
papaver, -eris *n.*	poppy-seed
***pars, partis** *f.*	a part
partim	(*adv.*) partly
partus, -us *m.*	offspring
parvulus, -a, -um	very small
passer, -eris *m.*	a sparrow
***passim** (*adv.*)	here and there, everywhere
passivus, -a, -um	random
pastus, -us *m.*	a pasture
***patior,** (3), **passus sum**	to allow
***paulisper**	(*adv.*) for only a short time
***pauper, pauperis** *m.*	a poor man
pectus, -oris *n.*	a heart
pecu, -us *n.*	a flock
peior, -us	worse
Penas, -atis *m.*	Penates, gods of home; dwelling
penetro, (1)	to enter
penitus, -a, -um	inner
***per**	through (+ *acc.*)
percolens, -entis (*gen.*)	honouring completely
percutio, (3), **percussi, percussum**	to strike
***perdo,** (3), **perdidi, perditum**	to lose
***pereo, -ire, -ivi, -itum**	to die
perfero, -ferre, -tuli, -latum	to carry through, bear
perfundo, (3), **-fusi, fusum**	to pour over
pergo, (3), **perrexi, perrectus**	to direct one's course right onward; go on

periclitor, (1), periclitatus sum	to put in peril
*periculum, -i *n.*	danger
perniciter	(*adv.*) briskly
perpetuus, -a, -um	perpetual
pertimesco, (3), -timui	to become very scared (of)
*pes, pedis *m.*	a foot
pessimus, -a, -um	worst
petitus, -us *m.*	entreaty, begging
*peto, (3), petivi, petitum	to ask (for), attack, seek, desire, make for
petulans, -antis (*gen.*)	wanton
Phrygius, -a, -um	Phrygian (Trojan)
pietas, -atis *f.*	loyalty, pity
piger, -a, -um	slow
*placeo, (2), placui, placitus	to please, give pleasure to (+ *dat.*)
platanus, -i *f.*	a plane tree
*plenus, -a, -um	full
plurifariam (*adv.*)	extensively
pocillator, -oris *m.*	a cupbearer
*poena, -ae *f.*	penalty
polenta, -ae *f.*	barley-meal
polentarius, -a, -um	of barley-meal
polluo, (3), pollui, pollutum	to stain, dishonour
*populus, -i *m.*	a host, group of people
porrigo, (3), porrexi, porrectum	to stretch out, extend, hand X (*acc.*) to Y (*dat.*)
*porta, -ae *f.*	a gate
portorium, -i *n.*	port duty, toll
possideo, (3), -sedi, -sessum	to seize
*possum, posse, potui	to be able, be possible
*postulo, (1)	to demand
potissimum	(*adv.*) before all
*potius	(*adv.*) more likely, rather
prae	(*adv.*) before
praealtus, -a, -um	very high

praeceps, -ipitis (*gen.*)	headlong
praeceptum, -i *n.*	order
praecipitium, -i *n.*	precipice, a falling headlong
praecipue	(*adv.*) especially
praeclarus, -a, -um	noble
praeconium, -i *n.*	a proclamation
*****praeda, -ae** *f.*	loot, prize
praedicatio, -onis *f.*	an announcement
praedicator, -oris *m.*	a herald, proclaimer
praedictus, -a, -um	previously named
praeditus, -a, -um	endowed with
praefectus, -i *m.*	a commander
praegrandis, -e	very large
praeministro, (1)	to attend to
praemino, (1)	to threaten thoroughly
*****praemium, -i** *n.*	reward
praesens, -entis (*gen.*)	present
praesentia, -ae *f.*	presence
*****praeterea**	besides, moreover
praetereo, -ire, -ivi, -itus	to pass by, escape
praevolo, (1)	to fly before
prandium, -i *n.*	lunch
pretiosus, -a, -um	costly, precious
prex, precis *f.*	prayers, entreaties
primum	at first, firstly
*****prior, -us**	former
*****pro**	for, on behalf of, in proportion to (+ *abl.*)
procerus, -a, -um	lofty
proclive, -is *n.*	a downward slope
profecto	(*adv.*) surely, certainly
*****progredior,** (3), **progressus sum**	to advance
proiicio, (3), **proieci, proiectus**	to throw down
promereor, (2), **promeritus sum**	to gain
promptus, -a, -um	eager, manifest, ready

A Level

pronuntio, (1)	to announce, proclaim
pronus, -a, -um	prone
propando, (3), **propansi, propansus**	to spread out
*****propter**	because of (+ *acc*.)
prorsus	(*adv*.) absolutely, entirely
prorumpo, (3), **-rupi, -ruptum**	to break out
proserpo, (3), **-serpsi, -serptum**	to creep forward
prospicuus, -a, -um	provident
protenus/protinus	(*adv*.) immediately
Providentia, -ae *f.*	Providence
proximo, (1)	to draw near
*****proximus/proxumus, -a, -um**	nearest
prudentia, -ae *f.*	good sense
publicitus	(*adv*.) publicly
*****puella, -ae** *f.*	a girl
pupula, -ae *f.*	a little girl; pupil (of an eye)
puter, -tris, -tre	decaying
*****puto**, (1)	to suppose
pyxis, -idis *f.*	a small box
*****quaero**, (3), **quaesivi, quaesitus**	to obtain, seek
*****quam**	how? (after comparative) than
quamvis	however you like; although
*****quanquam**	although
*****quantum**	(*adv*.) how much? how greatly? how much! how greatly! as much as
quare	whereby
*****quasi**	as if
quatio, (3), **quassum**	to shake
*****-que**	(*enclitic*) and (after comparatives) than
*****qui, quae, quod**	who, which, what
*****quidem**	certainly, at least; *****ne ... quidem**: not even

quidni	why not?
***quis**, **quid**	who? what? which?
quispiam, **quaepiam**, **quodpiam**	any
***quisquam**, **quicquam/quidquam**	any (single) person, anyone at all
***quo**	for which reason? to or in what place? to what end? for what purpose?
***quoad**	as long as
***quoque**	also, too
rabies, **-ei** *f.*	madness
rapax, **-acis** (*gen.*)	rapacious
raucus, **-a**, **-um**	raucous
recalco, (1)	to tread again
recte	(*adv.*) rightly
recurro, (3)	to run back
***reddo**, (3), **reddidi**, **redditus**	to deliver, render
***redeo**, **-ire**, **-ivi**, **-itus**	to return
redimo, (3)	to buy off
***refero**, **referre**, **rettuli**, **relatus**	to carry back
regalis, **-e**	royal
regia, **-ae** *f.*	a palace
regius, **-a**, **-um**	regal
reiicio, (3), **reieci**, **reiectus**	to throw back, remove
reliquus, **-a**, **-um**	remaining
remeo, (1)	to return
remigium, **-i** *n.*	rowing; oars; oarsmen
renideo, (2)	to gleam, smile
renitor, (3), **renisus sum**	to struggle
rennuo, (3), **rennui**	to refuse (by nodding)
reor, (2), **ratus sum**	to suppose
***repente**	(*adv.*) suddenly
reperio, (4), **repperi**, **repertum**	to find, obtain
repeto, (3), **repetivi**, **repetitum**	to return to
repleo, (2), **replevi**, **repletum**	to fill again
reporto, (1)	to carry back

A Level

requies, -ei *f.*	respite
res, rei *f.*	thing, affair
resero, (1)	to open up
reservo, (1)	to preserve, keep back
resideo, (2), **-sedi, -sessum**	to settle, sit down on
residuus, -a, -um	remaining
resono, (1)	to resound
retraho, (3)	to bring back
retro	behind (+ *acc.*)
revelo, (1)	to lay bare, uncover
revincio, (4), **revinxi, revinctus**	to bind fast
rigens, -entis (*gen.*)	freezing cold
*****ripa, -ae** *f.*	a bank
risus, -us *m.*	laughter
rite	(*adv.*) duly
*****rogo**, (1)	to ask
ros, roris *m.*	spray of water
rosa, -ae *f.*	a rose
ruo, (3)	to rush on
rupes, -is *f.*	a cliff
ruricola, -e *f.*	a country-dweller
*****rursus** (*adv.*)	again, back
saevio, (4), **saevivi, saevitum**	to rage
saevitia, -ae *f.*	cruelty, rage
*****saevus, -a, -um**	fierce
salebritas, -ates *f.*	ruggedness
saltem (*adv.*)	at least, even
*****salus, -utis** *f.*	salvation
*****saluto**, (1)	to greet
sanctus, -a, -um	venerable, sacred
sarcina, -ae *f.*	a burden
savium, -i *n.*	a kiss
saxeus, -a, -um	stony
saxum, -i *n.*	a stone
scaturrigo, -inis *f.*	bubbling

A Level

scilicet	certainly, of course
*scio, (4), scivi, scitus	to know
secedo, (3), -cessi, -cessum	to withdraw
secretum, -i *n*.	a secret
sectator, -oris *m*.	attendant, adherent, follower
*secundus, -a, -um	second, favourable
securus, -a, -um	untroubled
*sed, set	but
sedile, -is *n*.	seat
sedo, (1)	to allay, diminish
sedulo	(*adv*.) carefully
sedulus, -a, -um	attentive
seiugatus, -a, -um	separated
*semel	one time
semen, -inis *n*.	a seed
semita, -ae *f*.	a path
*semper	always, ever
senex, -is *m*.	an old man
sensus, -us *m*.	sense
*sentio, (4), sensi, sensum	feel
separatim	(*adv*.) apart
separo, (1)	to separate
sepes, sepedis	six-footed
sequens, -entis (*gen*.)	next, second
*sequor, (3), secutus sum	to obey
serenitas, -atis *f*.	peacefulness
sero, (3), serui, sertum	to compose
*servo, (1)	to guard
setius	comparative adverb from **secus**, otherwise; in phrase, **non setius**, just as much, likewise
*si	if
*sic	in this manner, thus; **sic ... ut**: in the same way as
sidus, -eris *n*.	a star

*silentium, -i *n.*	silence
sileo, (2)	to be silent, be still
*similis, -e	like, similar
simplex, -icis (*gen.*)	simple
*simul	(*adv.*) at same time
*simul atque	as soon as
singularis, -e	remarkable
singulus, -a, -um	each, apiece (*pl.*)
*sino, (3), sivi, situs	to allow
*sive	whether; sive ... sive: whether ... or
socrus, -us *f.*	mother-in-law
*sol, solis *m.*	sun
solacium, -i *n.*	solace
*soleo, (2), solitus sum	to be in the habit of, become accustomed to
solidus, -a, -um (1)	whole
sollicite	(*adv.*) anxiously
Sollicitudo, -inis *f.*	Anxiety
*sonus, -i *m.*	a noise, sound
sopio, (4), sopivi, sopitus	to render insensible
sopor, -oris *m.*	a deep sleep
sordidus, -a, -um	paltry
soror, -oris *f.*	a sister
*sperno, (3), sprevi, spretus	to spurn
*spero, (1)	to hope
*spes, -ei *f.*	hope
spiraculum, -i *n.*	vent, breathing-passage
spiritus, -us *m.*	breath, life, spirit
spurius, -i *m.*	a bastard
squalidus, -a, -um	filthy
*statim	immediately
stilla, -ae *f.*	a drop
stips, -ipis *f.*	a small offering (coin)
stirps, -irpis *f.*	a trunk (of a plant)

struo, (3), **struxi**, **structum**	to construct
studiose	(*adv.*) eagerly
*****studium**, -i *n.*	zeal
Stygius, -a, -um	Stygian, of the underworld
Styx, **Stygis** *f.*	the Styx River
suadeo, (2)	to persuade
suavis, -e	charming, pleasant, sweet
*****sub**	under, close to (+ *acc.* or *abl.*)
subdolus, -a, -um	treacherous
subeo, -ire, -ivi, -itus	to be placed under
subinde	(*adv.*) repeatedly
subitus, -a, -um	unexpected
sublatus, -a, -um	elated
suboles, -is *f.*	offspring
subrideo, (2)	to smile
succumbo, (3), **-cubui**, **-cubitum**	to break down
succurro, (3), **succurri**, **succursum**	to help
suffero, (3), **sustuli**, **sublatum**	bear
sufficio, (3), **-feci**, **-fectum**	to suffice
*****sui**, **sibi**, **se/sese**	him/her/itself
*****sum**, **esse**, **fui**, **futurus**	to be, exist
*****summus**, -a, -um	the top of
*****sumo**, (3), **sumpsi**, **sumptum**	to take up, obtain
super	over (*adv.* and *prep.* + *acc.*)
superbus, -a, -um	haughty
supercilium, -i *n.*	eyebrow
supernato, (1)	to float
*****supersum**, **-esse**	to be remaining
supremus, -a, -um	greatest
*****suscipio** (3), **-cepi**, **-ceptum**	to take up, accept, undertake
sustineo, (2), **sustinui**	to sustain, endure
sutilis, -e	patched, made by sewing
*****suus**, **sua**, **suum**	his/her/its (own); (*pl.*) their (own)
*****tacitus**, -a, -um	silent

A Level

Taenarus, -i *f.*	Taenarus, well-known entrance to the underworld
*****tam**	so, so much
*****tamen**	nevertheless, still
*****tandem**	finally
tantillus, -a, -um	so small a quantity
Tartarus, -i *m.*	Tartarus
*****tectum**, -i *n.*	a roof
tela, -ae *f.*	warp
temerarius, -a, -um	rash
temere	(*adv.*) blindly
temeritas, -atis *f.*	rashness
tempto, (1)	to test
*****tempus**, -oris *n.*	time
tenebra, -ae *f.*	darkness (*pl.*)
teriugus, -a, -um	threefold
termino, (1)	to conclude
territo, (1)	to intimidate
testimonium, -i *n.*	testimony
testis, -is *m.*	a witness
teter, -tra, -trum	horrible
textrix, -icis *f.*	a female weaver
theatrum, -i *n.*	a theatre
thensaurus, -i *m.*	treasure
*****tollo**, (3), **sustuli**, **sublatum**	raise, lift up, remove
tono, (1)	to thunder
tormentum, -i *n.*	a torture device
torqueo, (2), **torsi**, **tortum**	to torture
*****totus**, -a, -um	whole, entire
*****trado**, (3), **tradidi**, **traditum**	to deliver, hand over
*****traho**, (3), **traxi**, **tractum**	to haul, drag
trames, -itis *m.*	a track
transeo, -ire, -ivi, transitus	to go over, cross
transmeo, (1)	to cross
Tristities, -ei *f.*	Sadness

A Level

trisulcus, -a, -um	triple-forked
truculentus, -a, -um	ferocious
trux, -ucis	savage
*****tu, tui, tibi, te**	you (*sing.*)
tumulus, -i *m.*	mound
*****tunc**	then
turgidus, -a, -um	swollen
turris, -is *f.*	a tower
*****ubi**	where, when
ulterior, -ius	later
*****ultimus, -a, -um**	last, worst
ultro	(*adv.*) unaided, spontaneously
*****unda, -ae** *f.*	a wave
unicus, -a, -um	single
*****unquam**	ever
*****unus, -a, -um** (*gen.* **-ius**)	one
urnula, -ae *f.*	a little jar
usura, -ae *f.*	use
*****ut, uti**	as (+ *indic.*); so that, with the result that (+ *subj.*)
*****utique**	(*adv.*) certainly
utrimque	on each side
vacuus, -a, -um	empty
vagor, (1), vagatus sum	to roam
vallis, -is *f.*	a valley
vapor, -oris *m.*	a fever
vasculum, -i *n.*	a small vessel
vastus, -a, -um	monstrous
vaticinatio, -onis *f.*	prophecy
vaticinor, (1), vaticinatus sum	to prophesy
vector, -oris *m.*	a passenger
vegetus, -a, -um	vigorous
*****vel**	or else, or; even; **vel . . . vel**: either . . . or
velamentum, -i *n.*	a cover, veil

A Level

vellus, -eris *n.*	fleece
velocitas, -atis *f.*	speed
veneno, (1)	to imbue or infect with poison
*****venio,** (4), **veni**	to come
venter, ventris *m.*	a womb
vere	(*adv.*) truly
vero	in fact, certainly, without doubt
vertex, -icis *m.*	a peak
*****verus, -a, -um**	true, real, actual
*****vespera, -ae** *f.*	evening
vestigium, -i *n.*	a spot, track
*****vestis, -is** *f.*	a garment
*****vetus, veteris** (*gen.*)	long established
*****via, -ae** *f.*	a way, road, journey
viaticum, -i *n.*	a travelling allowance
vibramen, -inis *n.*	a quivering
vicinus, -a, -um	neighbouring
*****video, videre, vidi, visum**	to see, (*pass.*) to seem
vigilia, -ae *f.*	a watch, wakefulness
vilis, -e	common
*****villa, -ae** *f.*	a country home
vinum, -i *n.*	wine
viridis, -e	green
*****vita, -ae** *f.*	life
*****vivo,** (3), **vixi**	to live
vocalis, -e	causing speech, tuneful
*****voco,** (1)	to call, summon
volenter	(*adv.*) willingly
voluptas, -atis *f.*	delight
*****vos, vestrum, vobis, vos**	you (*pl.*)
*****vulnus, -eris** *n*	a wound
*****vultus, -us** *m.*	a look, expression, face

A Level